D1379467

THE PHOTOGRAPHER OF
Mauthausen

WRITER
SALVA RUBIO

ARTIST
PEDRO J. COLOMBO

COLORIST
AINTZANE LANDA

DEAD RECKONING
ANNAPOLIS, MARYLAND

GLOSSARY

Appellplatz: Roll call area where prisoners were assembled to be counted twice daily.

CNT: Confederation of National Workers (Confederación Nacional del Trabajo).

CTE: Company of Foreign Workers (Compagnies de travailleurs étrangers).

Erkennungsdienst: Identification service.

Fallschirmspringerwand, or "The Parachutists' Wall": A 120-foot-high cliff from which prisoners were thrown to their deaths.

Frontstalag (or stalag): Prisoner-of-war camp.

Garagenplatz: Square in front of the main camp building where vehicles were stored and where the mass disinfection took place.

Hauptlager: Main camp.

Himmlerstraße: Band shaved through the middle of the head to identify and humiliate prisoners who attempted to escape.

JSU: United Socialist Youth (Juventudes Socialistas Unificadas).

Kapos: Kamerad Polizei or Funktionshäftlinge, common law prisoners, usually very cruel, charged with leading and punishing the other prisoners.

Klagemauer: The Wailing Wall, so-called because of the beatings and torture inflicted on prisoners there.

Kommando: Work group within the camp.

Luftwaffe: German Air Force.

Nebenlager: Annexes connected to the main camp.

Oberscharführer: Senior squad leader.

PCE: Spanish Communist Party (Partido Comunista de España).

Pochacas or Poschacher: Spanish boys who work for the Poshcacher Kommando (named after the local granite company).

Politische Abteilung: Department of the Gestapo charged with the administration of the camp.

PSOE: Spanish Socialist Workers' Party (Partido Socialista Obrero Español).

RSHA: Reichssicherheitshauptamt, central security office of the Third Reich.

Schutzhaftlagerführer: SS in charge of detainees in the camps.

Spaniaker: Pejorative name given by Nazis to the Spaniards in the camp.

SS-Hauptscharführer: Head squad leader.

Strafkompanie: Group of prisoners who were given the toughest tasks with the goal of killing them off more quickly.

Totenkopf: "Death's Head," insignia of the SS.

Volkssturm: Militia created by Hitler in 1944 bringing together all men deemed useful between 16 and 60 years old.

Wehrmacht: German army.

Wiener Graben: Granite quarry.

Winkel: Any sign marking a prisoner's status (a yellow star for Jews, a red triangle for Communists, a blue triangle for Spaniards...).

Sometimes it's hard to be both a historian and a writer. The historian in me insists that the only events I can write about are those based on actual facts that can be corroborated by multiple sources. The writer in me wants to take these more-or-less well-known historical facts and transform them into a fictional tale, changing my task into adaptation, a job which often entails filling in the gaps of history with my imagination.

This push and pull is all the more difficult to manage considering that the events I'm relating touch on a theme as delicate as concentration camp survivors. Although there is no lack of reliable sources, a story like the one we're telling here also depends—and it was often the case, in fact—on testimonies that are impossible to verify, incomplete stories and decades-old memories, even if they are faithful to reality. What's more, it was often impossible for us to get in touch with the survivors in question or, more sadly still, they are no longer among us to tell their stories*.

Salva Rubio

PREFACE

*The script was reviewed by Gregor Holzinger and Ralf Lechner (of the Archiv der KZ-Gedenkstätte Mauthausen), Margarida Sala (of the Museu d'Història de Catalunya) and Rosa Toran (of the Amical de Mauthausen y otros campos); I am profoundly grateful for their advice and correction which were taken into account except in cases where the adaptation demanded otherwise.

"The Spaniards were
the hardest ones to kill."

FRANZ ZIEREIS,
COMMANDANT OF
MAUTHAUSEN

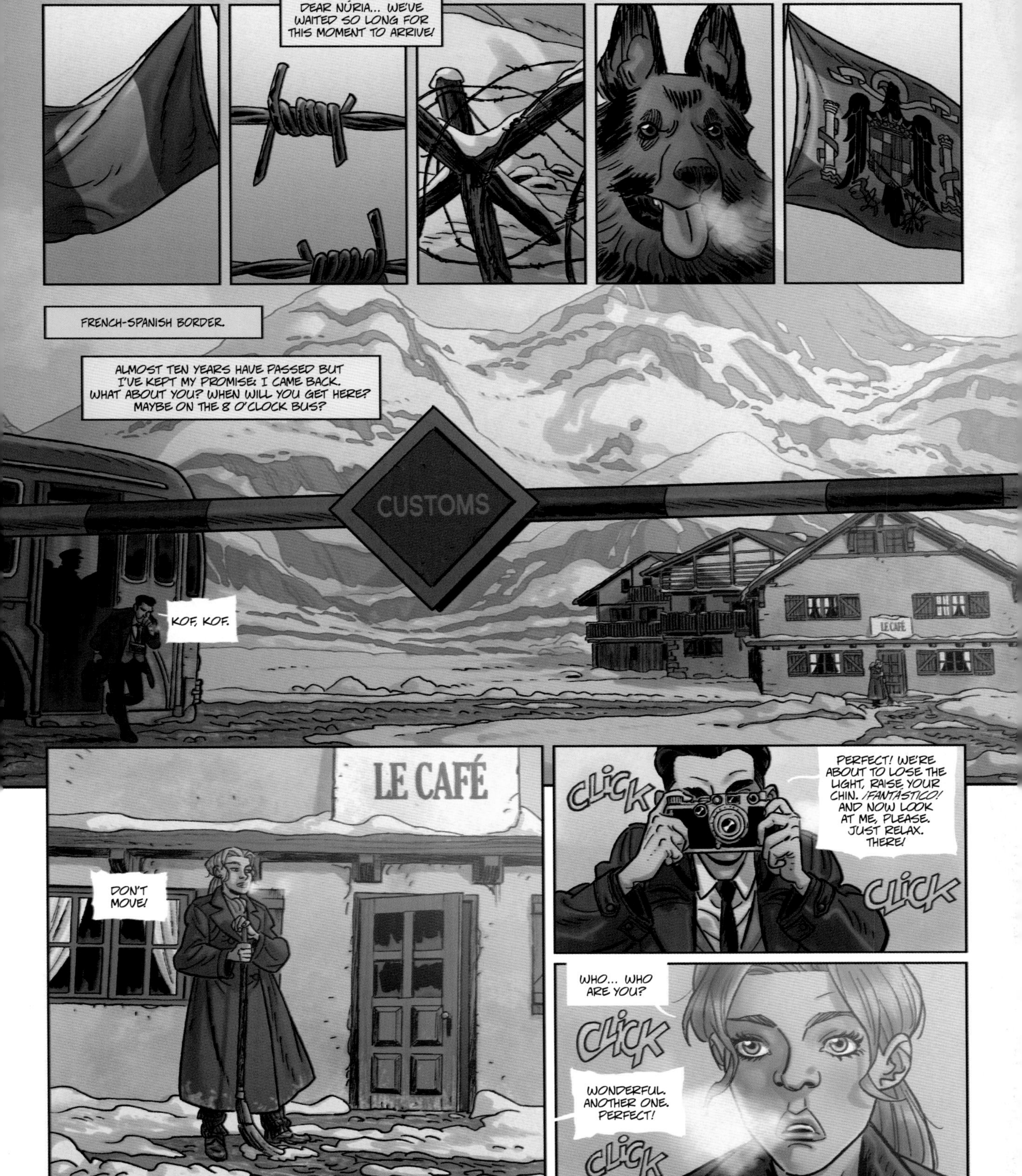
DEAR NÚRIA... WE'VE WAITED SO LONG FOR THIS MOMENT TO ARRIVE!
FRENCH-SPANISH BORDER.
ALMOST TEN YEARS HAVE PASSED BUT I'VE KEPT MY PROMISE: I CAME BACK. WHAT ABOUT YOU? WHEN WILL YOU GET HERE? MAYBE ON THE 8 O'CLOCK BUS?
CUSTOMS
KOF, KOF.
LE CAFÉ
LE CAFÉ
DON'T MOVE!
CLICK
PERFECT! WE'RE ABOUT TO LOSE THE LIGHT, RAISE YOUR CHIN. *¡FANTÁSTICO!* AND NOW LOOK AT ME, PLEASE. JUST RELAX. THERE!
CLICK
WHO... WHO ARE YOU?
CLICK
WONDERFUL. ANOTHER ONE. PERFECT!
CLICK

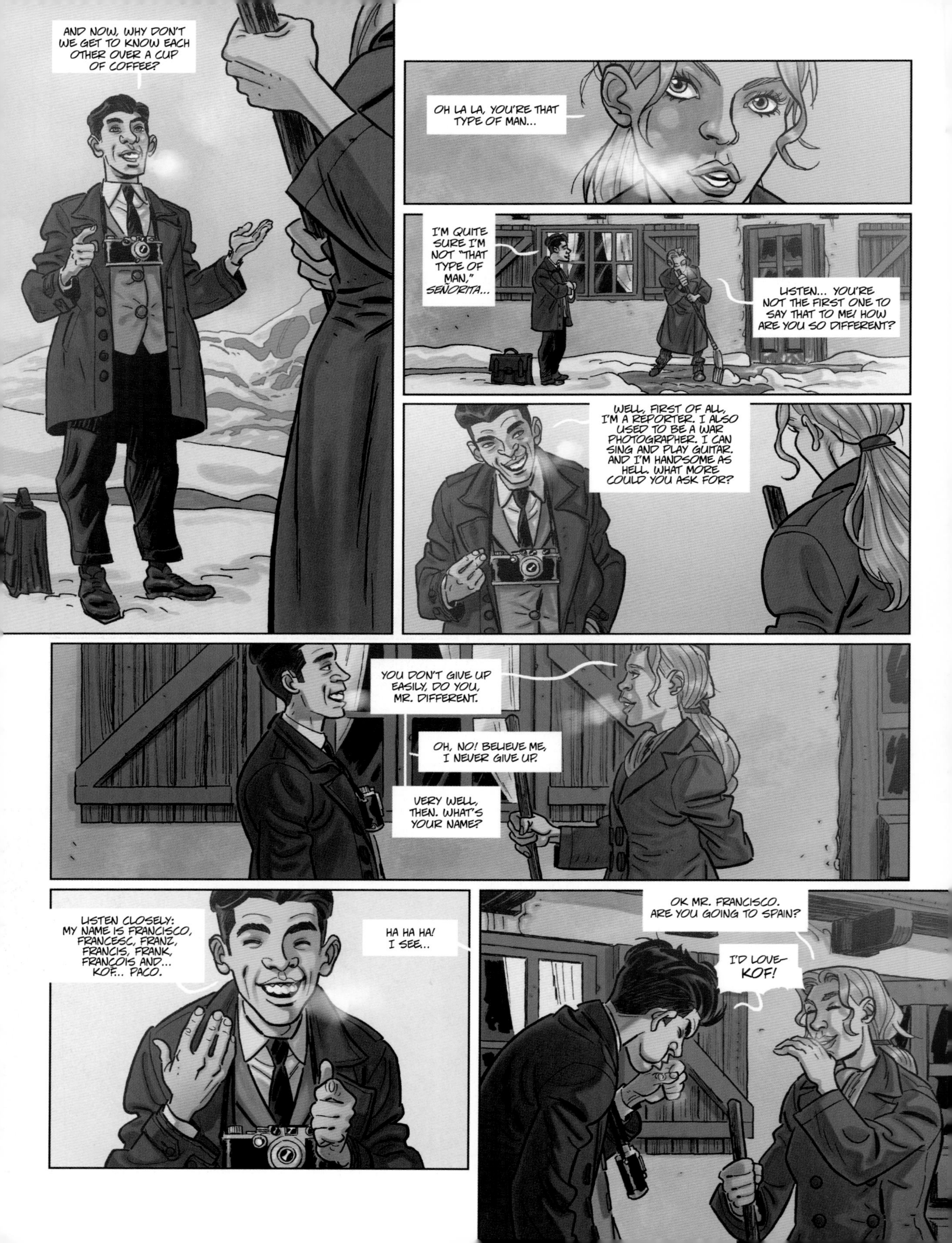
AND NOW, WHY DON'T WE GET TO KNOW EACH OTHER OVER A CUP OF COFFEE?
OH LA LA, YOU'RE THAT TYPE OF MAN...
I'M QUITE SURE I'M NOT "THAT TYPE OF MAN," SEÑORITA...
LISTEN... YOU'RE NOT THE FIRST ONE TO SAY THAT TO ME! HOW ARE YOU SO DIFFERENT?
WELL, FIRST OF ALL, I'M A REPORTER. I ALSO USED TO BE A WAR PHOTOGRAPHER. I CAN SING AND PLAY GUITAR. AND I'M HANDSOME AS HELL. WHAT MORE COULD YOU ASK FOR?
YOU DON'T GIVE UP EASILY, DO YOU, MR. DIFFERENT.
OH, NO! BELIEVE ME, I NEVER GIVE UP.
VERY WELL, THEN. WHAT'S YOUR NAME?
LISTEN CLOSELY: MY NAME IS FRANCISCO, FRANCESC, FRANZ, FRANCIS, FRANK, FRANCOIS AND... KOF... PACO.
HA HA HA! I SEE...
OK MR. FRANCISCO. ARE YOU GOING TO SPAIN?
I'D LOVE- KOF!

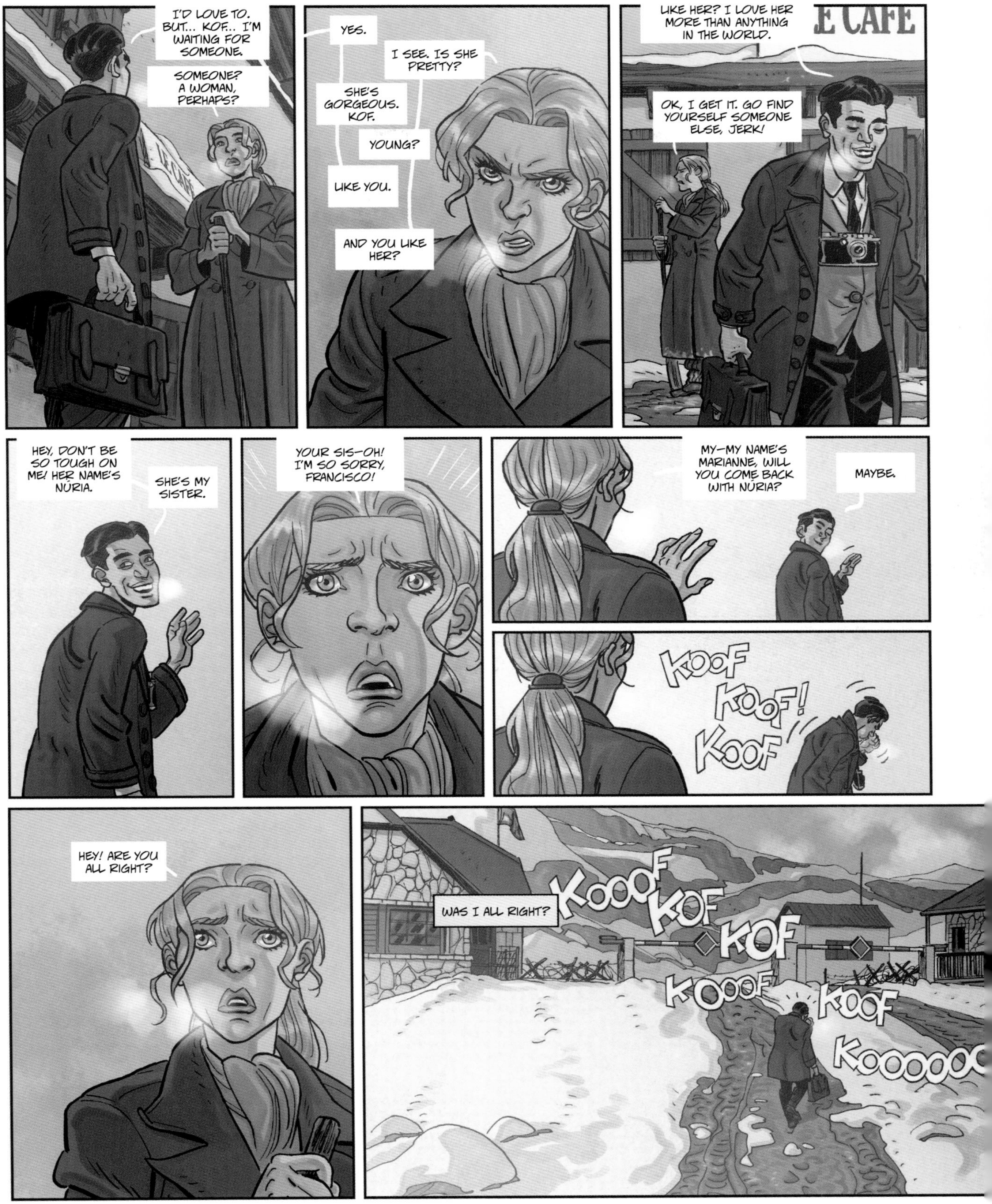
I'D LOVE TO. BUT... KOF... I'M WAITING FOR SOMEONE.
SOMEONE? A WOMAN, PERHAPS?
LE CAFÉ
YES.
I SEE. IS SHE PRETTY?
SHE'S GORGEOUS. KOF.
YOUNG?
LIKE YOU.
AND YOU LIKE HER?
LIKE HER? I LOVE HER MORE THAN ANYTHING IN THE WORLD.
E CAFE
OK, I GET IT. GO FIND YOURSELF SOMEONE ELSE, JERK!
HEY, DON'T BE SO TOUGH ON ME! HER NAME'S NÚRIA.
SHE'S MY SISTER.
YOUR SIS—OH! I'M SO SORRY, FRANCISCO!
MY—MY NAME'S MARIANNE, WILL YOU COME BACK WITH NÚRIA?
MAYBE.
KOOF
KOOF!
KOOF
HEY! ARE YOU ALL RIGHT?
WAS I ALL RIGHT?
KOOOF
KOF
KOF
KOOOF
KOOF
KOOOOOO

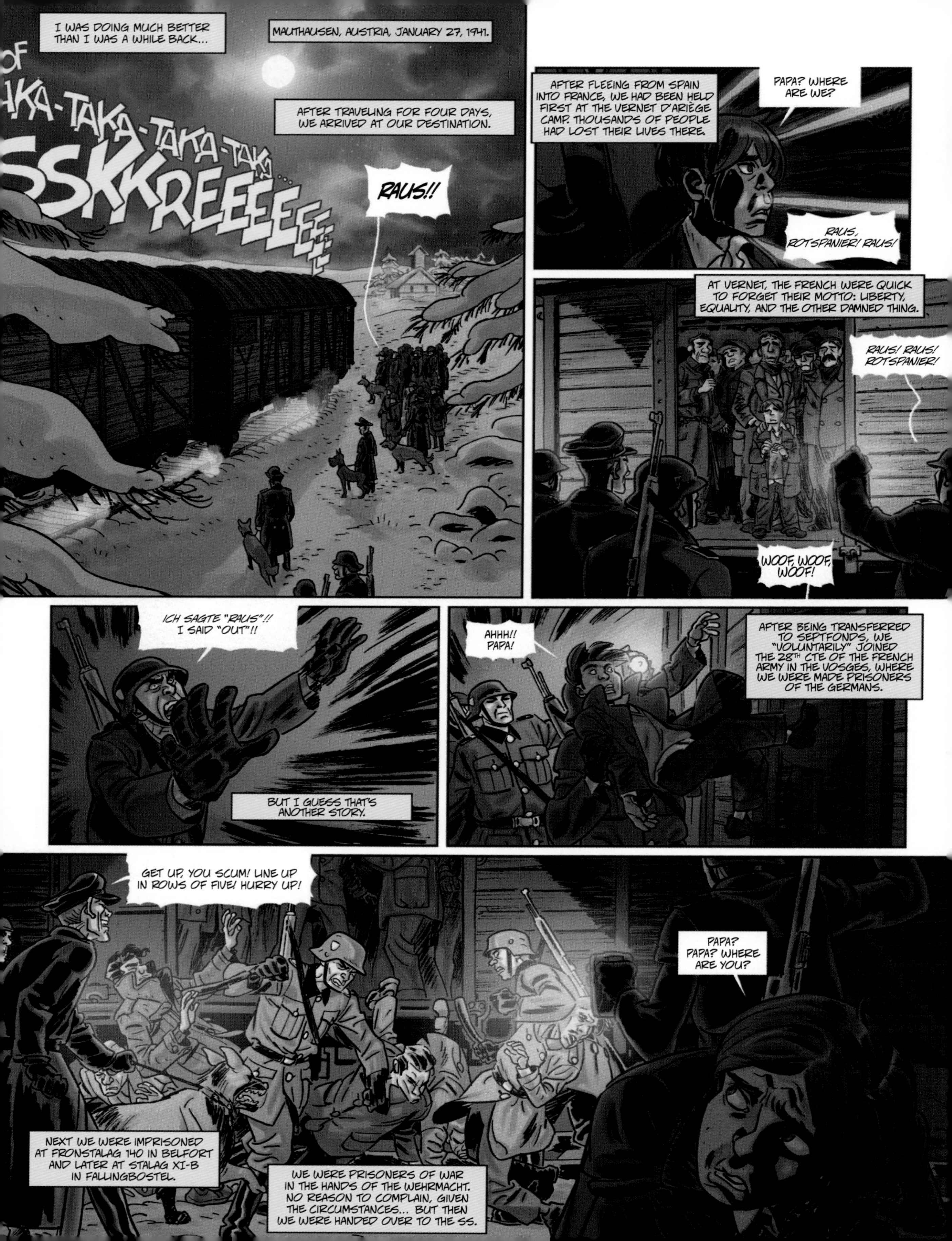
I WAS DOING MUCH BETTER THAN I WAS A WHILE BACK...
MAUTHAUSEN, AUSTRIA, JANUARY 27, 1941.
...AKA-TAKA-TAKA-TAKA...
SSKKREEEEEEE
AFTER TRAVELING FOR FOUR DAYS, WE ARRIVED AT OUR DESTINATION.
RAUS!!
AFTER FLEEING FROM SPAIN INTO FRANCE, WE HAD BEEN HELD FIRST AT THE VERNET D'ARIÈGE CAMP. THOUSANDS OF PEOPLE HAD LOST THEIR LIVES THERE.
PAPA? WHERE ARE WE?
RAUS, ROTSPANIER! RAUS!
AT VERNET, THE FRENCH WERE QUICK TO FORGET THEIR MOTTO: LIBERTY, EQUALITY, AND THE OTHER DAMNED THING.
RAUS! RAUS! ROTSPANIER!
WOOF, WOOF, WOOF!
ICH SAGTE "RAUS"!! I SAID "OUT"!!
BUT I GUESS THAT'S ANOTHER STORY.
AHHH!! PAPA!
AFTER BEING TRANSFERRED TO SEPTFONDS, WE "VOLUNTARILY" JOINED THE 28TH CTE OF THE FRENCH ARMY IN THE VOSGES, WHERE WE WERE MADE PRISONERS OF THE GERMANS.
GET UP, YOU SCUM! LINE UP IN ROWS OF FIVE! HURRY UP!
PAPA? PAPA? WHERE ARE YOU?
NEXT WE WERE IMPRISONED AT FRONSTALAG 140 IN BELFORT AND LATER AT STALAG XI-B IN FALLINGBOSTEL.
WE WERE PRISONERS OF WAR IN THE HANDS OF THE WEHRMACHT. NO REASON TO COMPLAIN, GIVEN THE CIRCUMSTANCES... BUT THEN WE WERE HANDED OVER TO THE SS.

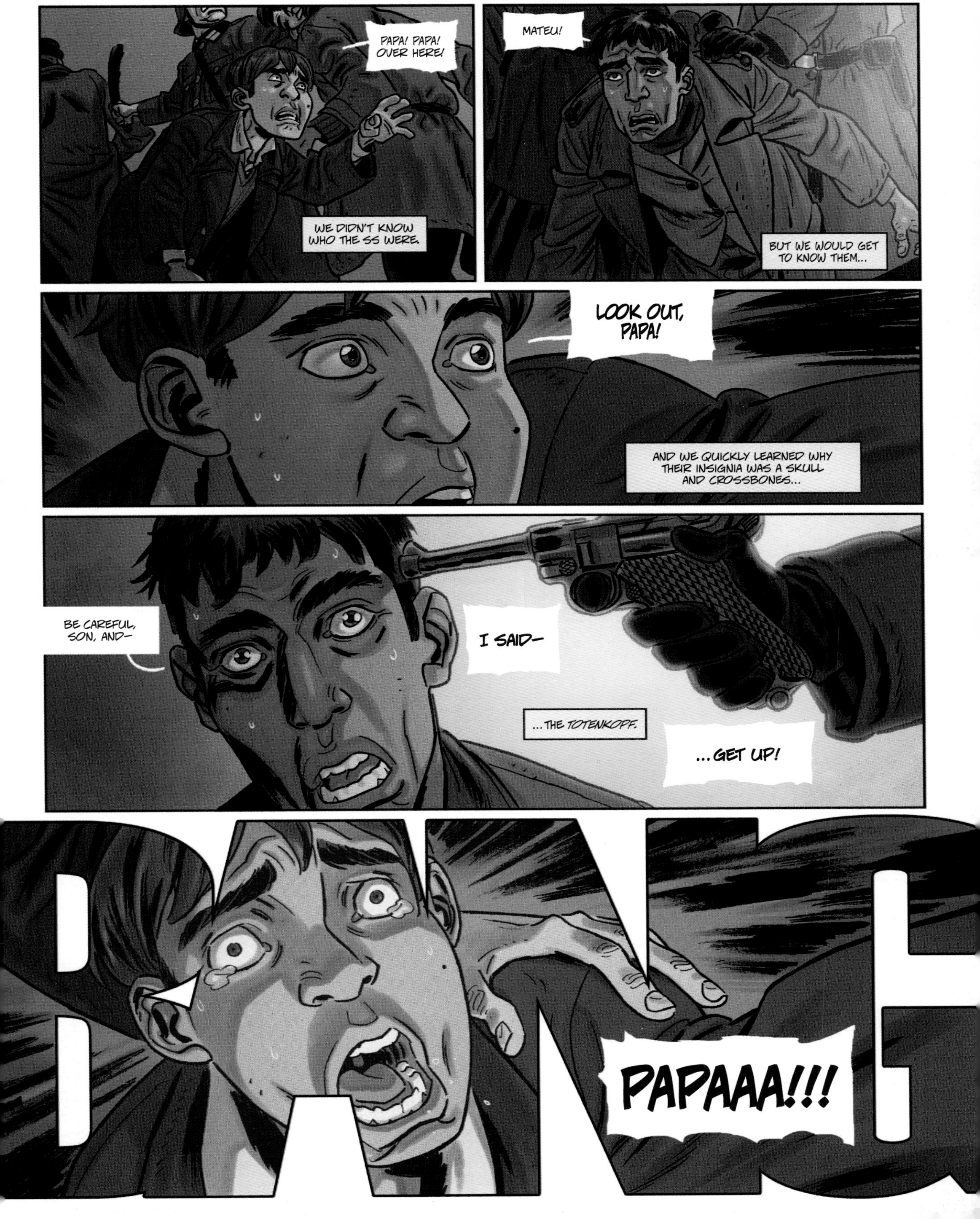
PAPA! PAPA! OVER HERE!
WE DIDN'T KNOW WHO THE SS WERE.
MATEU!
BUT WE WOULD GET TO KNOW THEM...
LOOK OUT, PAPA!
AND WE QUICKLY LEARNED WHY THEIR INSIGNIA WAS A SKULL AND CROSSBONES...
BE CAREFUL, SON, AND—
I SAID—
...THE *TOTENKOPF*.
...GET UP!
BANG
PAPAAA!!!

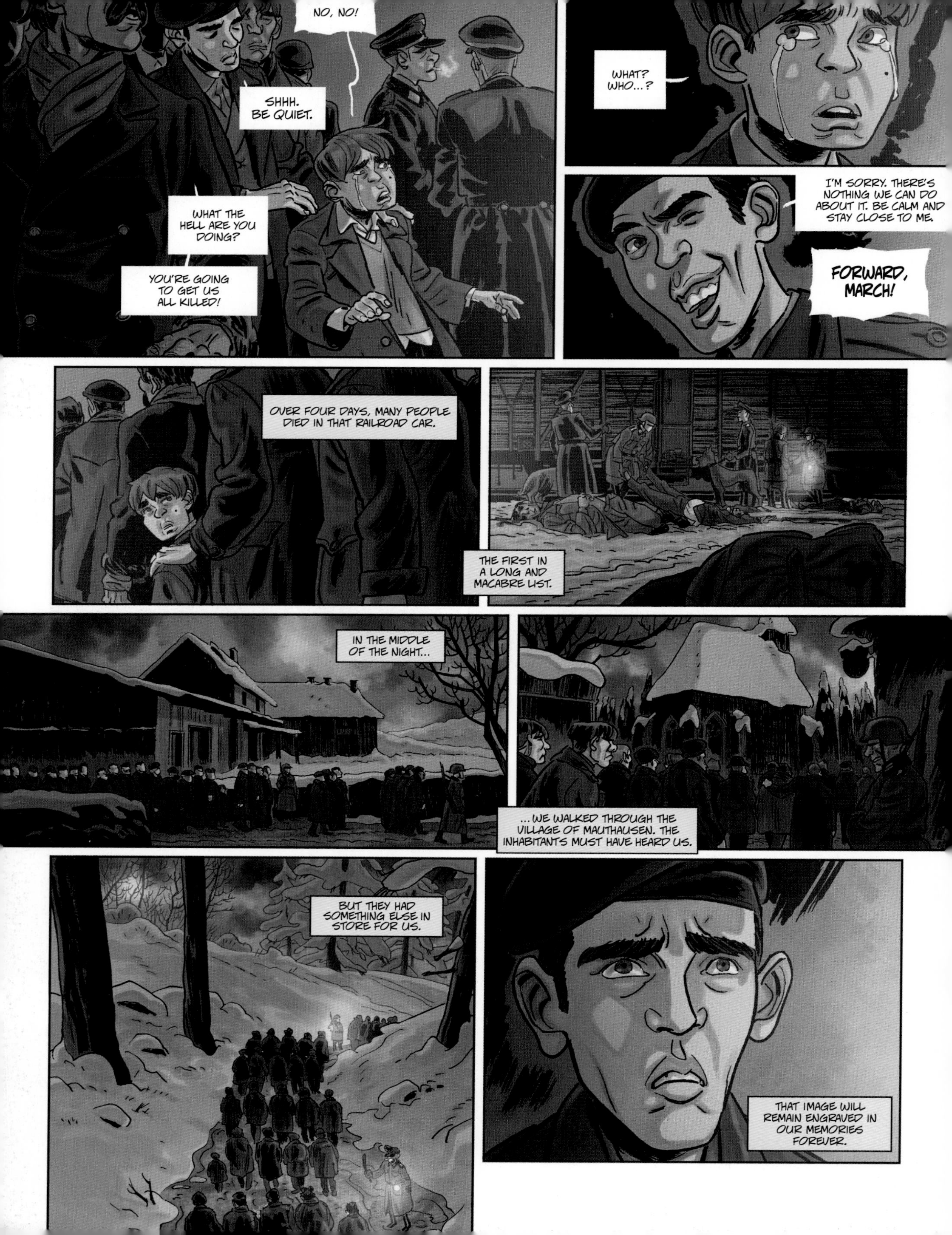
NO, NO!
SHHH. BE QUIET.
WHAT THE HELL ARE YOU DOING?
YOU'RE GOING TO GET US ALL KILLED!
WHAT? WHO...?
I'M SORRY. THERE'S NOTHING WE CAN DO ABOUT IT. BE CALM AND STAY CLOSE TO ME.
FORWARD, MARCH!
OVER FOUR DAYS, MANY PEOPLE DIED IN THAT RAILROAD CAR.
THE FIRST IN A LONG AND MACABRE LIST.
IN THE MIDDLE OF THE NIGHT...
...WE WALKED THROUGH THE VILLAGE OF MAUTHAUSEN. THE INHABITANTS MUST HAVE HEARD US.
BUT THEY HAD SOMETHING ELSE IN STORE FOR US.
THAT IMAGE WILL REMAIN ENGRAVED IN OUR MEMORIES FOREVER.

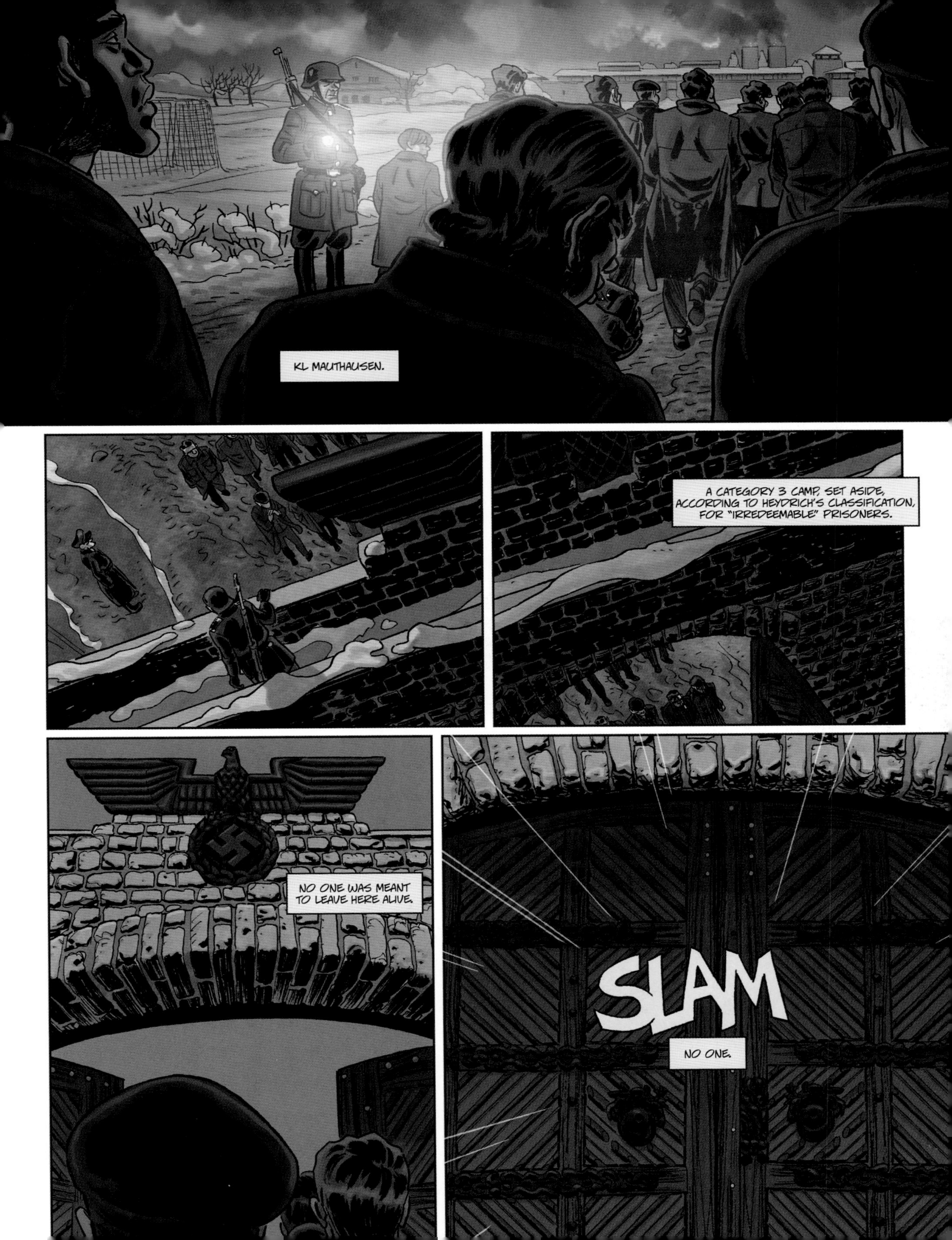
KL MAUTHAUSEN.
A CATEGORY 3 CAMP, SET ASIDE, ACCORDING TO HEYDRICH'S CLASSIFICATION, FOR "IRREDEEMABLE" PRISONERS.
NO ONE WAS MEANT TO LEAVE HERE ALIVE.
SLAM
NO ONE.

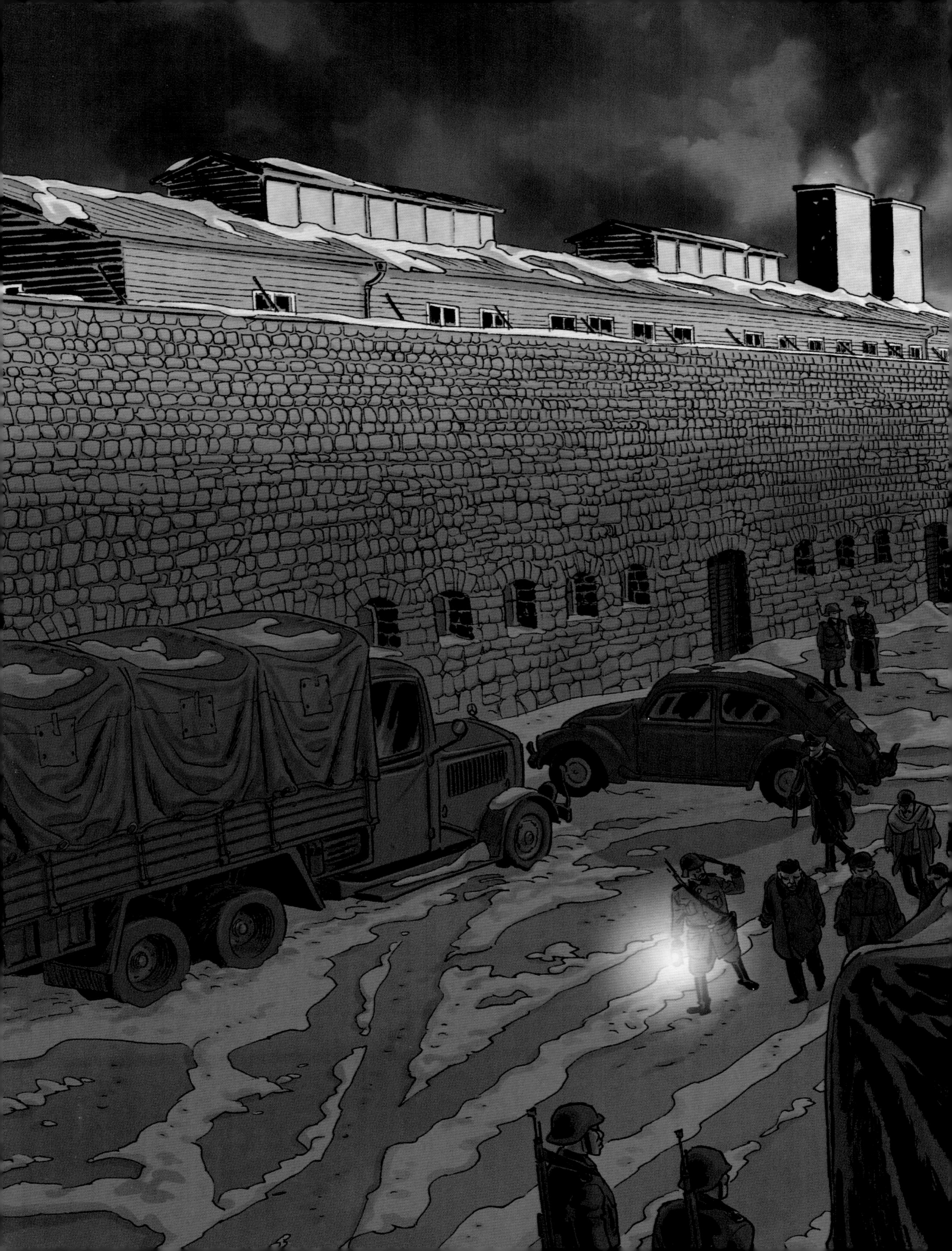

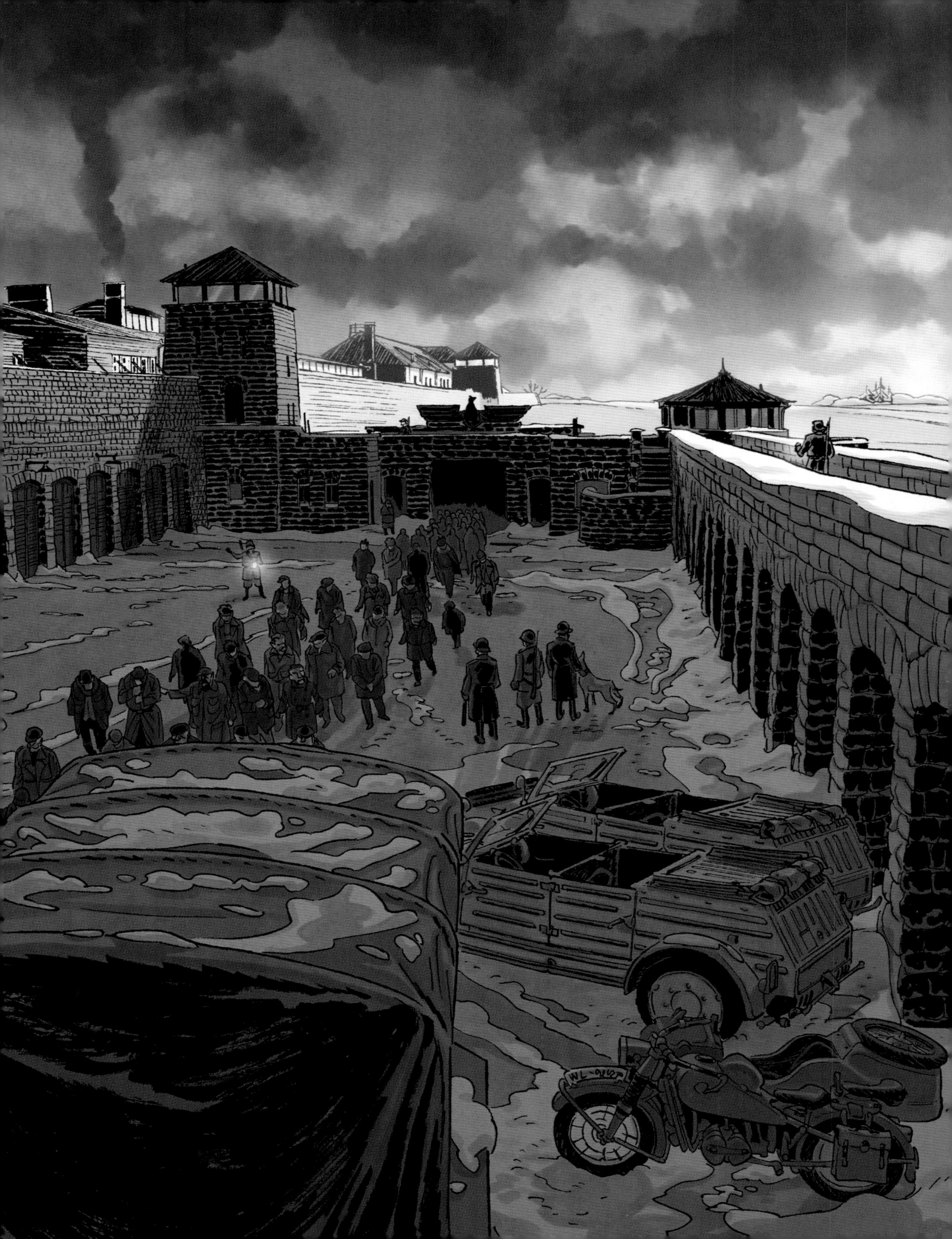

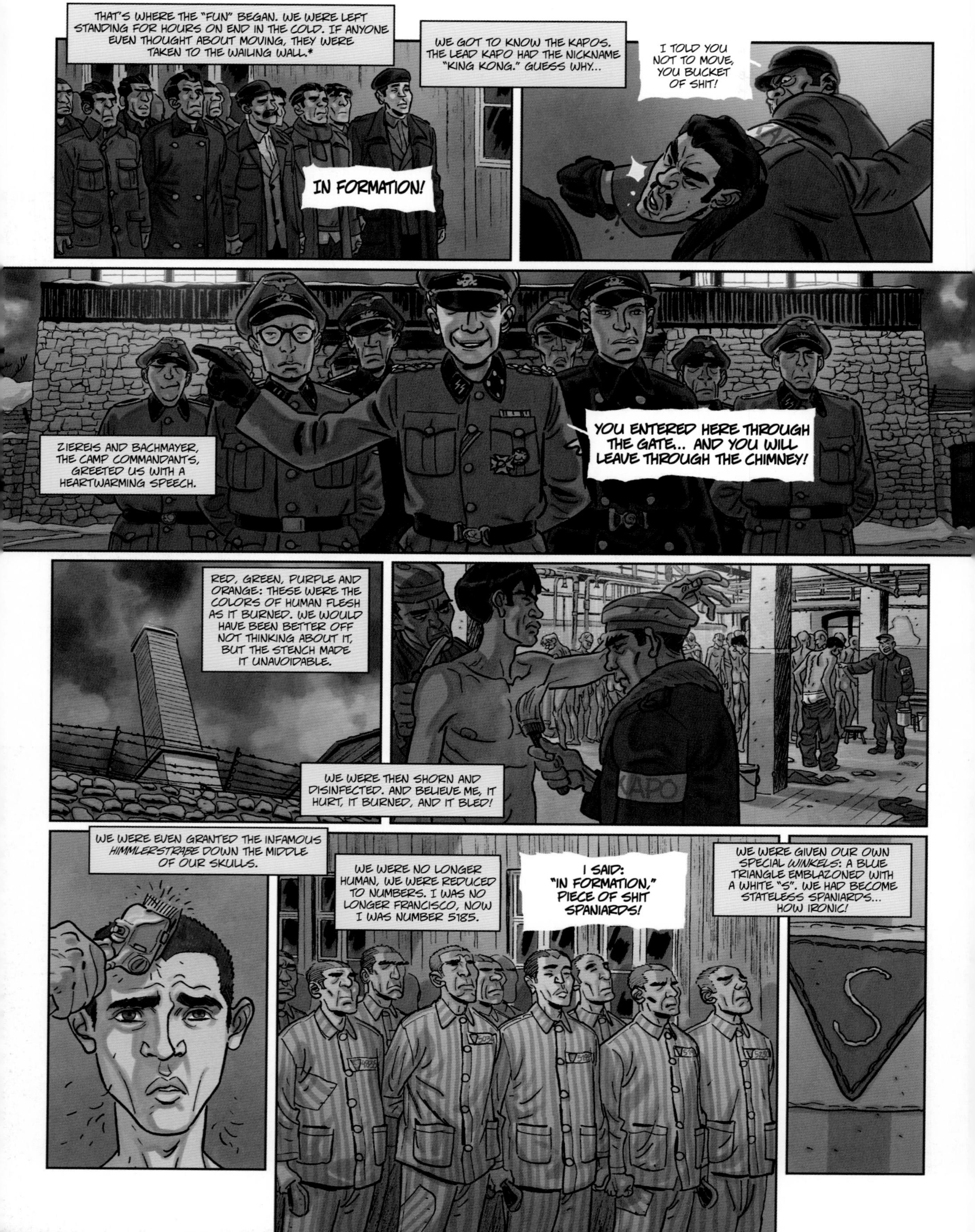
THAT'S WHERE THE "FUN" BEGAN. WE WERE LEFT STANDING FOR HOURS ON END IN THE COLD. IF ANYONE EVEN THOUGHT ABOUT MOVING, THEY WERE TAKEN TO THE WAILING WALL.*
IN FORMATION!
WE GOT TO KNOW THE KAPOS. THE LEAD KAPO HAD THE NICKNAME "KING KONG." GUESS WHY...
I TOLD YOU NOT TO MOVE, YOU BUCKET OF SHIT!
ZIEREIS AND BACHMAYER, THE CAMP COMMANDANTS, GREETED US WITH A HEARTWARMING SPEECH.
YOU ENTERED HERE THROUGH THE GATE... AND YOU WILL LEAVE THROUGH THE CHIMNEY!
RED, GREEN, PURPLE AND ORANGE: THESE WERE THE COLORS OF HUMAN FLESH AS IT BURNED. WE WOULD HAVE BEEN BETTER OFF NOT THINKING ABOUT IT, BUT THE STENCH MADE IT UNAVOIDABLE.
WE WERE THEN SHORN AND DISINFECTED. AND BELIEVE ME, IT HURT, IT BURNED, AND IT BLED!
KAPO
WE WERE EVEN GRANTED THE INFAMOUS *HIMMLERSTRAßE* DOWN THE MIDDLE OF OUR SKULLS.
WE WERE NO LONGER HUMAN, WE WERE REDUCED TO NUMBERS. I WAS NO LONGER FRANCISCO, NOW I WAS NUMBER 5185.
I SAID: "IN FORMATION," PIECE OF SHIT SPANIARDS!
WE WERE GIVEN OUR OWN SPECIAL *WINKELS*: A BLUE TRIANGLE EMBLAZONED WITH A WHITE "S". WE HAD BECOME STATELESS SPANIARDS... HOW IRONIC!
S

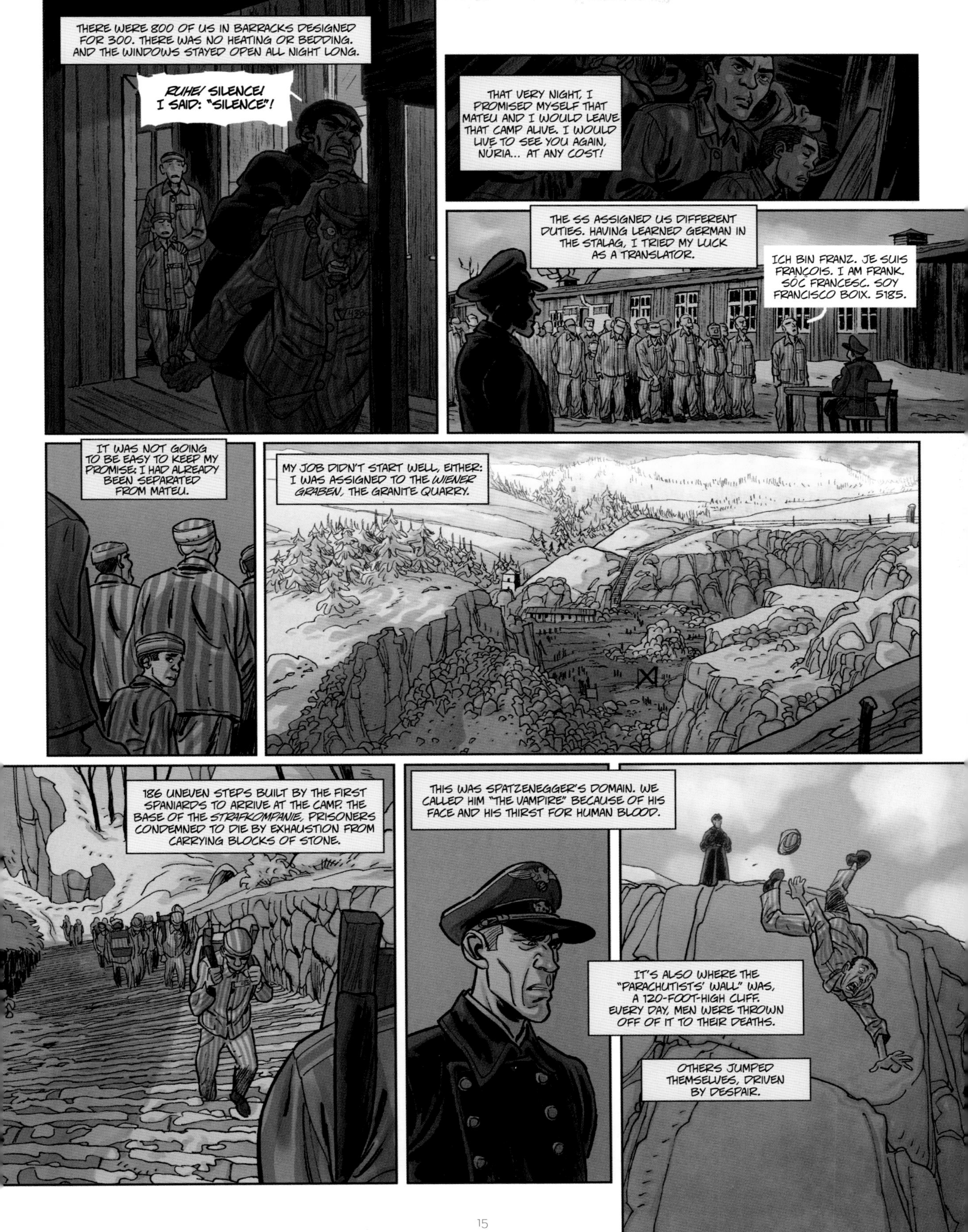
THERE WERE 800 OF US IN BARRACKS DESIGNED FOR 300. THERE WAS NO HEATING OR BEDDING. AND THE WINDOWS STAYED OPEN ALL NIGHT LONG.
RUHE! SILENCE! I SAID: "SILENCE"!
THAT VERY NIGHT, I PROMISED MYSELF THAT MATEU AND I WOULD LEAVE THAT CAMP ALIVE. I WOULD LIVE TO SEE YOU AGAIN, NÚRIA... AT ANY COST!
THE SS ASSIGNED US DIFFERENT DUTIES. HAVING LEARNED GERMAN IN THE STALAG, I TRIED MY LUCK AS A TRANSLATOR.
ICH BIN FRANZ. JE SUIS FRANÇOIS. I AM FRANK. SÓC FRANCESC. SOY FRANCISCO BOIX. 5185.
IT WAS NOT GOING TO BE EASY TO KEEP MY PROMISE: I HAD ALREADY BEEN SEPARATED FROM MATEU.
MY JOB DIDN'T START WELL, EITHER: I WAS ASSIGNED TO THE *WIENER GRABEN*, THE GRANITE QUARRY.
186 UNEVEN STEPS BUILT BY THE FIRST SPANIARDS TO ARRIVE AT THE CAMP. THE BASE OF THE *STRAFKOMPANIE*, PRISONERS CONDEMNED TO DIE BY EXHAUSTION FROM CARRYING BLOCKS OF STONE.
THIS WAS SPATZENEGGER'S DOMAIN. WE CALLED HIM "THE VAMPIRE" BECAUSE OF HIS FACE AND HIS THIRST FOR HUMAN BLOOD.
IT'S ALSO WHERE THE "PARACHUTISTS' WALL" WAS, A 120-FOOT-HIGH CLIFF. EVERY DAY, MEN WERE THROWN OFF OF IT TO THEIR DEATHS.
OTHERS JUMPED THEMSELVES, DRIVEN BY DESPAIR.

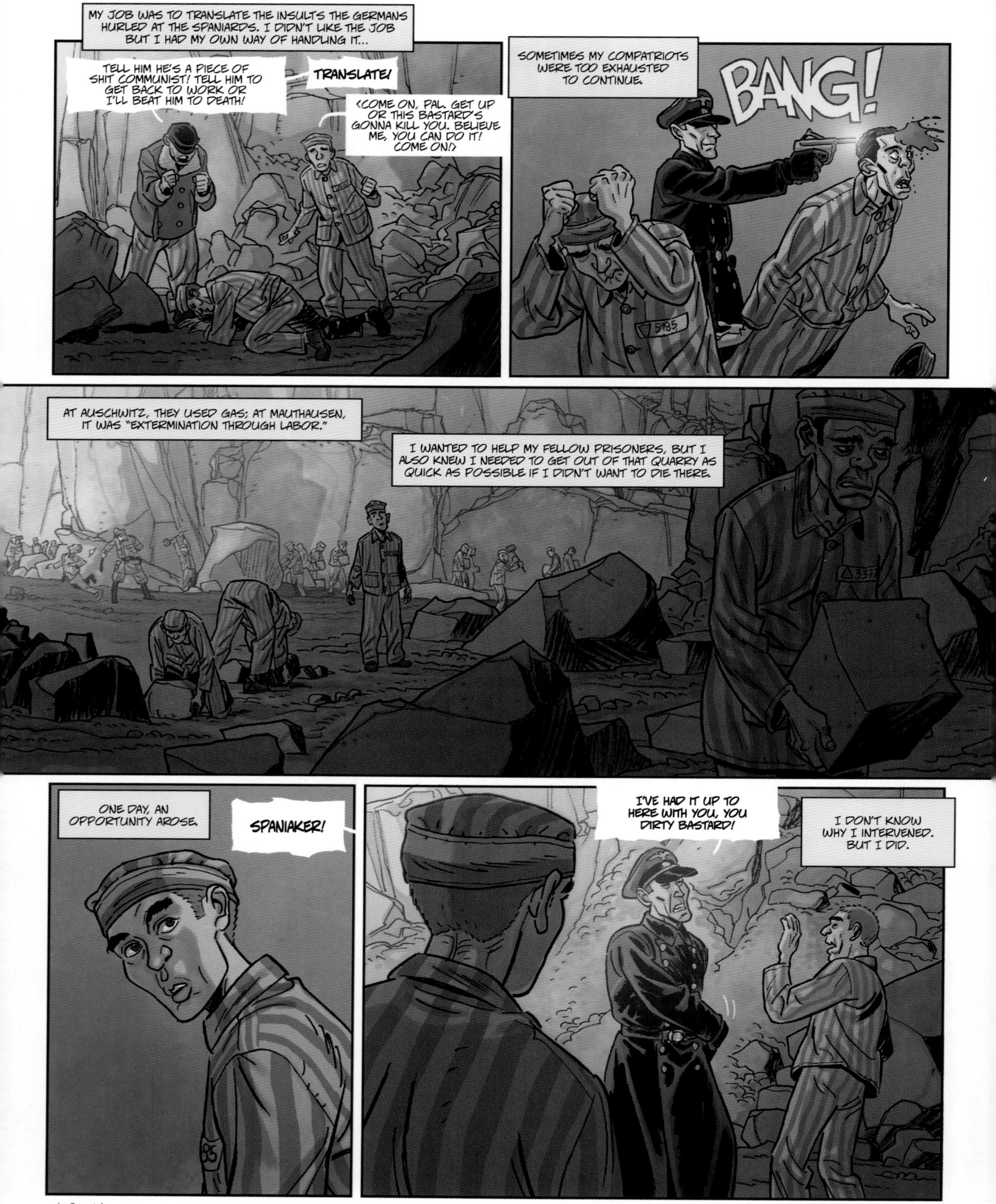
MY JOB WAS TO TRANSLATE THE INSULTS THE GERMANS HURLED AT THE SPANIARDS. I DIDN'T LIKE THE JOB BUT I HAD MY OWN WAY OF HANDLING IT...
TELL HIM HE'S A PIECE OF SHIT COMMUNIST! TELL HIM TO GET BACK TO WORK OR I'LL BEAT HIM TO DEATH!
TRANSLATE!
<COME ON, PAL. GET UP OR THIS BASTARD'S GONNA KILL YOU. BELIEVE ME, YOU CAN DO IT! COME ON!>
SOMETIMES MY COMPATRIOTS WERE TOO EXHAUSTED TO CONTINUE.
BANG!
5185
AT AUSCHWITZ, THEY USED GAS; AT MAUTHAUSEN, IT WAS "EXTERMINATION THROUGH LABOR."
I WANTED TO HELP MY FELLOW PRISONERS, BUT I ALSO KNEW I NEEDED TO GET OUT OF THAT QUARRY AS QUICK AS POSSIBLE IF I DIDN'T WANT TO DIE THERE.
ONE DAY, AN OPPORTUNITY AROSE.
SPANIAKER!
I'VE HAD IT UP TO HERE WITH YOU, YOU DIRTY BASTARD!
I DON'T KNOW WHY I INTERVENED. BUT I DID.

<In Spanish>

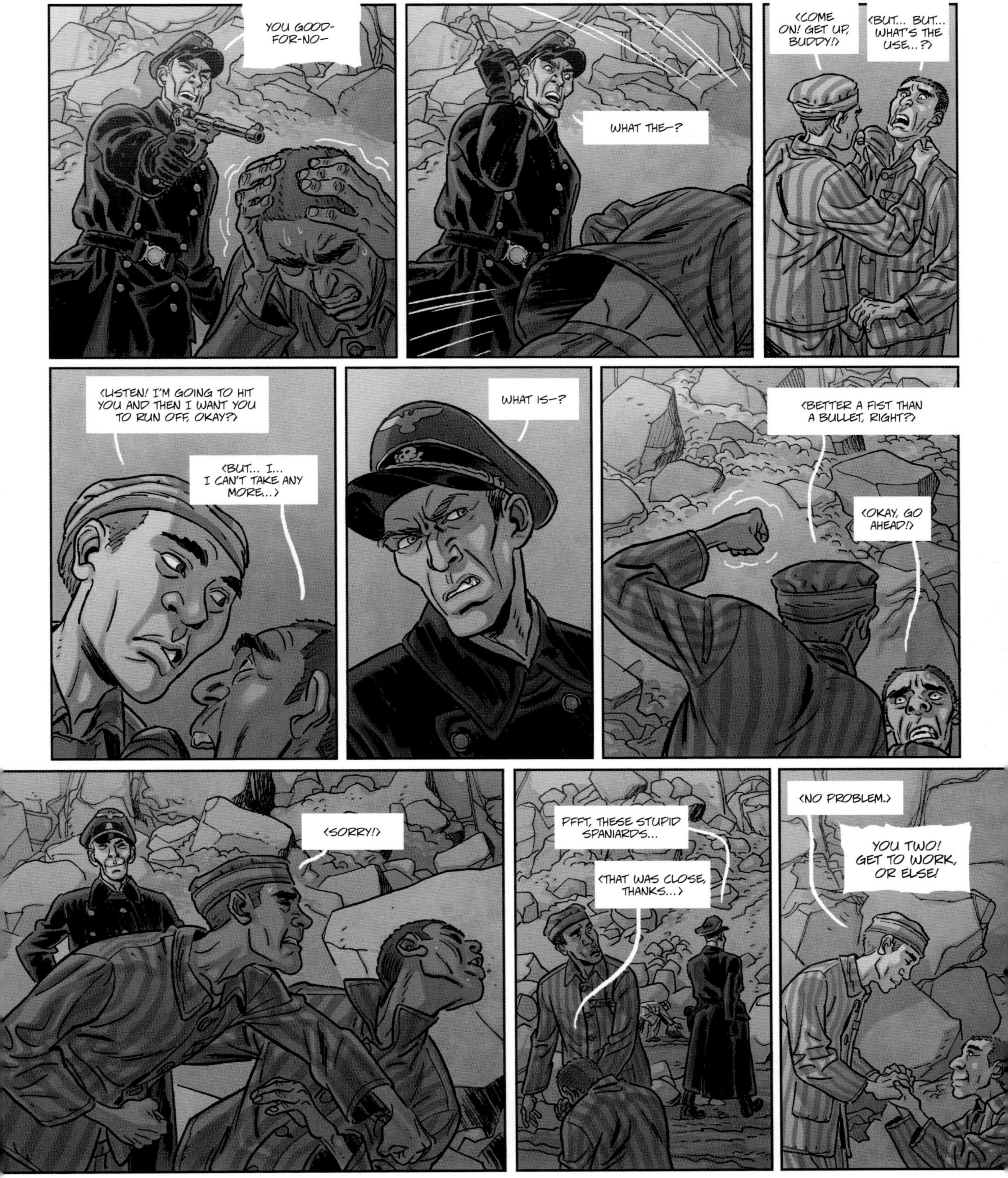
YOU GOOD-FOR-NO-
WHAT THE-?
<COME ON! GET UP, BUDDY!>
<BUT... BUT... WHAT'S THE USE...?>
<LISTEN! I'M GOING TO HIT YOU AND THEN I WANT YOU TO RUN OFF, OKAY?>
<BUT... I... I CAN'T TAKE ANY MORE...>
WHAT IS-?
<BETTER A FIST THAN A BULLET, RIGHT?>
<OKAY, GO AHEAD!>
<SORRY!>
PFFT, THESE STUPID SPANIARDS...
<THAT WAS CLOSE, THANKS...>
<NO PROBLEM.>
YOU TWO! GET TO WORK, OR ELSE!

<in spanish>

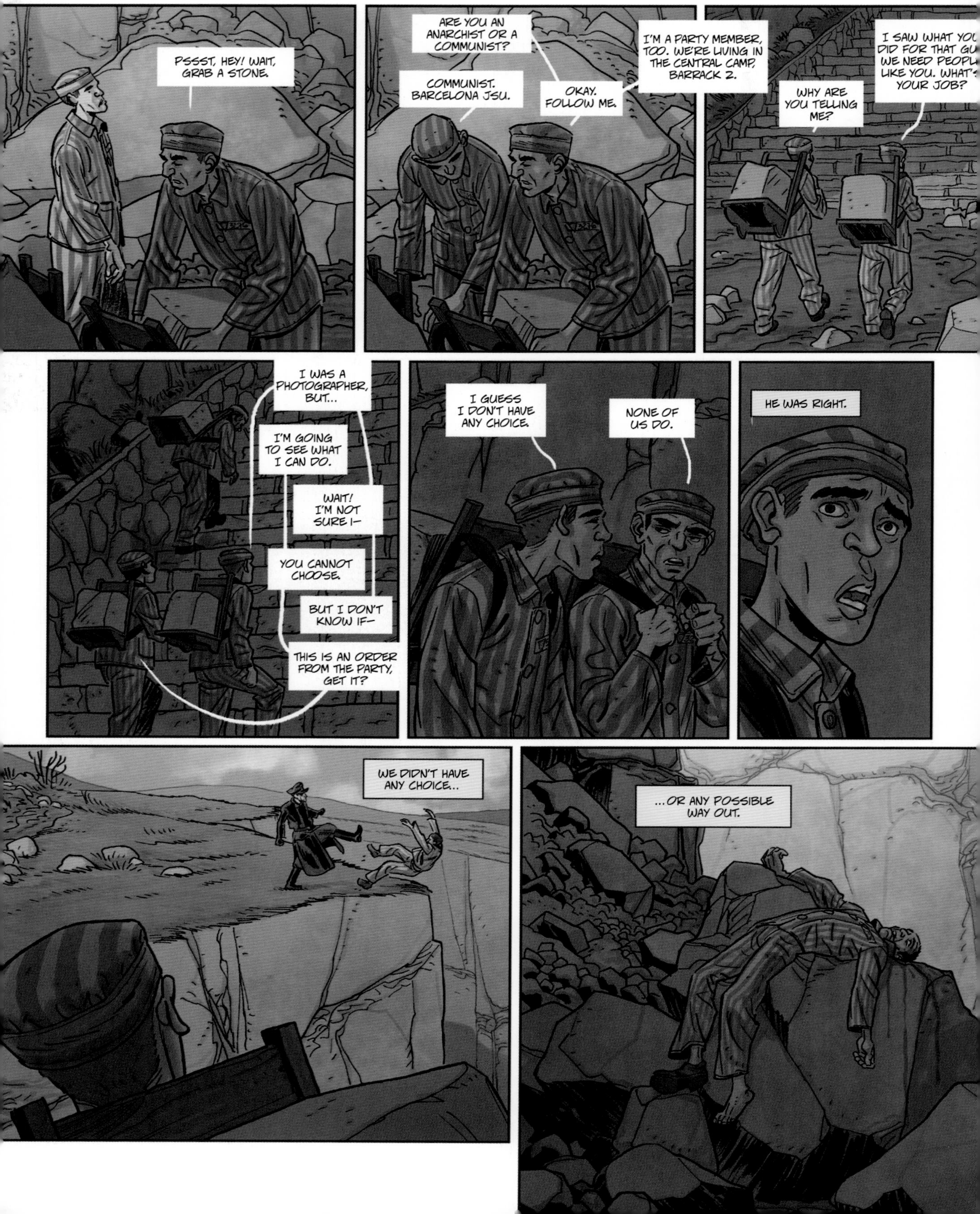
PSSST, HEY! WAIT, GRAB A STONE.
ARE YOU AN ANARCHIST OR A COMMUNIST?
COMMUNIST. BARCELONA JSU.
OKAY. FOLLOW ME.
I'M A PARTY MEMBER, TOO. WE'RE LIVING IN THE CENTRAL CAMP, BARRACK 2.
WHY ARE YOU TELLING ME?
I SAW WHAT YOU DID FOR THAT GU WE NEED PEOPL LIKE YOU. WHAT'S YOUR JOB?
I WAS A PHOTOGRAPHER, BUT...
I'M GOING TO SEE WHAT I CAN DO.
WAIT! I'M NOT SURE I—
YOU CANNOT CHOOSE.
BUT I DON'T KNOW IF—
THIS IS AN ORDER FROM THE PARTY, GET IT?
I GUESS I DON'T HAVE ANY CHOICE.
NONE OF US DO.
HE WAS RIGHT.
WE DIDN'T HAVE ANY CHOICE...
...OR ANY POSSIBLE WAY OUT.

A FEW DAYS LATER, I WAS SUMMONED TO BARRACK 2.

THAT'S WHERE THE *PROMINENTEN* LIVED -- PRISONERS WHO ENJOYED CERTAIN PRIVILEGES DUE TO THEIR PROFESSIONS: SECRETARIES, CHEFS, BARBERS, ENGINEERS....

A NUMBER OF THEM WERE SPANIARDS WHO HAD BEEN AMONG THE FIRST TO ARRIVE AT THE CAMP.

THEY DID THEIR BEST TO HELP THEIR COMPATRIOTS.

IT WAS ALSO THE SECRET HEADQUARTERS OF THE COMMUNIST PARTY, AND THAT'S HOW I MET CARLOS, THE HEAD OF THE ORGANIZATION.

WELCOME TO BARRACK 2, CATALAN COMRADE.

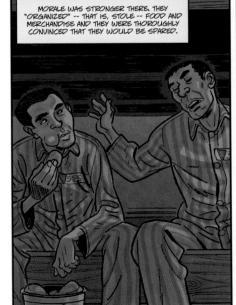

MORALE WAS STRONGER THERE. THEY "ORGANIZED" -- THAT IS, STOLE -- FOOD AND MERCHANDISE AND THEY WERE THOROUGHLY CONVINCED THAT THEY WOULD BE SPARED.

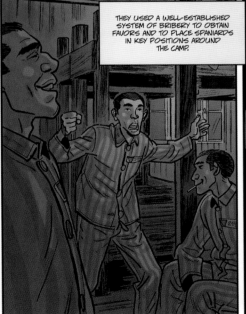

THEY USED A WELL-ESTABLISHED SYSTEM OF BRIBERY TO OBTAIN FAVORS AND TO PLACE SPANIARDS IN KEY POSITIONS AROUND THE CAMP.

BUT ABOVE ALL, THEY LAUGHED, THEY SANG, AND JOKED AROUND AS ONLY SPANIARDS CAN. IT WAS THE FIRST TIME SINCE MY ARRIVAL AT THE CAMP THAT I WAS ONCE AGAIN FRANCISCO.

EVEN MORE SIGNIFICANTLY, THEY GOT ME ASSIGNED TO ONE OF THOSE PRIVILEGED AND COVETED POSTS: I WAS NOW GOING TO WORK IN THE *ERKENNUNGSDIENST* -- THE IDENTIFICATION DEPARTMENT.

I WAS A PHOTOGRAPHER AGAIN!

THAT'S WHERE I MET ROVIRA. THE FORMER COMEDIAN AND FLAMENCO DANCER FROM ANDALUSIA WAS THE FUNNIEST GUY IN THE CAMP.

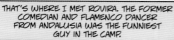

PACO, I BET YOU'RE AN UTTER LIAR AND THAT YOU'VE NEVER PICKED UP A CAMERA IN YOUR WHOLE LIFE!

I'M GUESSING YOU'RE HERE FOR THE SAME REASON, RIGHT?

HA HA HA! YOU GOT ME! COME ON, I'LL SHOW YOU THE LAB.

THE IDENTIFICATION DEPARTMENT WAS MUCH MORE THAN A SIMPLE PHOTOGRAPHY LAB.

IT WAS RUN BY THE GESTAPO. OFFICIALLY, OUR JOB WAS TO IDENTIFY THE PRISONERS WHEN THEY ARRIVED AT THE CAMP, AS HAD BEEN DONE TO ME WHEN I ARRIVED.

UNOFFICIALLY, THE SS HAD US DEVELOPING THEIR PERSONAL PHOTOS WHICH THEY WOULD THEN SEND TO THEIR GIRLFRIENDS.

WE WERE EXPECTED TO PARTICIPATE IN THIS LOW KEY CORRUPTION, DEVELOPING THEIR PRIVATE PHOTOS WHEN ASKED.

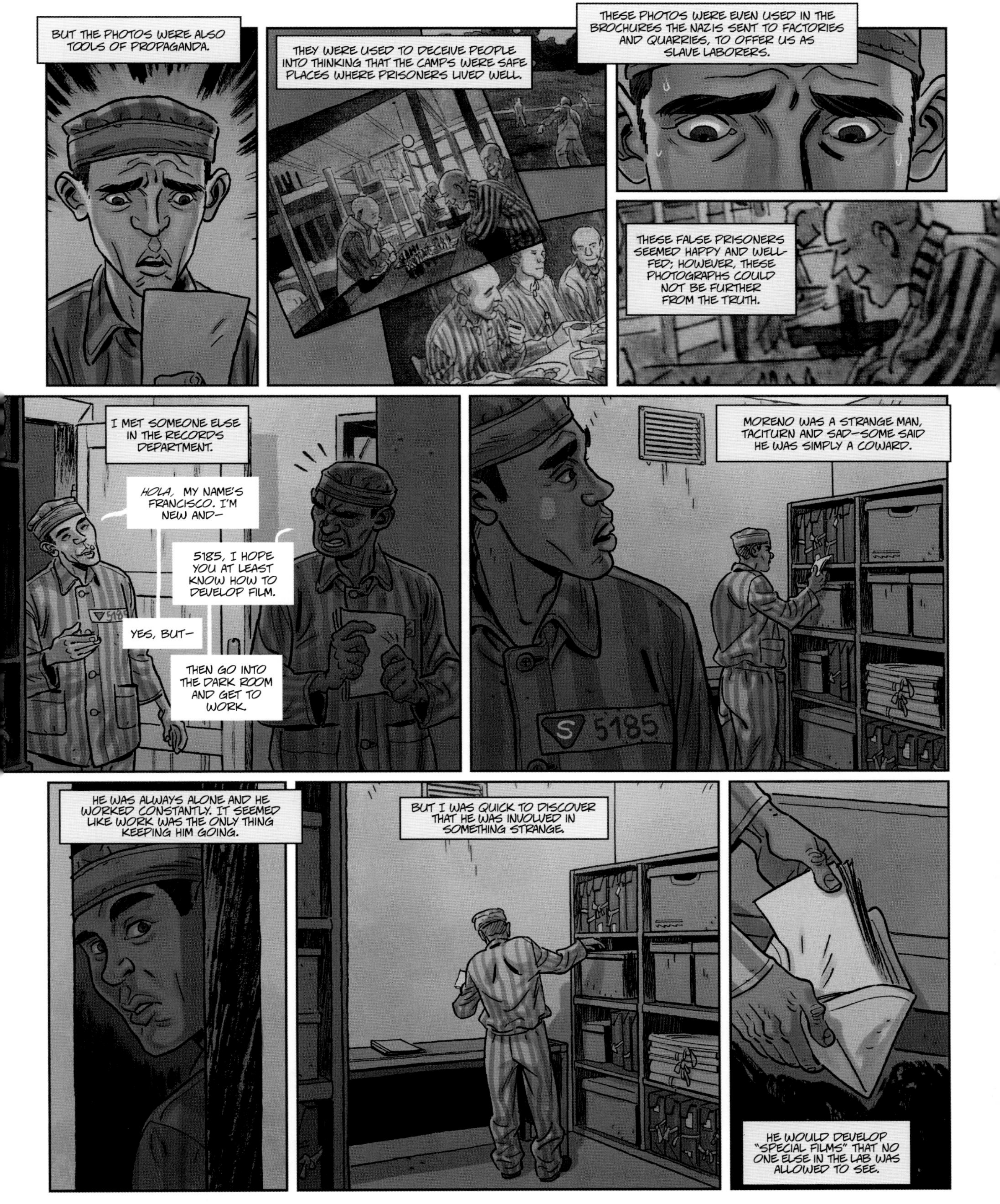
BUT THE PHOTOS WERE ALSO TOOLS OF PROPAGANDA.
THEY WERE USED TO DECEIVE PEOPLE INTO THINKING THAT THE CAMPS WERE SAFE PLACES WHERE PRISONERS LIVED WELL.
THESE PHOTOS WERE EVEN USED IN THE BROCHURES THE NAZIS SENT TO FACTORIES AND QUARRIES, TO OFFER US AS SLAVE LABORERS.
THESE FALSE PRISONERS SEEMED HAPPY AND WELL-FED; HOWEVER, THESE PHOTOGRAPHS COULD NOT BE FURTHER FROM THE TRUTH.
I MET SOMEONE ELSE IN THE RECORDS DEPARTMENT.
HOLA, MY NAME'S FRANCISCO. I'M NEW AND–
5185, I HOPE YOU AT LEAST KNOW HOW TO DEVELOP FILM.
YES, BUT–
THEN GO INTO THE DARK ROOM AND GET TO WORK.
MORENO WAS A STRANGE MAN, TACITURN AND SAD—SOME SAID HE WAS SIMPLY A COWARD.
S 5185
HE WAS ALWAYS ALONE AND HE WORKED CONSTANTLY. IT SEEMED LIKE WORK WAS THE ONLY THING KEEPING HIM GOING.
BUT I WAS QUICK TO DISCOVER THAT HE WAS INVOLVED IN SOMETHING STRANGE.
HE WOULD DEVELOP "SPECIAL FILMS" THAT NO ONE ELSE IN THE LAB WAS ALLOWED TO SEE.

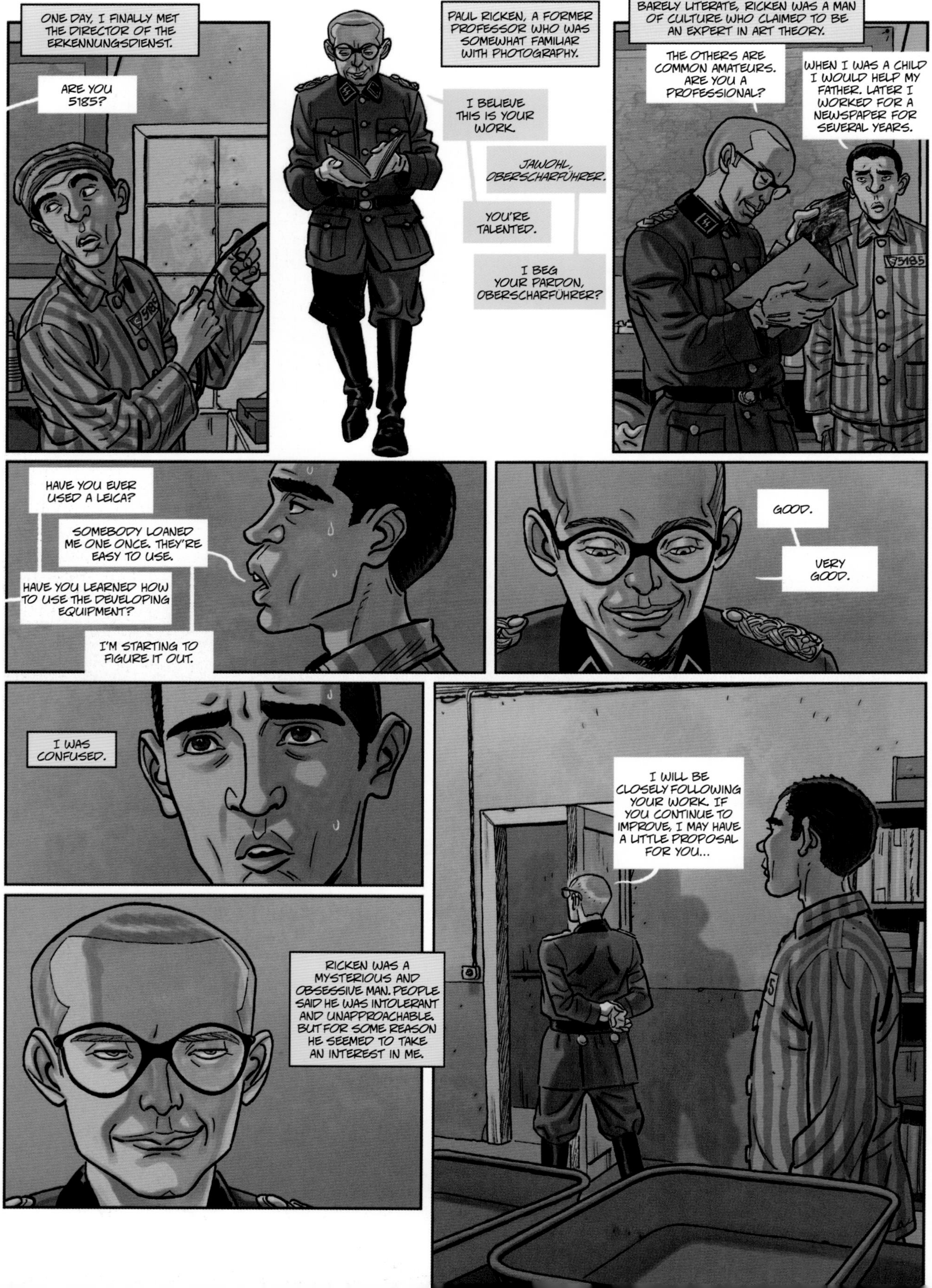
ONE DAY, I FINALLY MET THE DIRECTOR OF THE ERKENNUNGSDIENST.
ARE YOU 5185?
PAUL RICKEN, A FORMER PROFESSOR WHO WAS SOMEWHAT FAMILIAR WITH PHOTOGRAPHY.
I BELIEVE THIS IS YOUR WORK.
JAWOHL, OBERSCHARFÜHRER.
YOU'RE TALENTED.
I BEG YOUR PARDON, OBERSCHARFÜHRER?
COMPARED TO THE SS, WHO WERE BARELY LITERATE, RICKEN WAS A MAN OF CULTURE WHO CLAIMED TO BE AN EXPERT IN ART THEORY.
THE OTHERS ARE COMMON AMATEURS. ARE YOU A PROFESSIONAL?
WHEN I WAS A CHILD I WOULD HELP MY FATHER. LATER I WORKED FOR A NEWSPAPER FOR SEVERAL YEARS.
5185
HAVE YOU EVER USED A LEICA?
SOMEBODY LOANED ME ONE ONCE. THEY'RE EASY TO USE.
HAVE YOU LEARNED HOW TO USE THE DEVELOPING EQUIPMENT?
I'M STARTING TO FIGURE IT OUT.
GOOD.
VERY GOOD.
I WAS CONFUSED.
I WILL BE CLOSELY FOLLOWING YOUR WORK. IF YOU CONTINUE TO IMPROVE, I MAY HAVE A LITTLE PROPOSAL FOR YOU...
RICKEN WAS A MYSTERIOUS AND OBSESSIVE MAN. PEOPLE SAID HE WAS INTOLERANT AND UNAPPROACHABLE. BUT FOR SOME REASON HE SEEMED TO TAKE AN INTEREST IN ME.

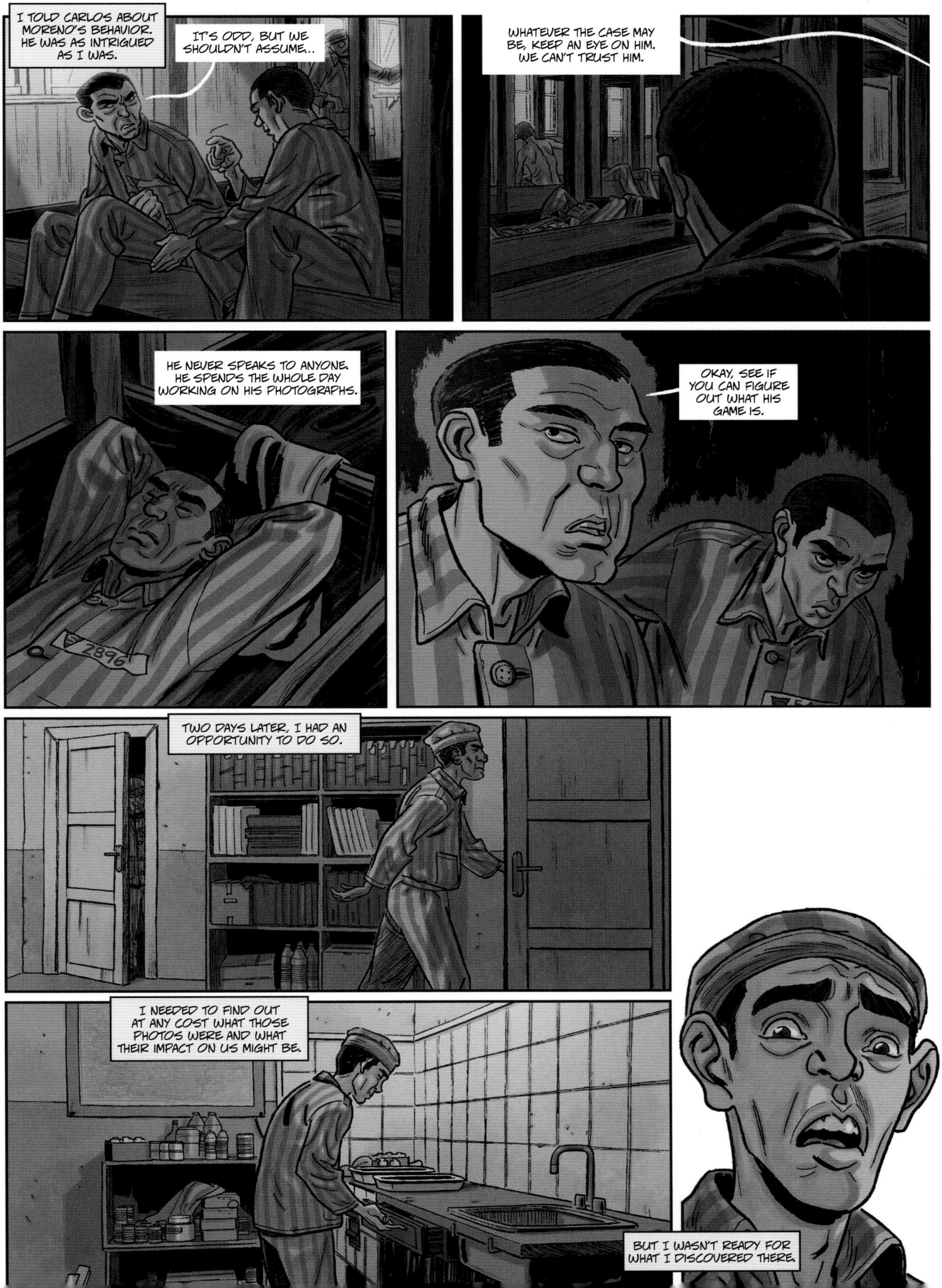
I TOLD CARLOS ABOUT MORENO'S BEHAVIOR. HE WAS AS INTRIGUED AS I WAS.
IT'S ODD, BUT WE SHOULDN'T ASSUME...
WHATEVER THE CASE MAY BE, KEEP AN EYE ON HIM. WE CAN'T TRUST HIM.
HE NEVER SPEAKS TO ANYONE. HE SPENDS THE WHOLE DAY WORKING ON HIS PHOTOGRAPHS.
2896
OKAY, SEE IF YOU CAN FIGURE OUT WHAT HIS GAME IS.
TWO DAYS LATER, I HAD AN OPPORTUNITY TO DO SO.
I NEEDED TO FIND OUT AT ANY COST WHAT THOSE PHOTOS WERE AND WHAT THEIR IMPACT ON US MIGHT BE.
BUT I WASN'T READY FOR WHAT I DISCOVERED THERE.

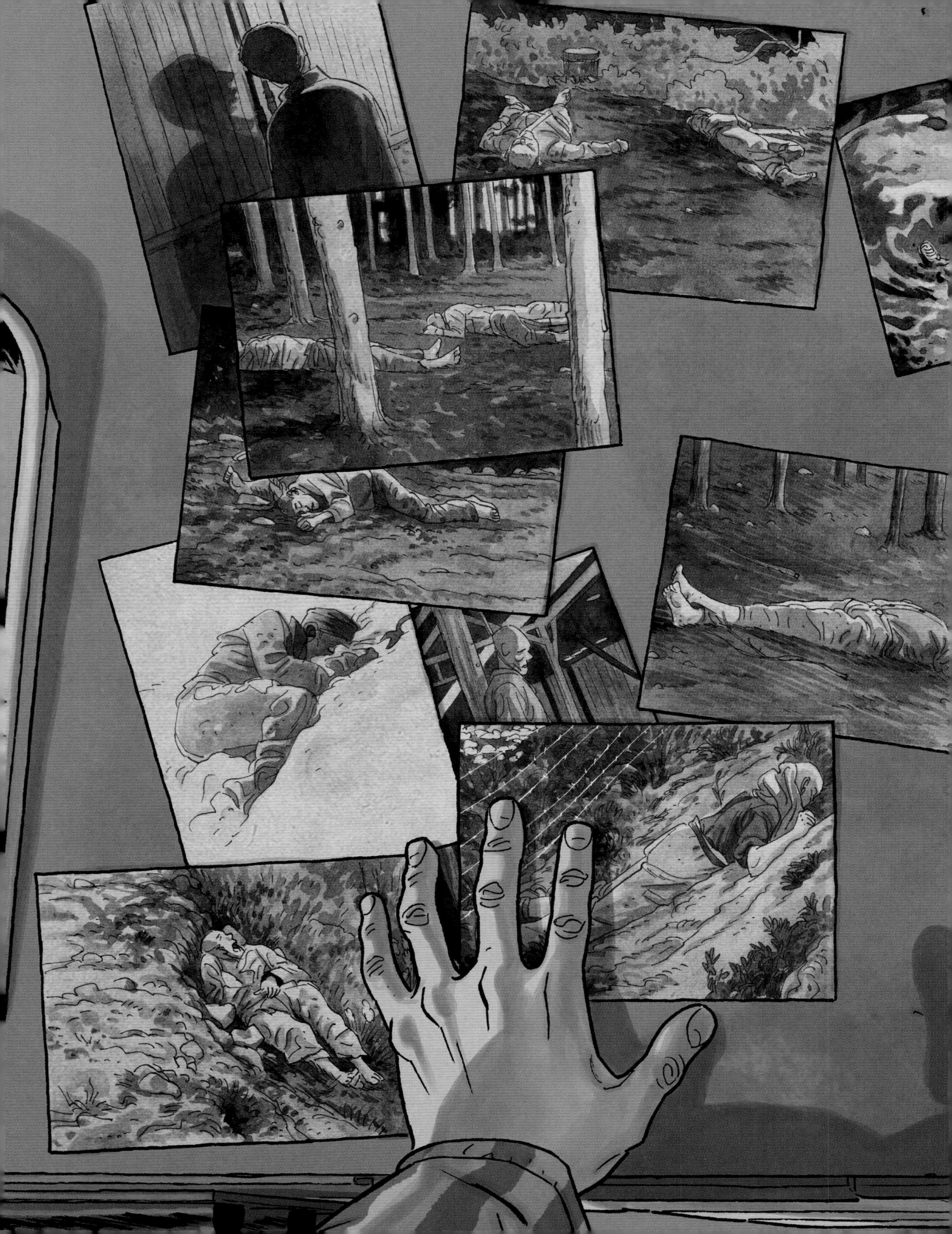

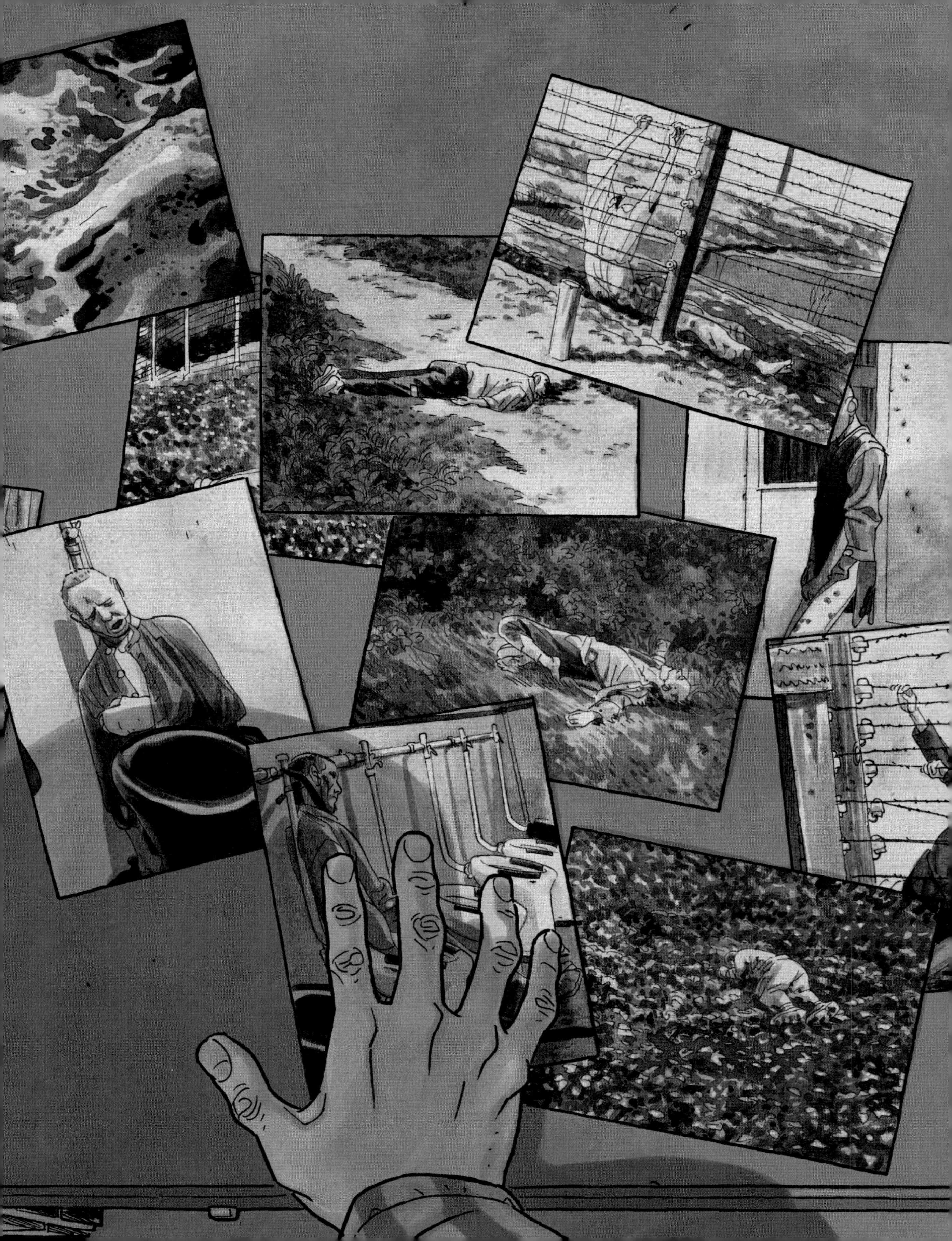

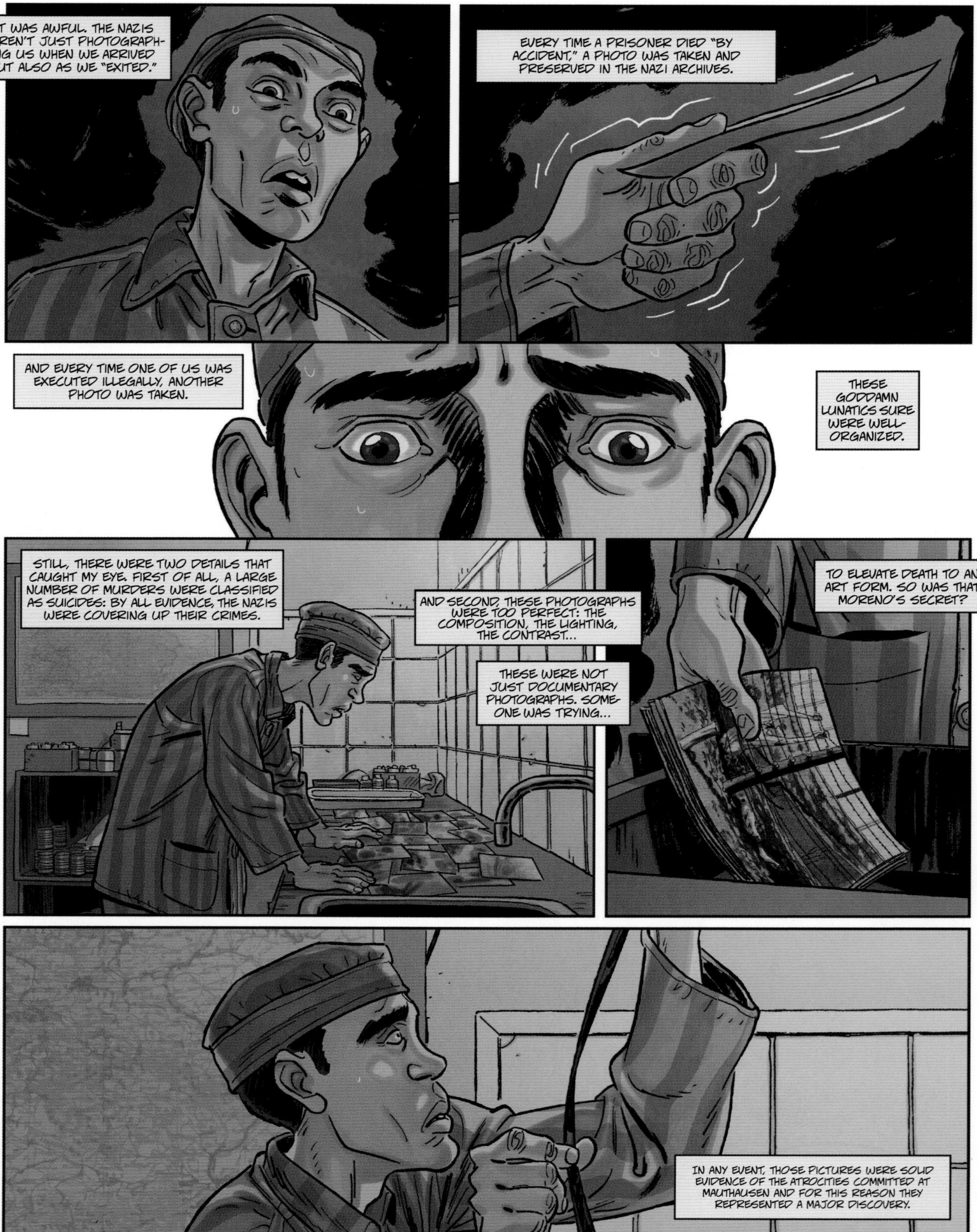
IT WAS AWFUL. THE NAZIS WEREN'T JUST PHOTOGRAPHING US WHEN WE ARRIVED BUT ALSO AS WE "EXITED."
EVERY TIME A PRISONER DIED "BY ACCIDENT," A PHOTO WAS TAKEN AND PRESERVED IN THE NAZI ARCHIVES.
AND EVERY TIME ONE OF US WAS EXECUTED ILLEGALLY, ANOTHER PHOTO WAS TAKEN.
THESE GODDAMN LUNATICS SURE WERE WELL-ORGANIZED.
STILL, THERE WERE TWO DETAILS THAT CAUGHT MY EYE. FIRST OF ALL, A LARGE NUMBER OF MURDERS WERE CLASSIFIED AS SUICIDES: BY ALL EVIDENCE, THE NAZIS WERE COVERING UP THEIR CRIMES.
AND SECOND, THESE PHOTOGRAPHS WERE TOO PERFECT: THE COMPOSITION, THE LIGHTING, THE CONTRAST...
THESE WERE NOT JUST DOCUMENTARY PHOTOGRAPHS. SOMEONE WAS TRYING...
TO ELEVATE DEATH TO AN ART FORM. SO WAS THAT MORENO'S SECRET?
IN ANY EVENT, THOSE PICTURES WERE SOLID EVIDENCE OF THE ATROCITIES COMMITTED AT MAUTHAUSEN AND FOR THIS REASON THEY REPRESENTED A MAJOR DISCOVERY.

I TRIED TO REMEMBER WHY I HAD WANTED TO BECOME A PHOTOGRAPHER.

SURE, PHOTOGRAPHY HAD BEEN A FUN HOBBY WHEN I WAS A KID.

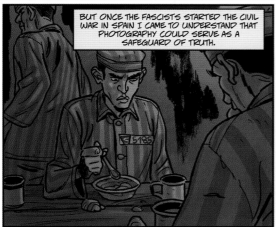

BUT ONCE THE FASCISTS STARTED THE CIVIL WAR IN SPAIN I CAME TO UNDERSTAND THAT PHOTOGRAPHY COULD SERVE AS A SAFEGUARD OF TRUTH.

EVEN IF THESE PEOPLE HAD DIED, THEIR TRUTH AND THEIR MEMORY WOULD REMAIN RECORDED ON MY FILM.

BREAK IT UP! BACK TO YOUR BARRACKS, YOU COMMUNIST SHITS!

BUT AT MAUTHAUSEN, PHOTOGRAPHY WAS A LIE. WE WEREN'T DYING BECAUSE OF OUR IDEALS. WE WERE DYING BECAUSE WE WERE NOTHING.

EVEN THOUGH THEY REPRESENTED A FLAGRANT LIE, THE PHOTOS I HAD FOUND COULD MAKE US IMMORTAL.

BECAUSE A PHOTO GRANTS YOU ETERNAL LIFE, EVEN IF YOU DIE AT MAUTHAUSEN.

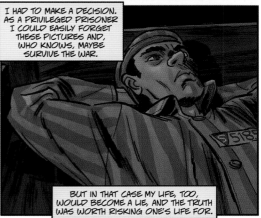

I HAD TO MAKE A DECISION. AS A PRIVILEGED PRISONER I COULD EASILY FORGET THESE PICTURES AND, WHO KNOWS, MAYBE SURVIVE THE WAR.

BUT IN THAT CASE MY LIFE, TOO, WOULD BECOME A LIE, AND THE TRUTH WAS WORTH RISKING ONE'S LIFE FOR.

I HAD MADE UP MY MIND.

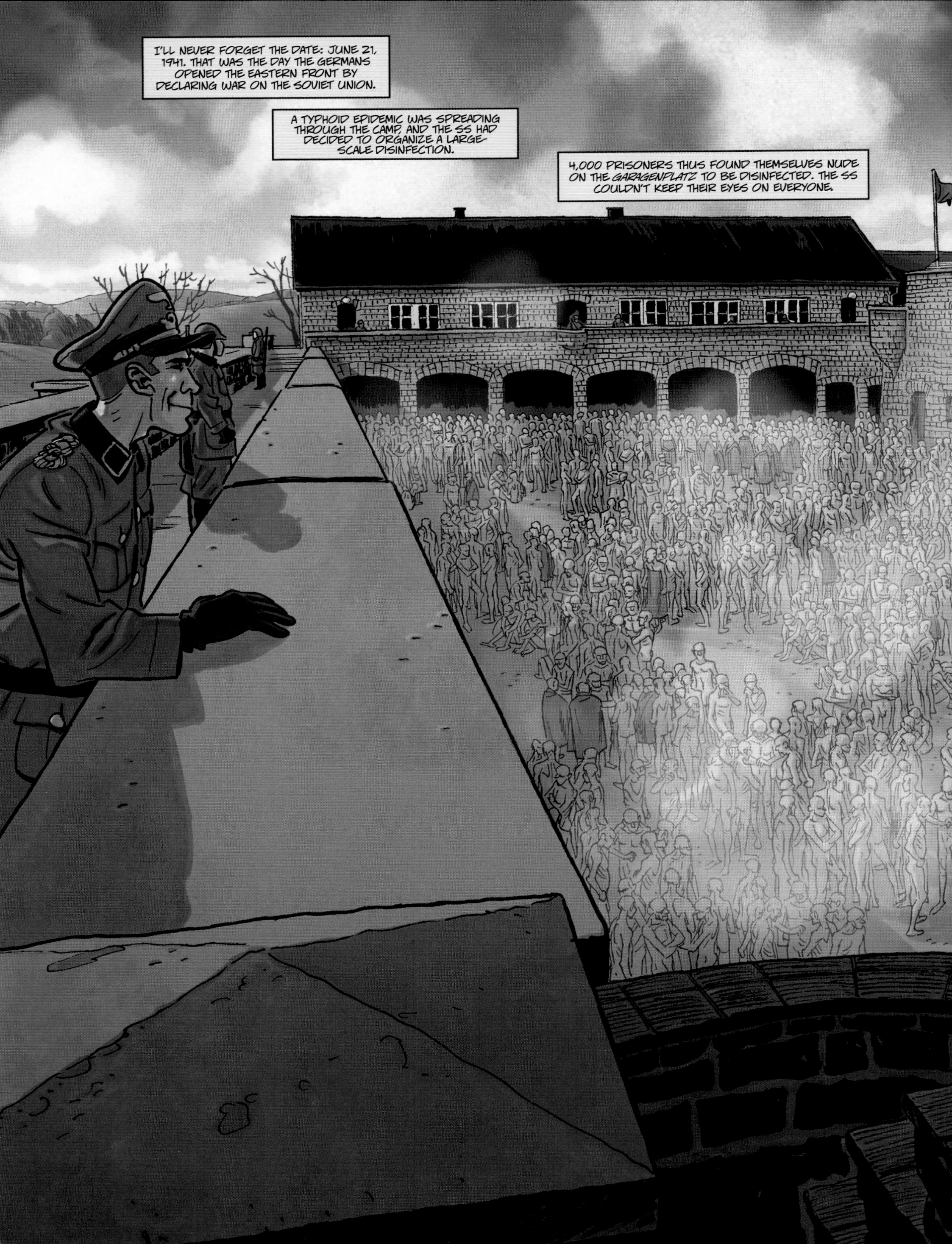
I'LL NEVER FORGET THE DATE: JUNE 21, 1941. THAT WAS THE DAY THE GERMANS OPENED THE EASTERN FRONT BY DECLARING WAR ON THE SOVIET UNION.
A TYPHOID EPIDEMIC WAS SPREADING THROUGH THE CAMP, AND THE SS HAD DECIDED TO ORGANIZE A LARGE-SCALE DISINFECTION.
4,000 PRISONERS THUS FOUND THEMSELVES NUDE ON THE *GARAGENPLATZ* TO BE DISINFECTED. THE SS COULDN'T KEEP THEIR EYES ON EVERYONE.

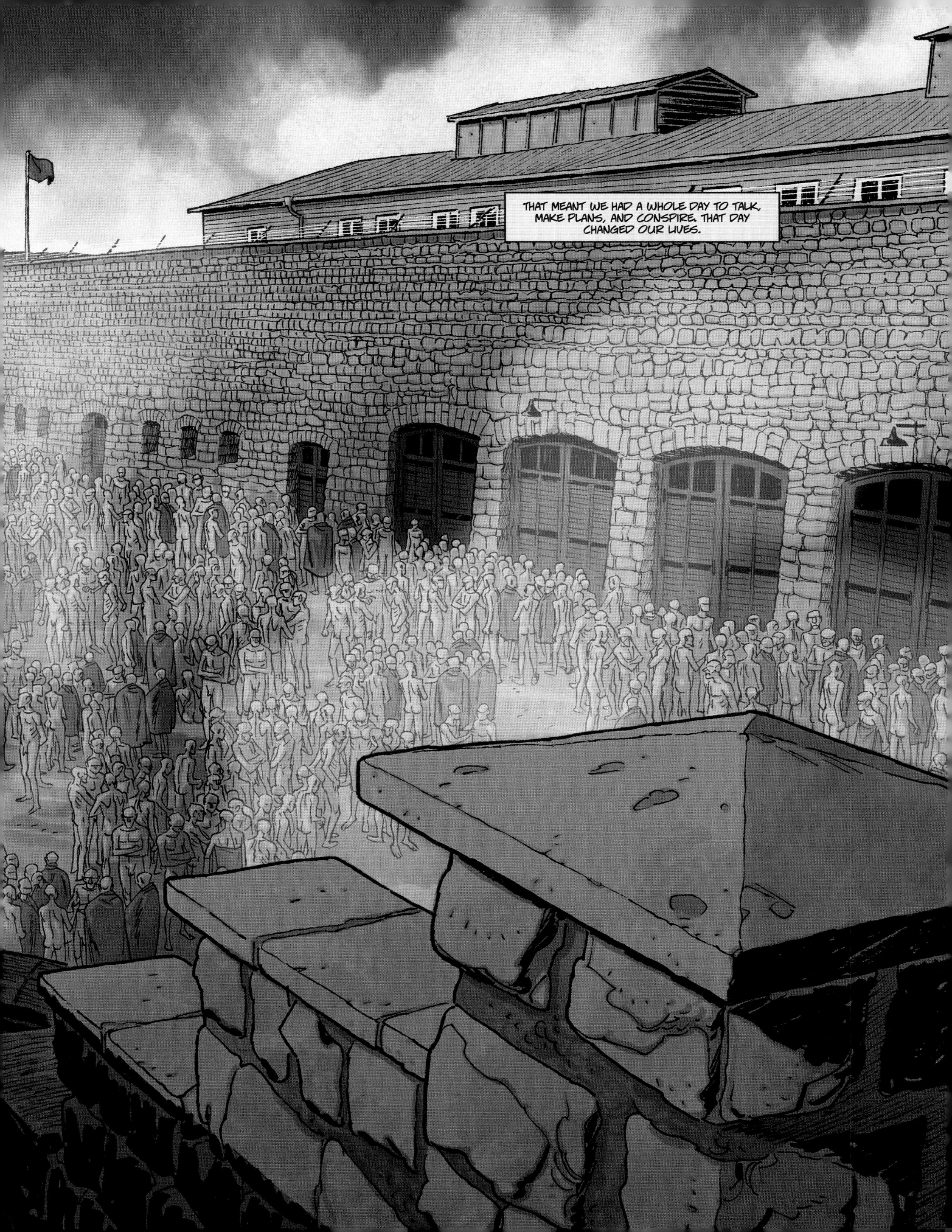
THAT MEANT WE HAD A WHOLE DAY TO TALK, MAKE PLANS, AND CONSPIRE. THAT DAY CHANGED OUR LIVES.

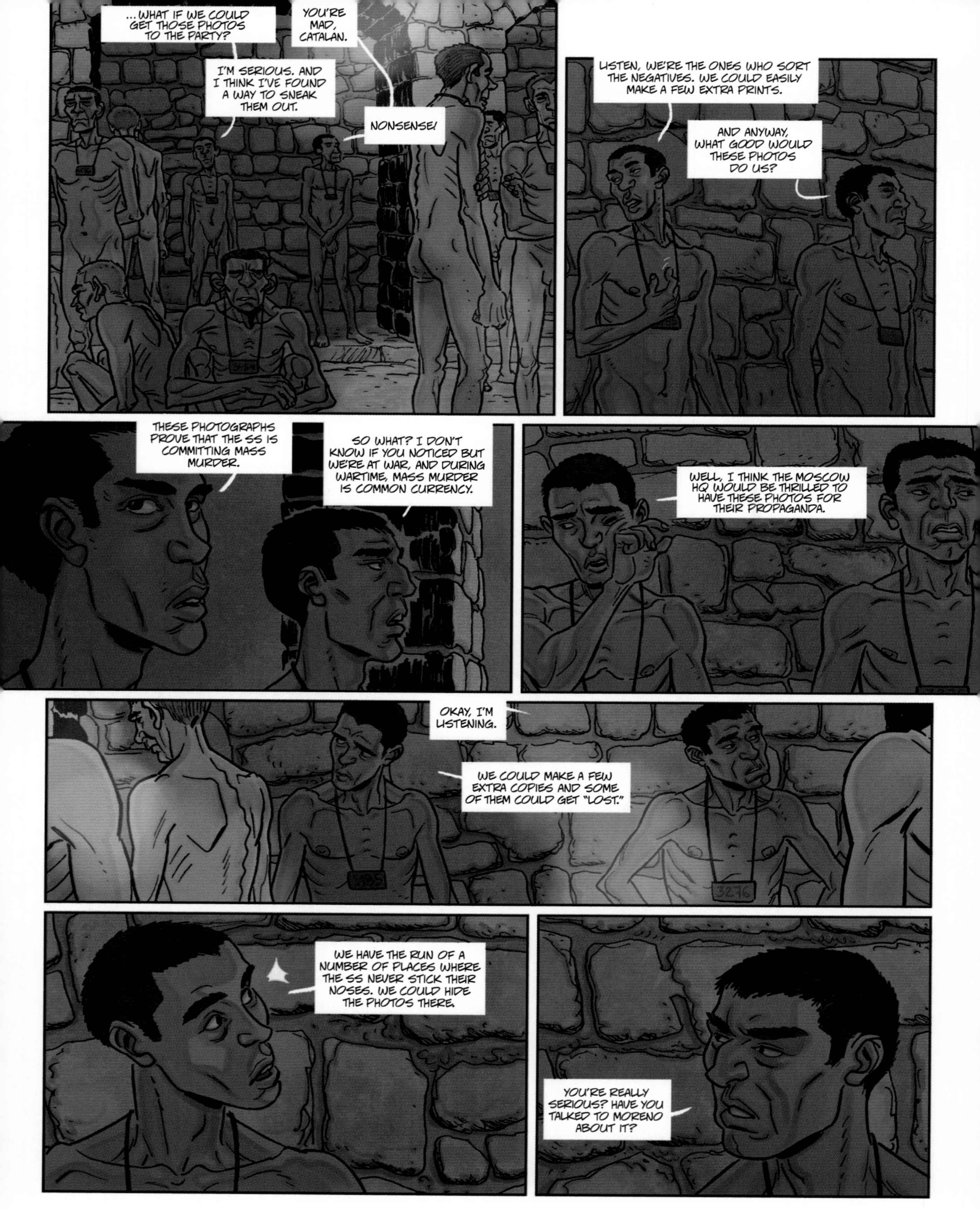

... WHAT IF WE COULD GET THOSE PHOTOS TO THE PARTY?
YOU'RE MAD, CATALAN.
I'M SERIOUS. AND I THINK I'VE FOUND A WAY TO SNEAK THEM OUT.
NONSENSE!
LISTEN, WE'RE THE ONES WHO SORT THE NEGATIVES. WE COULD EASILY MAKE A FEW EXTRA PRINTS.
AND ANYWAY, WHAT GOOD WOULD THESE PHOTOS DO US?
THESE PHOTOGRAPHS PROVE THAT THE SS IS COMMITTING MASS MURDER.
SO WHAT? I DON'T KNOW IF YOU NOTICED BUT WE'RE AT WAR, AND DURING WARTIME, MASS MURDER IS COMMON CURRENCY.
WELL, I THINK THE MOSCOW HQ WOULD BE THRILLED TO HAVE THESE PHOTOS FOR THEIR PROPAGANDA.
OKAY, I'M LISTENING.
WE COULD MAKE A FEW EXTRA COPIES AND SOME OF THEM COULD GET "LOST."
WE HAVE THE RUN OF A NUMBER OF PLACES WHERE THE SS NEVER STICK THEIR NOSES. WE COULD HIDE THE PHOTOS THERE.
YOU'RE REALLY SERIOUS? HAVE YOU TALKED TO MORENO ABOUT IT?

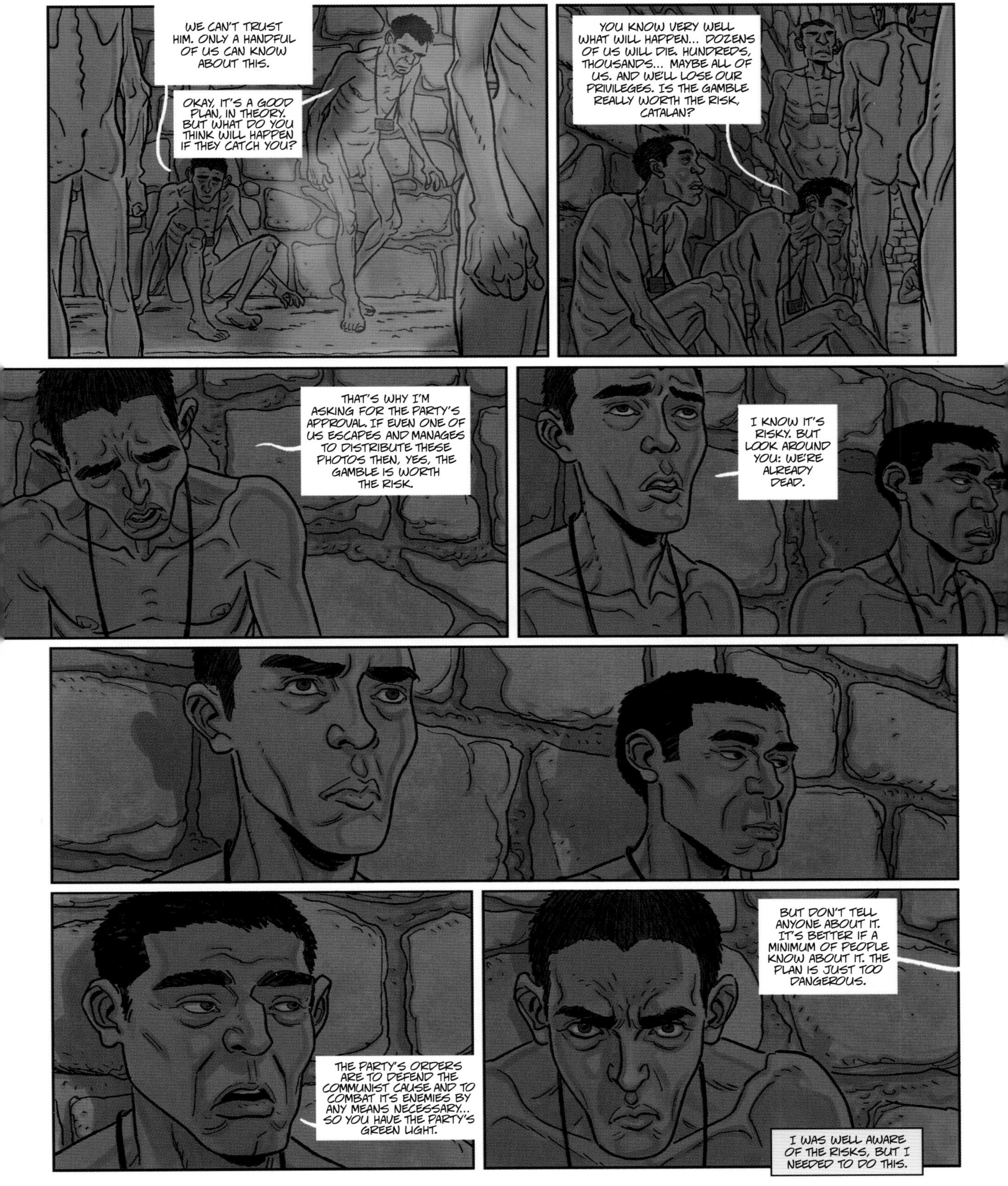
WE CAN'T TRUST HIM. ONLY A HANDFUL OF US CAN KNOW ABOUT THIS.
OKAY, IT'S A GOOD PLAN, IN THEORY. BUT WHAT DO YOU THINK WILL HAPPEN IF THEY CATCH YOU?
YOU KNOW VERY WELL WHAT WILL HAPPEN... DOZENS OF US WILL DIE. HUNDREDS, THOUSANDS... MAYBE ALL OF US. AND WE'LL LOSE OUR PRIVILEGES. IS THE GAMBLE REALLY WORTH THE RISK, CATALAN?
THAT'S WHY I'M ASKING FOR THE PARTY'S APPROVAL. IF EVEN ONE OF US ESCAPES AND MANAGES TO DISTRIBUTE THESE PHOTOS THEN, YES, THE GAMBLE IS WORTH THE RISK.
I KNOW IT'S RISKY. BUT LOOK AROUND YOU: WE'RE ALREADY DEAD.
THE PARTY'S ORDERS ARE TO DEFEND THE COMMUNIST CAUSE AND TO COMBAT IT'S ENEMIES BY ANY MEANS NECESSARY... SO YOU HAVE THE PARTY'S GREEN LIGHT.
BUT DON'T TELL ANYONE ABOUT IT. IT'S BETTER IF A MINIMUM OF PEOPLE KNOW ABOUT IT. THE PLAN IS JUST TOO DANGEROUS.
I WAS WELL AWARE OF THE RISKS, BUT I NEEDED TO DO THIS.

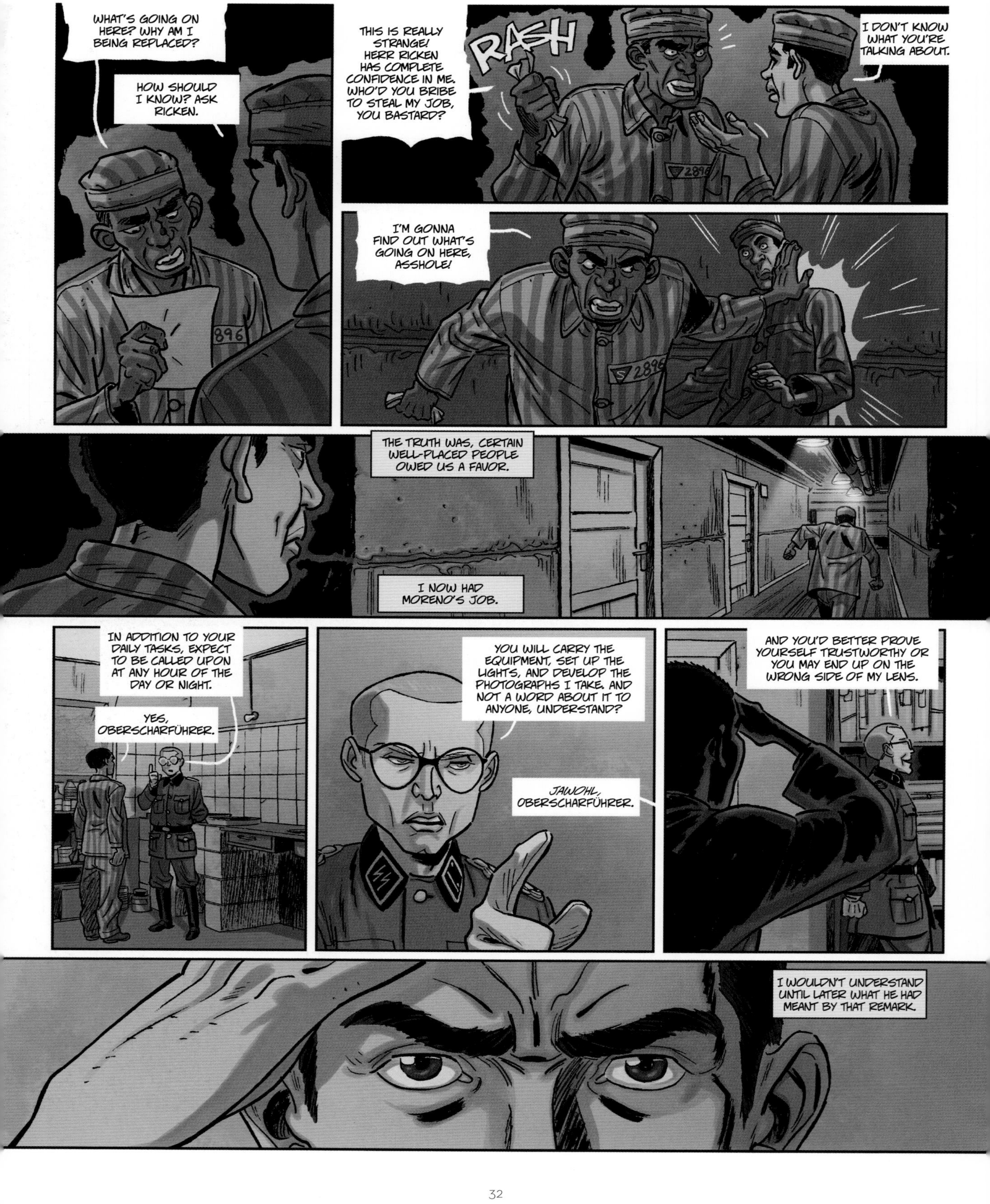
WHAT'S GOING ON HERE? WHY AM I BEING REPLACED?
HOW SHOULD I KNOW? ASK RICKEN.
THIS IS REALLY STRANGE! HERR RICKEN HAS COMPLETE CONFIDENCE IN ME. WHO'D YOU BRIBE TO STEAL MY JOB, YOU BASTARD?
RASH
I DON'T KNOW WHAT YOU'RE TALKING ABOUT.
I'M GONNA FIND OUT WHAT'S GOING ON HERE, ASSHOLE!
THE TRUTH WAS, CERTAIN WELL-PLACED PEOPLE OWED US A FAVOR.
I NOW HAD MORENO'S JOB.
IN ADDITION TO YOUR DAILY TASKS, EXPECT TO BE CALLED UPON AT ANY HOUR OF THE DAY OR NIGHT.
YES, OBERSCHARFÜHRER.
YOU WILL CARRY THE EQUIPMENT, SET UP THE LIGHTS, AND DEVELOP THE PHOTOGRAPHS I TAKE. AND NOT A WORD ABOUT IT TO ANYONE, UNDERSTAND?
JAWOHL, OBERSCHARFÜHRER.
AND YOU'D BETTER PROVE YOURSELF TRUSTWORTHY OR YOU MAY END UP ON THE WRONG SIDE OF MY LENS.
I WOULDN'T UNDERSTAND UNTIL LATER WHAT HE HAD MEANT BY THAT REMARK.

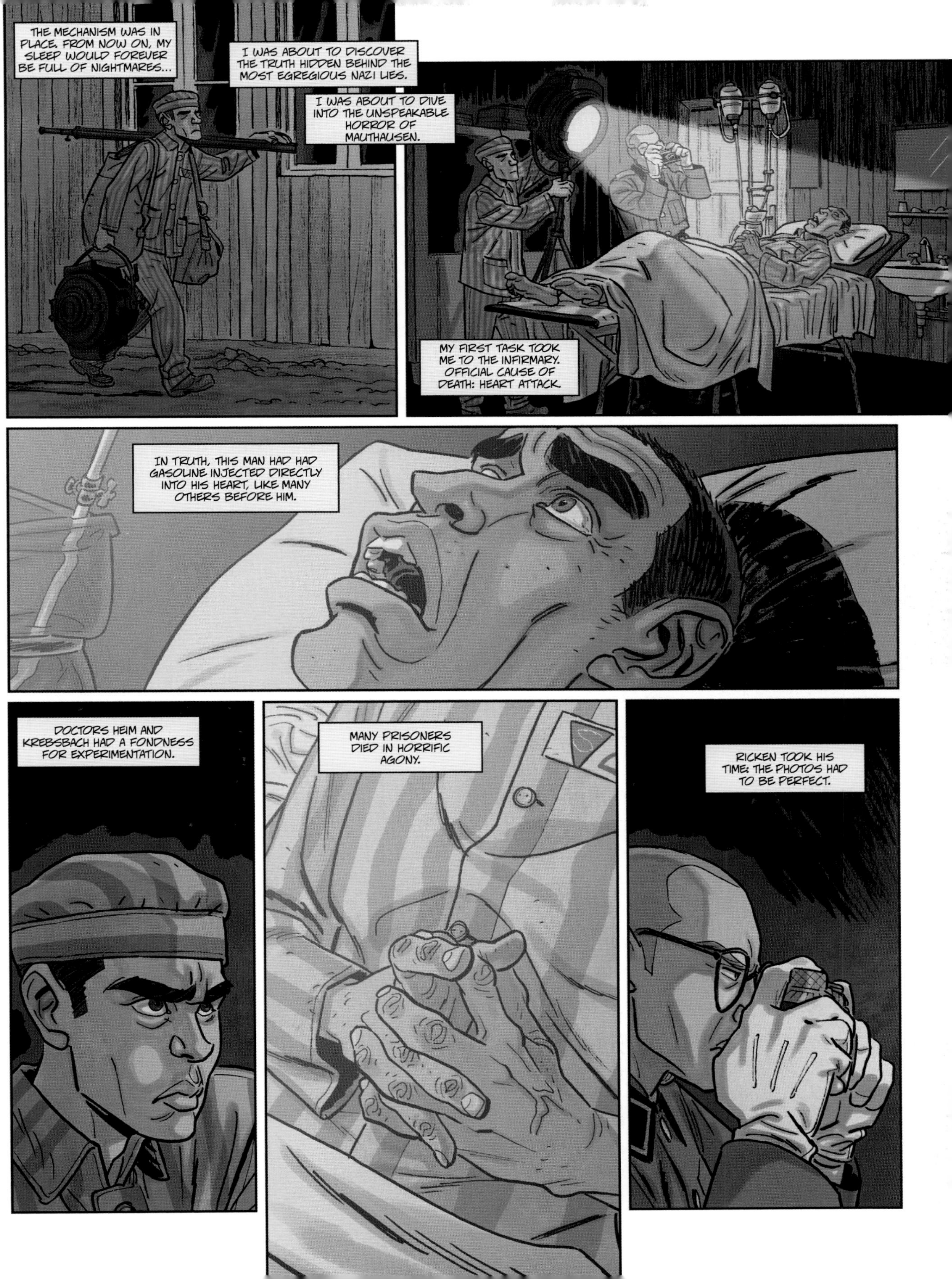
THE MECHANISM WAS IN PLACE. FROM NOW ON, MY SLEEP WOULD FOREVER BE FULL OF NIGHTMARES...
I WAS ABOUT TO DISCOVER THE TRUTH HIDDEN BEHIND THE MOST EGREGIOUS NAZI LIES.
I WAS ABOUT TO DIVE INTO THE UNSPEAKABLE HORROR OF MAUTHAUSEN.
MY FIRST TASK TOOK ME TO THE INFIRMARY. OFFICIAL CAUSE OF DEATH: HEART ATTACK.
IN TRUTH, THIS MAN HAD HAD GASOLINE INJECTED DIRECTLY INTO HIS HEART, LIKE MANY OTHERS BEFORE HIM.
DOCTORS HEIM AND KREBSBACH HAD A FONDNESS FOR EXPERIMENTATION.
MANY PRISONERS DIED IN HORRIFIC AGONY.
RICKEN TOOK HIS TIME: THE PHOTOS HAD TO BE PERFECT.

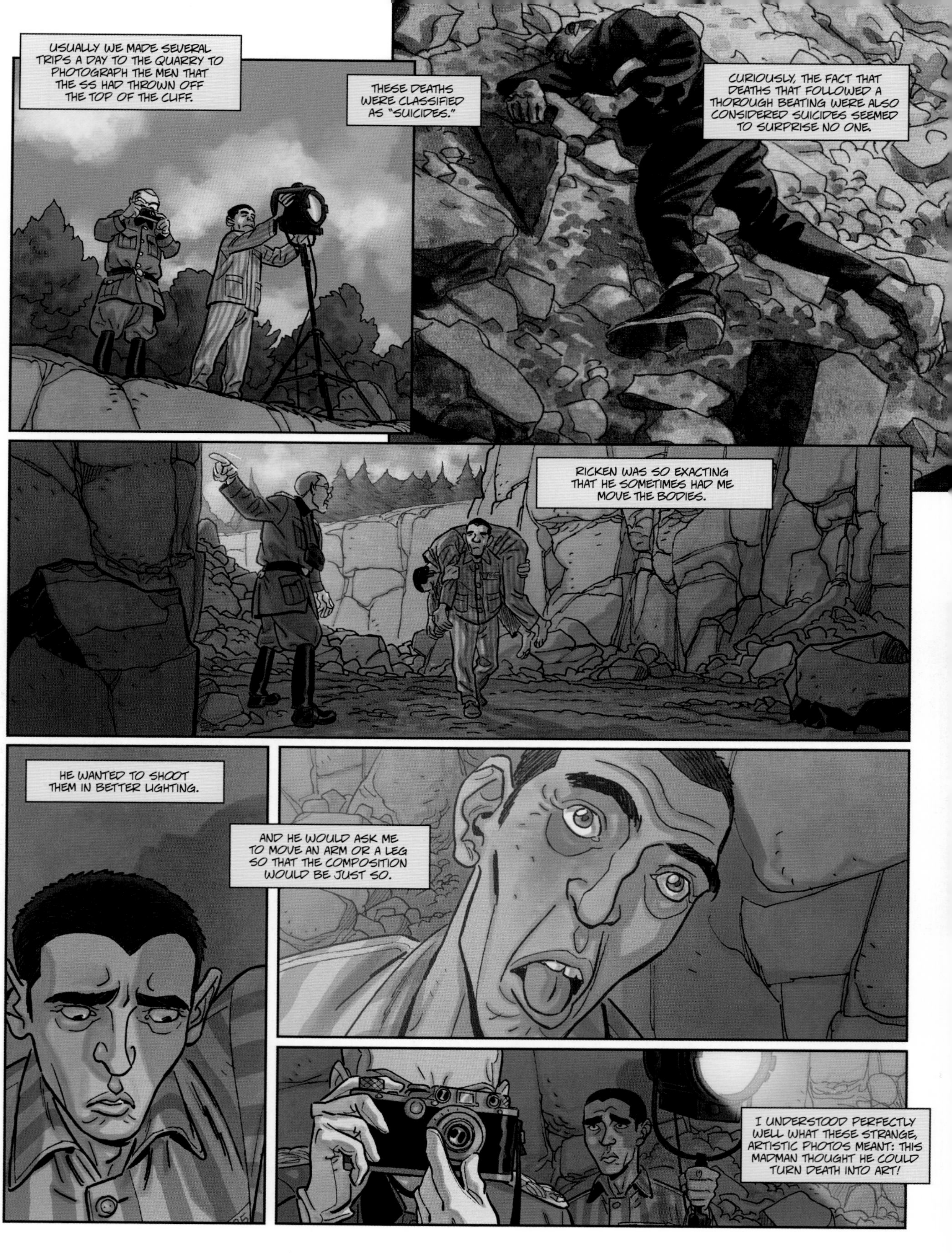
USUALLY WE MADE SEVERAL TRIPS A DAY TO THE QUARRY TO PHOTOGRAPH THE MEN THAT THE SS HAD THROWN OFF THE TOP OF THE CLIFF.
THESE DEATHS WERE CLASSIFIED AS "SUICIDES."
CURIOUSLY, THE FACT THAT DEATHS THAT FOLLOWED A THOROUGH BEATING WERE ALSO CONSIDERED SUICIDES SEEMED TO SURPRISE NO ONE.
RICKEN WAS SO EXACTING THAT HE SOMETIMES HAD ME MOVE THE BODIES.
HE WANTED TO SHOOT THEM IN BETTER LIGHTING.
AND HE WOULD ASK ME TO MOVE AN ARM OR A LEG SO THAT THE COMPOSITION WOULD BE JUST SO.
I UNDERSTOOD PERFECTLY WELL WHAT THESE STRANGE, ARTISTIC PHOTOS MEANT: THIS MADMAN THOUGHT HE COULD TURN DEATH INTO ART!

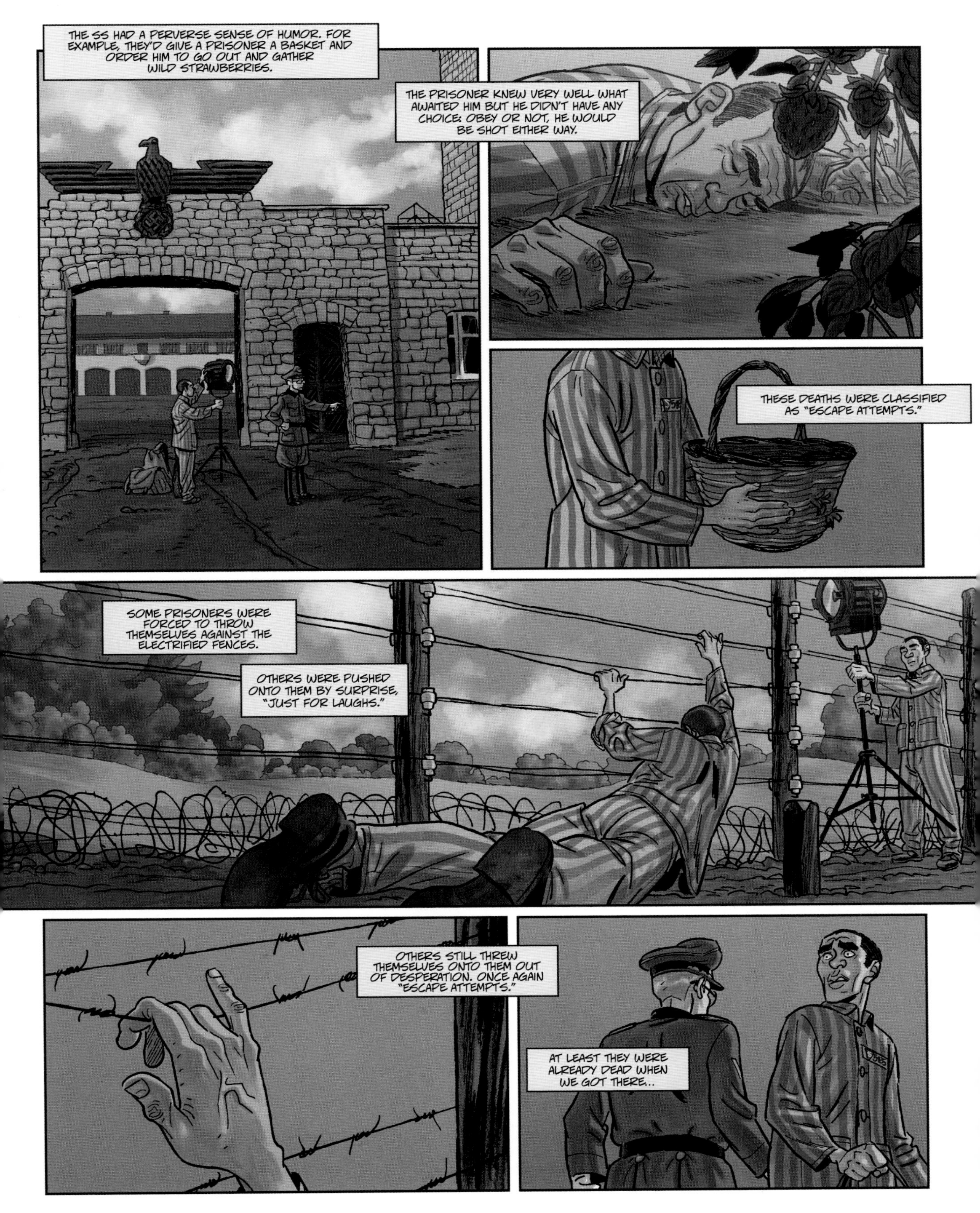
THE SS HAD A PERVERSE SENSE OF HUMOR. FOR EXAMPLE, THEY'D GIVE A PRISONER A BASKET AND ORDER HIM TO GO OUT AND GATHER WILD STRAWBERRIES.
THE PRISONER KNEW VERY WELL WHAT AWAITED HIM BUT HE DIDN'T HAVE ANY CHOICE: OBEY OR NOT, HE WOULD BE SHOT EITHER WAY.
THESE DEATHS WERE CLASSIFIED AS "ESCAPE ATTEMPTS."
SOME PRISONERS WERE FORCED TO THROW THEMSELVES AGAINST THE ELECTRIFIED FENCES.
OTHERS WERE PUSHED ONTO THEM BY SURPRISE, "JUST FOR LAUGHS."
OTHERS STILL THREW THEMSELVES ONTO THEM OUT OF DESPERATION. ONCE AGAIN "ESCAPE ATTEMPTS."
AT LEAST THEY WERE ALREADY DEAD WHEN WE GOT THERE...

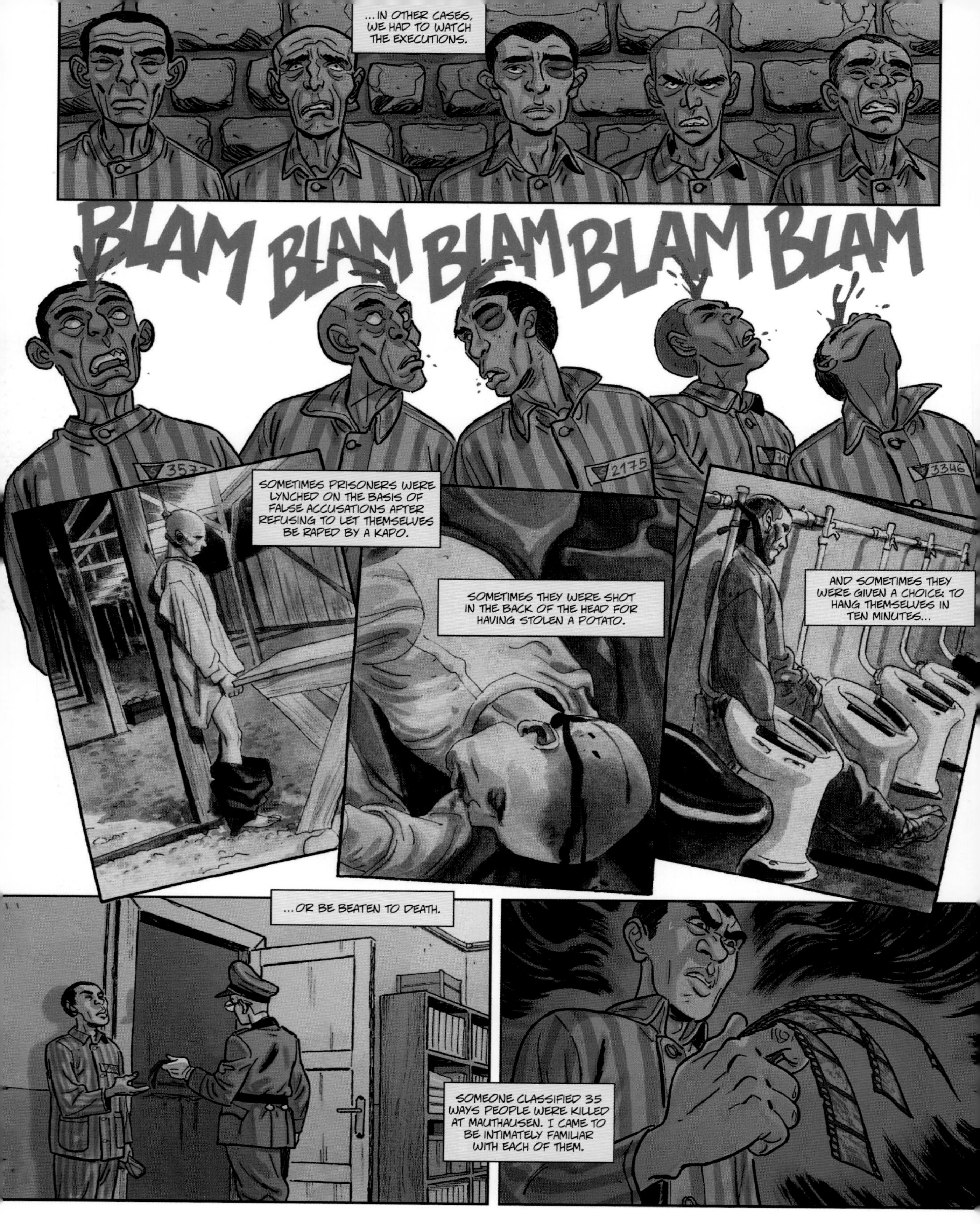
...IN OTHER CASES, WE HAD TO WATCH THE EXECUTIONS.
BLAM BLAM BLAM BLAM BLAM
3577
2175
3346
SOMETIMES PRISONERS WERE LYNCHED ON THE BASIS OF FALSE ACCUSATIONS AFTER REFUSING TO LET THEMSELVES BE RAPED BY A KAPO.
SOMETIMES THEY WERE SHOT IN THE BACK OF THE HEAD FOR HAVING STOLEN A POTATO.
AND SOMETIMES THEY WERE GIVEN A CHOICE: TO HANG THEMSELVES IN TEN MINUTES...
...OR BE BEATEN TO DEATH.
SOMEONE CLASSIFIED 35 WAYS PEOPLE WERE KILLED AT MAUTHAUSEN. I CAME TO BE INTIMATELY FAMILIAR WITH EACH OF THEM.

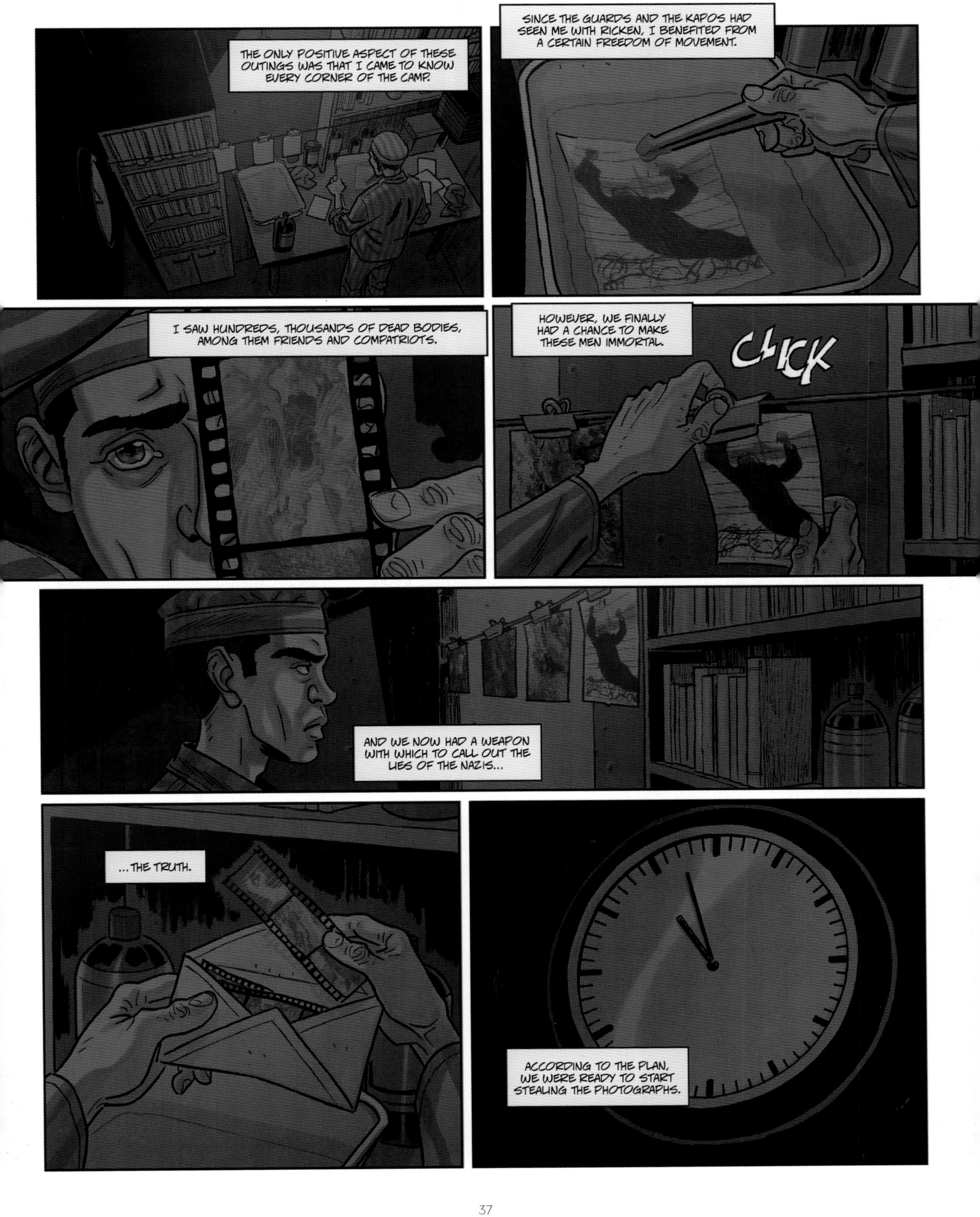
THE ONLY POSITIVE ASPECT OF THESE OUTINGS WAS THAT I CAME TO KNOW EVERY CORNER OF THE CAMP.
SINCE THE GUARDS AND THE KAPOS HAD SEEN ME WITH RICKEN, I BENEFITED FROM A CERTAIN FREEDOM OF MOVEMENT.
I SAW HUNDREDS, THOUSANDS OF DEAD BODIES, AMONG THEM FRIENDS AND COMPATRIOTS.
HOWEVER, WE FINALLY HAD A CHANCE TO MAKE THESE MEN IMMORTAL.
CLICK
AND WE NOW HAD A WEAPON WITH WHICH TO CALL OUT THE LIES OF THE NAZIS...
...THE TRUTH.
ACCORDING TO THE PLAN, WE WERE READY TO START STEALING THE PHOTOGRAPHS.

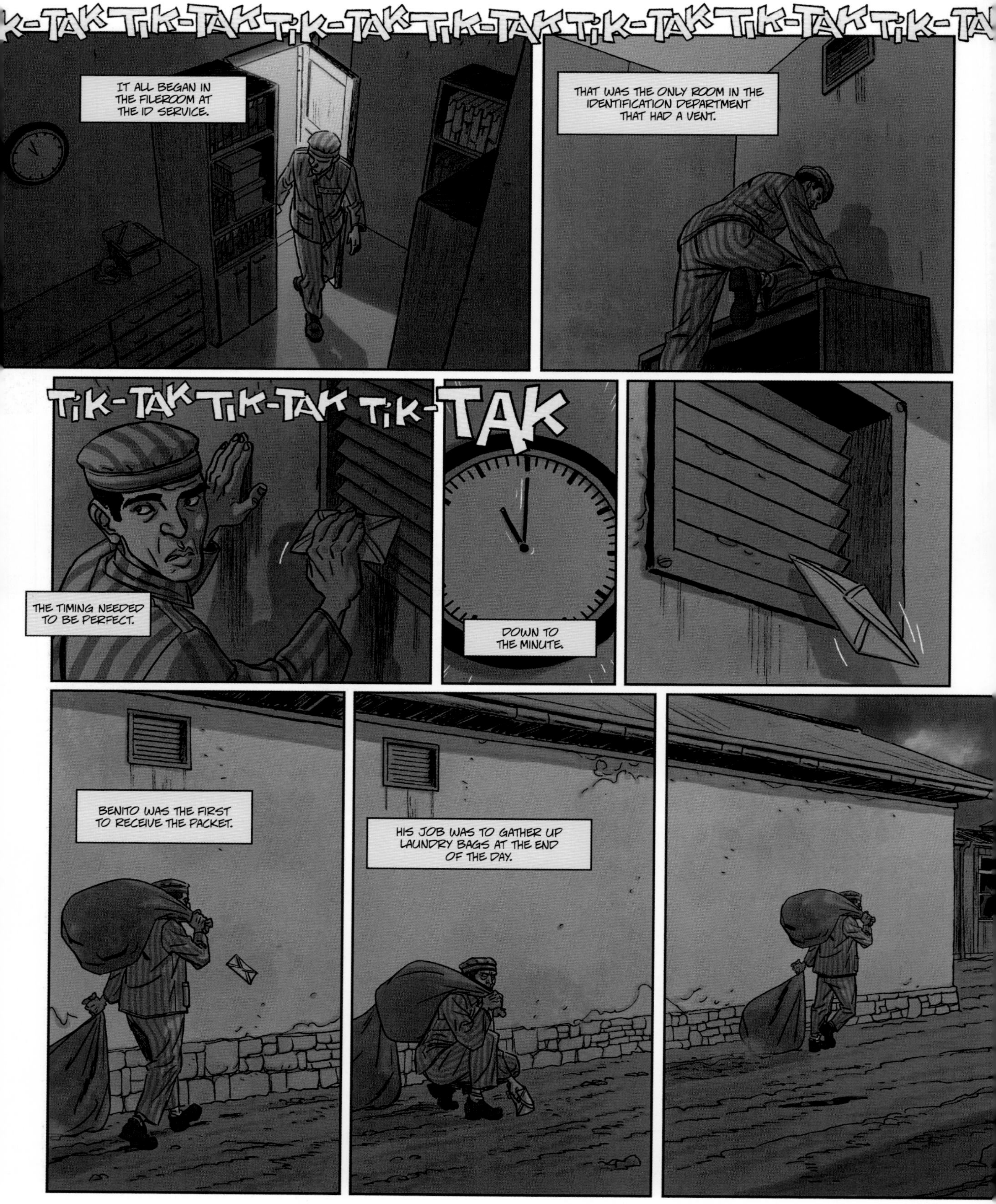

K-TAK TIK-TAK TIK-TAK TIK-TAK TIK-TAK TIK-TAK TIK-TA
IT ALL BEGAN IN THE FILEROOM AT THE ID SERVICE.
THAT WAS THE ONLY ROOM IN THE IDENTIFICATION DEPARTMENT THAT HAD A VENT.
TIK-TAK TIK-TAK TIK-TAK
THE TIMING NEEDED TO BE PERFECT.
DOWN TO THE MINUTE.
BENITO WAS THE FIRST TO RECEIVE THE PACKET.
HIS JOB WAS TO GATHER UP LAUNDRY BAGS AT THE END OF THE DAY.

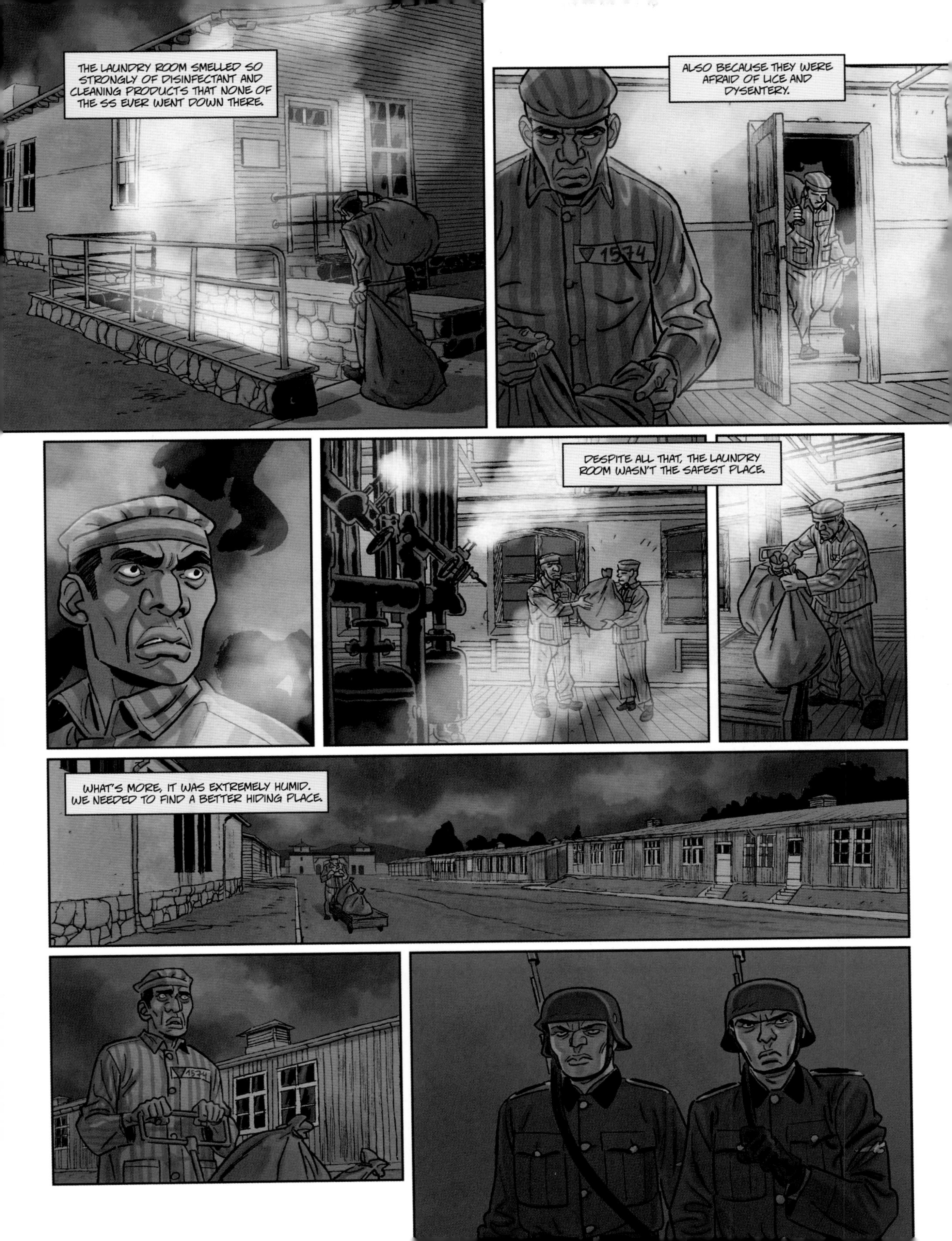
THE LAUNDRY ROOM SMELLED SO STRONGLY OF DISINFECTANT AND CLEANING PRODUCTS THAT NONE OF THE SS EVER WENT DOWN THERE.
ALSO BECAUSE THEY WERE AFRAID OF LICE AND DYSENTERY.
1574
DESPITE ALL THAT, THE LAUNDRY ROOM WASN'T THE SAFEST PLACE.
WHAT'S MORE, IT WAS EXTREMELY HUMID. WE NEEDED TO FIND A BETTER HIDING PLACE.
1574

THEN CAME STAGE TWO.

THE AWFUL CREMATORIUM: ANOTHER PLACE THE SS AVOIDED.

PRISCILIANO CAME TO GATHER THE CLOTHES TO DISINFECT THEM.

JOSEP KEPT THE NEGATIVES ON SITE ALL NIGHT LONG.

HIS JOB WAS TO OPERATE THE OVENS...

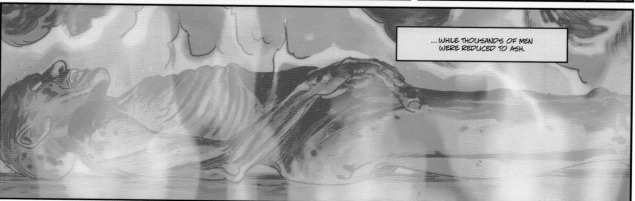

...WHILE THOUSANDS OF MEN WERE REDUCED TO ASH.

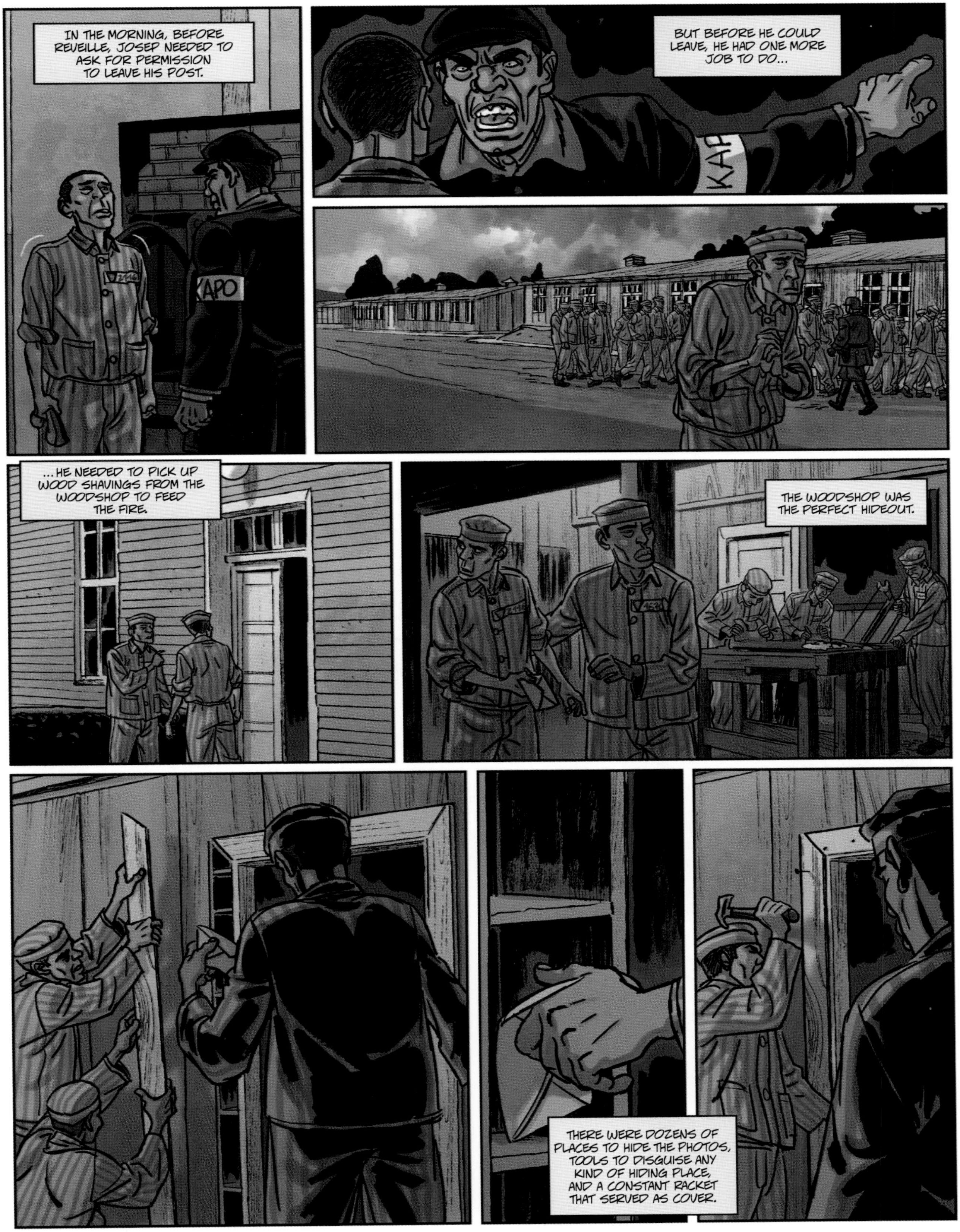
IN THE MORNING, BEFORE REVEILLE, JOSEP NEEDED TO ASK FOR PERMISSION TO LEAVE HIS POST.
KAPO
BUT BEFORE HE COULD LEAVE, HE HAD ONE MORE JOB TO DO...
...HE NEEDED TO PICK UP WOOD SHAVINGS FROM THE WOODSHOP TO FEED THE FIRE.
THE WOODSHOP WAS THE PERFECT HIDEOUT.
THERE WERE DOZENS OF PLACES TO HIDE THE PHOTOS, TOOLS TO DISGUISE ANY KIND OF HIDING PLACE, AND A CONSTANT RACKET THAT SERVED AS COVER.

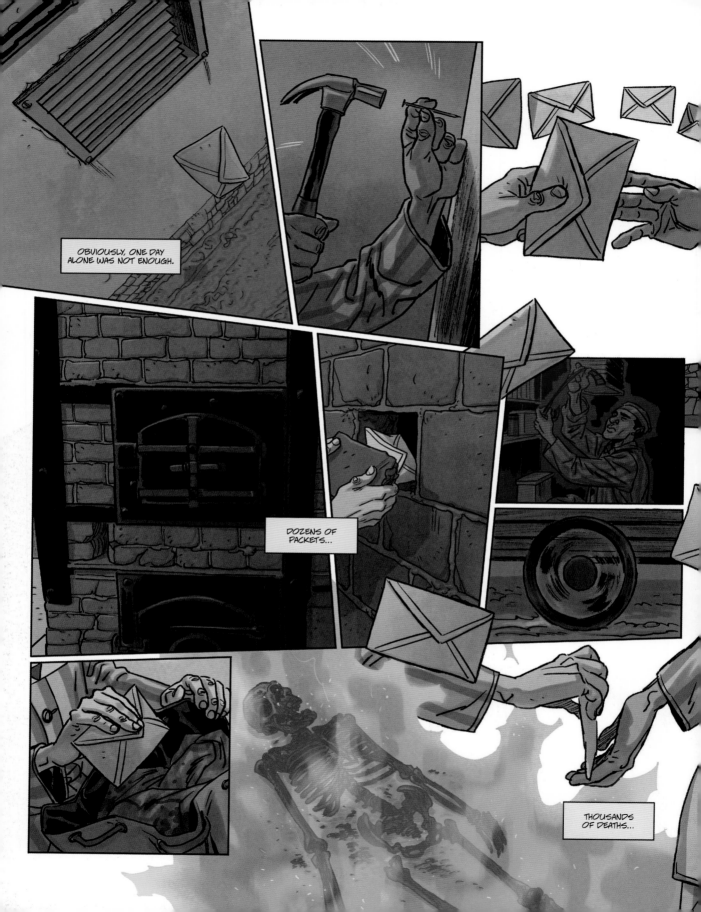

OBVIOUSLY, ONE DAY ALONE WAS NOT ENOUGH.

DOZENS OF PACKETS...

THOUSANDS OF DEATHS...

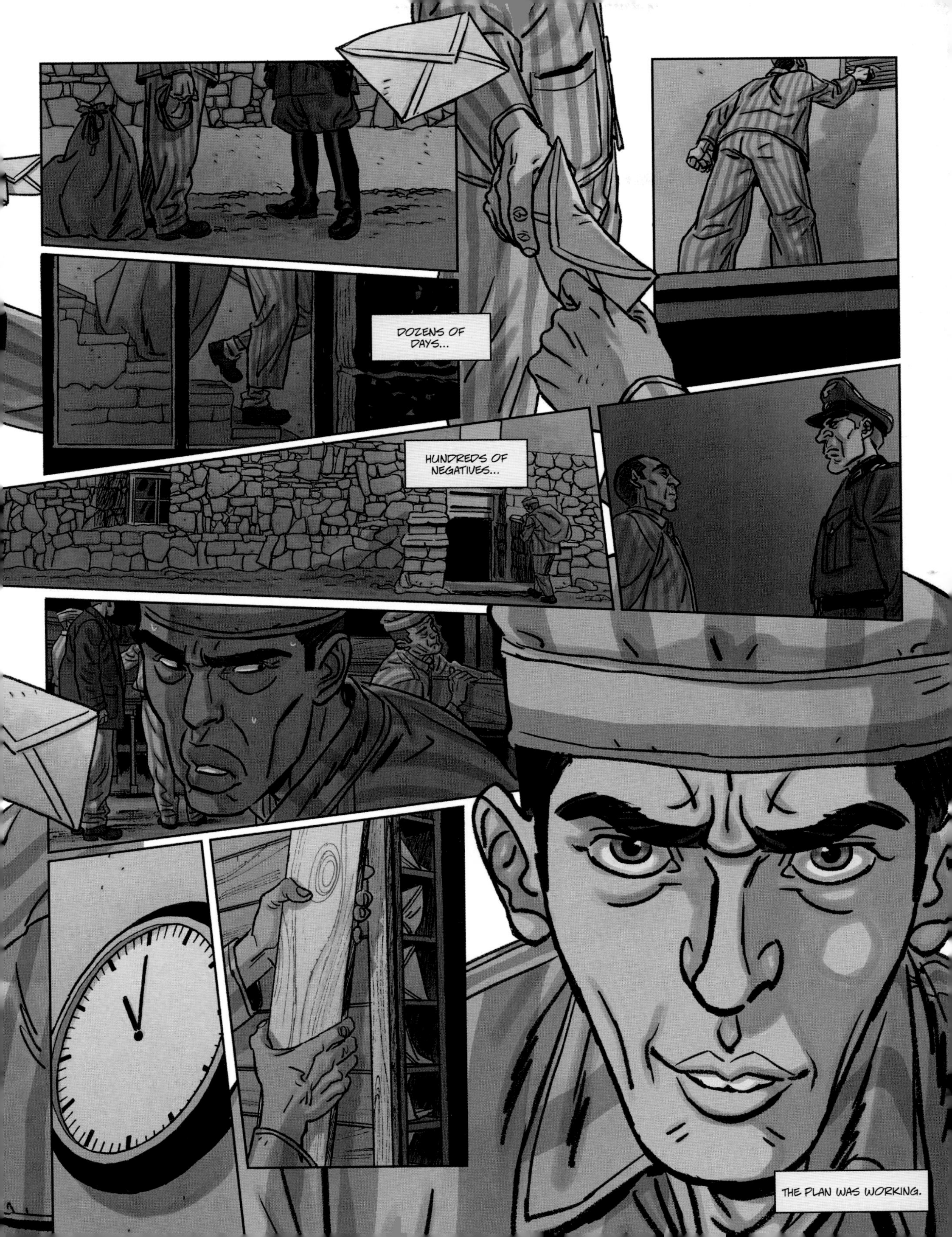
DOZENS OF DAYS...
HUNDREDS OF NEGATIVES...
THE PLAN WAS WORKING.

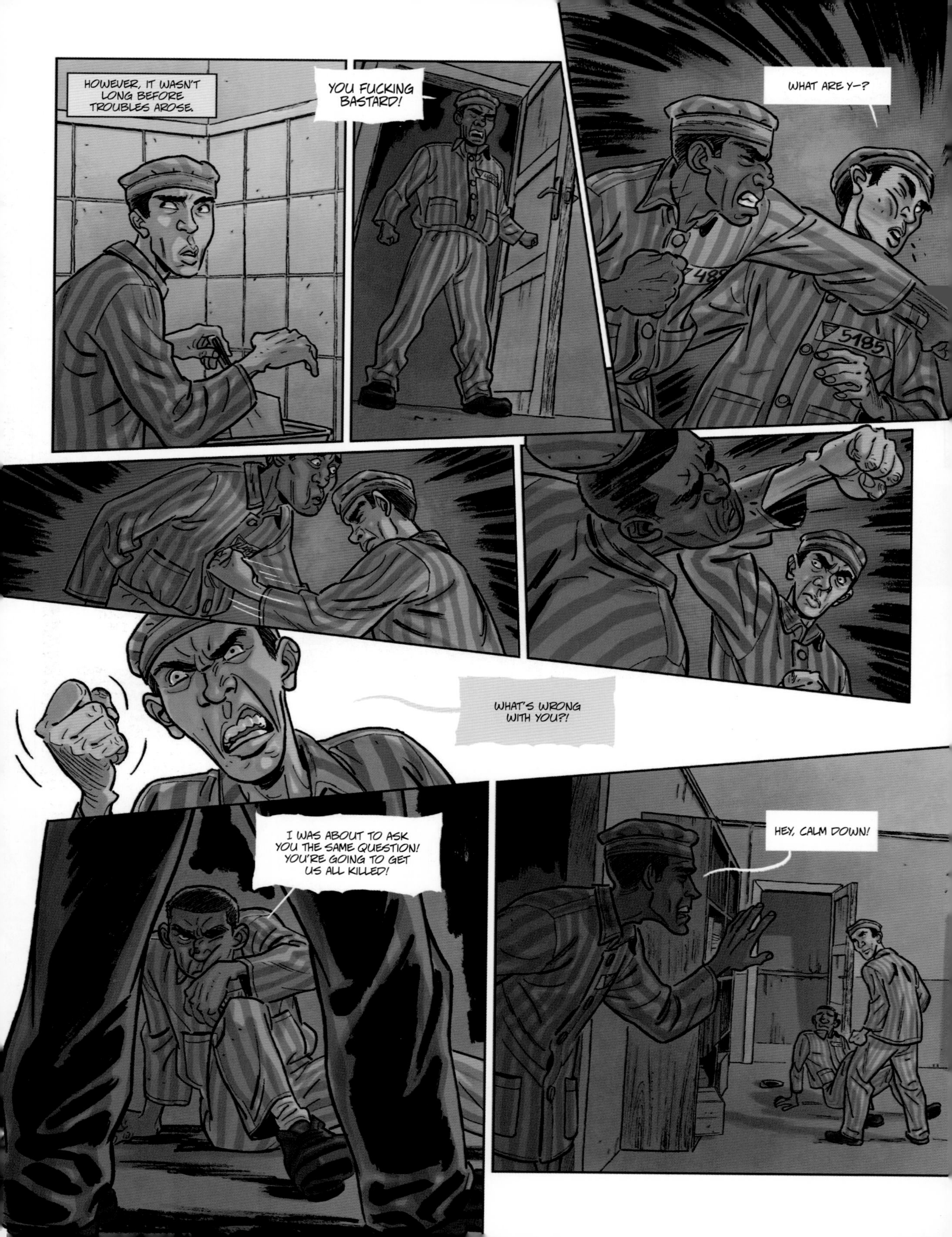
HOWEVER, IT WASN'T LONG BEFORE TROUBLES AROSE.
YOU FUCKING BASTARD!
WHAT ARE Y—?
5185
WHAT'S WRONG WITH YOU?!
I WAS ABOUT TO ASK YOU THE SAME QUESTION! YOU'RE GOING TO GET US ALL KILLED!
HEY, CALM DOWN!

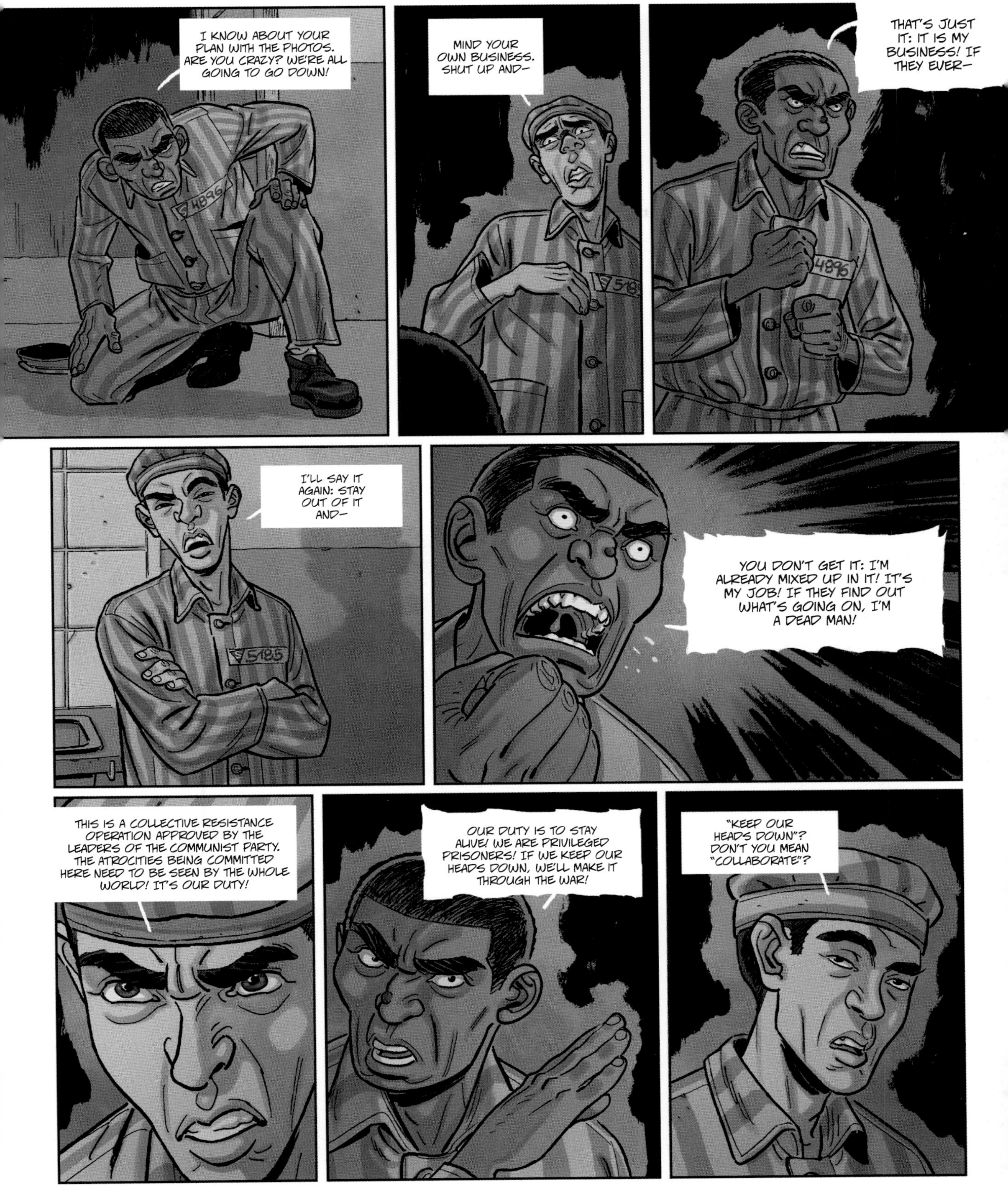

I KNOW ABOUT YOUR PLAN WITH THE PHOTOS. ARE YOU CRAZY? WE'RE ALL GOING TO GO DOWN!
MIND YOUR OWN BUSINESS. SHUT UP AND–
THAT'S JUST IT: IT IS MY BUSINESS! IF THEY EVER–
I'LL SAY IT AGAIN: STAY OUT OF IT AND–
YOU DON'T GET IT: I'M ALREADY MIXED UP IN IT! IT'S MY JOB! IF THEY FIND OUT WHAT'S GOING ON, I'M A DEAD MAN!
THIS IS A COLLECTIVE RESISTANCE OPERATION APPROVED BY THE LEADERS OF THE COMMUNIST PARTY. THE ATROCITIES BEING COMMITTED HERE NEED TO BE SEEN BY THE WHOLE WORLD! IT'S OUR DUTY!
OUR DUTY IS TO STAY ALIVE! WE ARE PRIVILEGED PRISONERS! IF WE KEEP OUR HEADS DOWN, WE'LL MAKE IT THROUGH THE WAR!
"KEEP OUR HEADS DOWN"? DON'T YOU MEAN "COLLABORATE"?

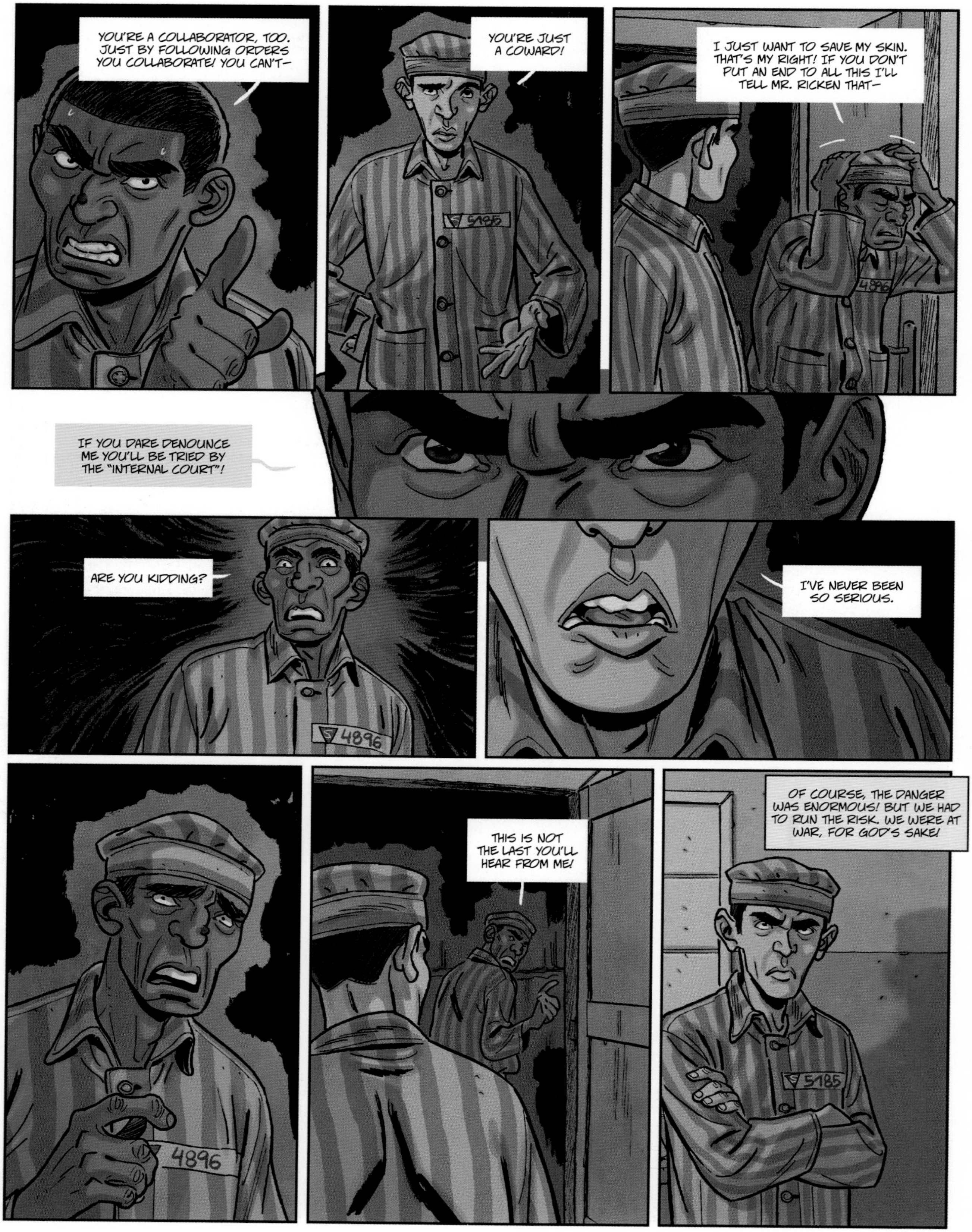
YOU'RE A COLLABORATOR, TOO. JUST BY FOLLOWING ORDERS YOU COLLABORATE! YOU CAN'T–
YOU'RE JUST A COWARD!
5185
I JUST WANT TO SAVE MY SKIN. THAT'S MY RIGHT! IF YOU DON'T PUT AN END TO ALL THIS I'LL TELL MR. RICKEN THAT–
4896
IF YOU DARE DENOUNCE ME YOU'LL BE TRIED BY THE "INTERNAL COURT"!
ARE YOU KIDDING?
4896
I'VE NEVER BEEN SO SERIOUS.
4896
THIS IS NOT THE LAST YOU'LL HEAR FROM ME!
OF COURSE, THE DANGER WAS ENORMOUS! BUT WE HAD TO RUN THE RISK. WE WERE AT WAR, FOR GOD'S SAKE!
5185

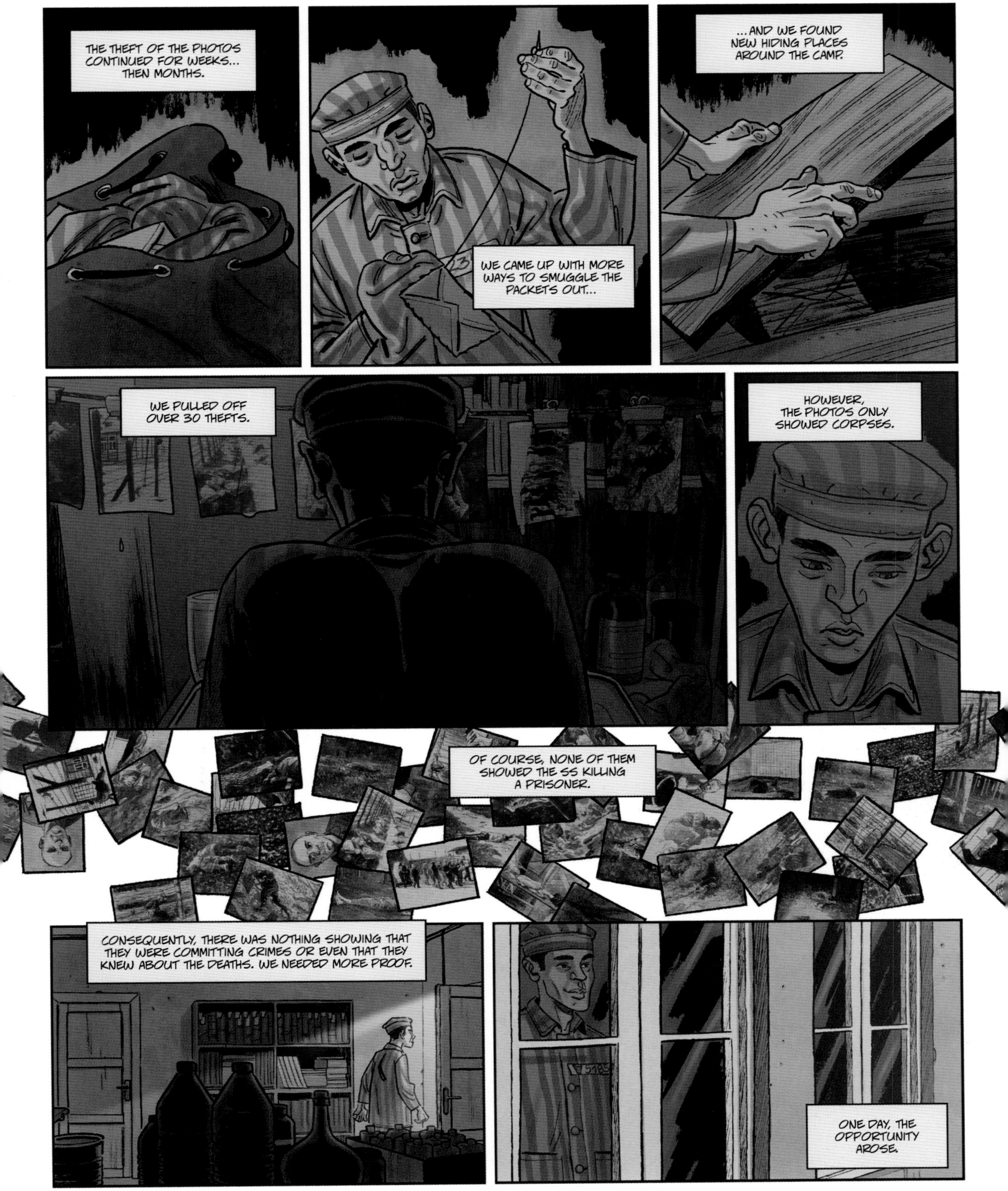
THE THEFT OF THE PHOTOS CONTINUED FOR WEEKS... THEN MONTHS.
WE CAME UP WITH MORE WAYS TO SMUGGLE THE PACKETS OUT...
...AND WE FOUND NEW HIDING PLACES AROUND THE CAMP.
WE PULLED OFF OVER 30 THEFTS.
HOWEVER, THE PHOTOS ONLY SHOWED CORPSES.
OF COURSE, NONE OF THEM SHOWED THE SS KILLING A PRISONER.
CONSEQUENTLY, THERE WAS NOTHING SHOWING THAT THEY WERE COMMITTING CRIMES OR EVEN THAT THEY KNEW ABOUT THE DEATHS. WE NEEDED MORE PROOF.
ONE DAY, THE OPPORTUNITY AROSE.

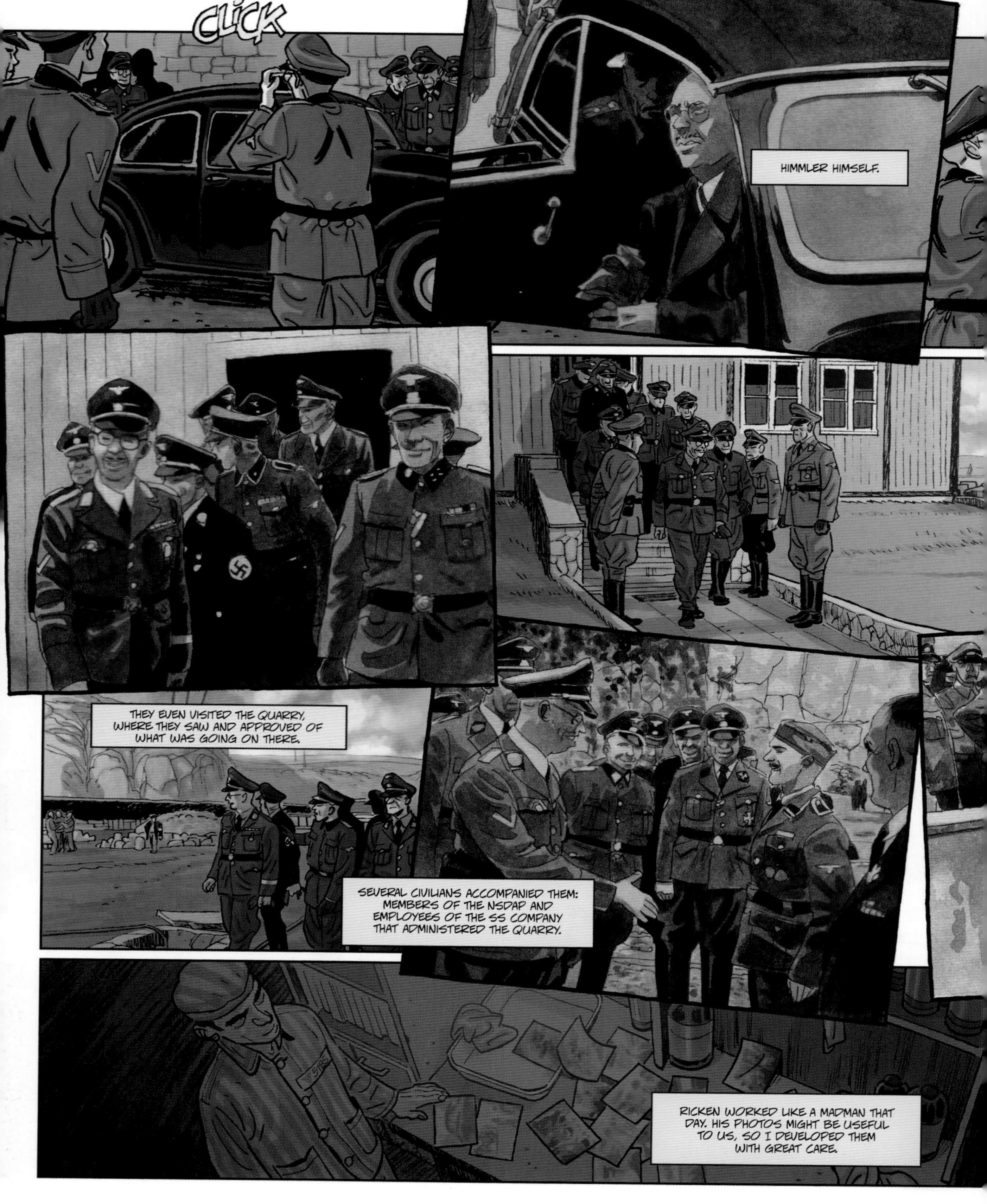
CLICK
HIMMLER HIMSELF.
THEY EVEN VISITED THE QUARRY, WHERE THEY SAW AND APPROVED OF WHAT WAS GOING ON THERE.
SEVERAL CIVILIANS ACCOMPANIED THEM: MEMBERS OF THE NSDAP AND EMPLOYEES OF THE SS COMPANY THAT ADMINISTERED THE QUARRY.
RICKEN WORKED LIKE A MADMAN THAT DAY. HIS PHOTOS MIGHT BE USEFUL TO US, SO I DEVELOPED THEM WITH GREAT CARE.

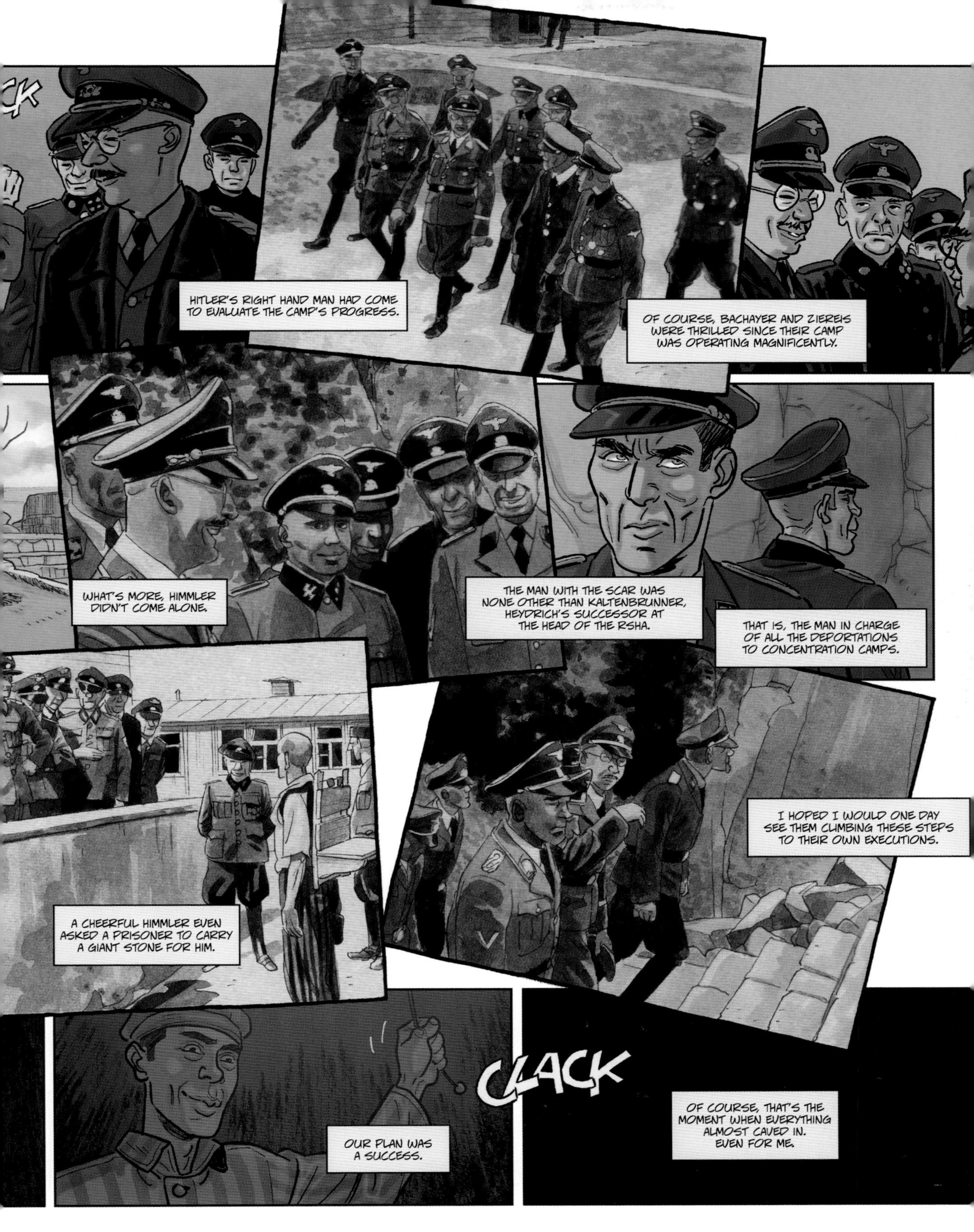

CK
HITLER'S RIGHT HAND MAN HAD COME TO EVALUATE THE CAMP'S PROGRESS.
OF COURSE, BACHAYER AND ZIEREIS WERE THRILLED SINCE THEIR CAMP WAS OPERATING MAGNIFICENTLY.
WHAT'S MORE, HIMMLER DIDN'T COME ALONE.
THE MAN WITH THE SCAR WAS NONE OTHER THAN KALTENBRUNNER, HEYDRICH'S SUCCESSOR AT THE HEAD OF THE RSHA.
THAT IS, THE MAN IN CHARGE OF ALL THE DEPORTATIONS TO CONCENTRATION CAMPS.
A CHEERFUL HIMMLER EVEN ASKED A PRISONER TO CARRY A GIANT STONE FOR HIM.
I HOPED I WOULD ONE DAY SEE THEM CLIMBING THESE STEPS TO THEIR OWN EXECUTIONS.
OUR PLAN WAS A SUCCESS.
CLACK
OF COURSE, THAT'S THE MOMENT WHEN EVERYTHING ALMOST CAVED IN. EVEN FOR ME.

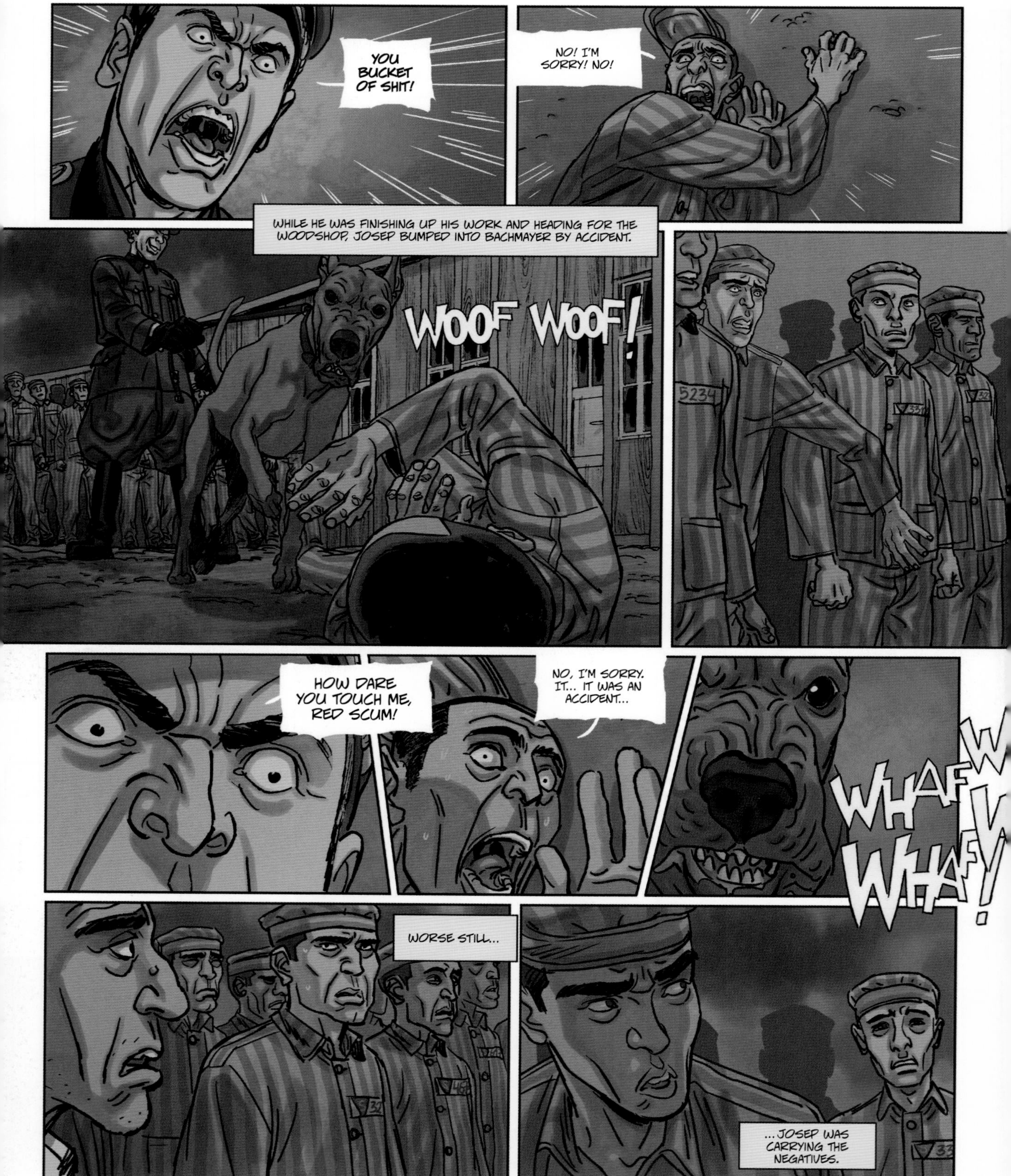
YOU BUCKET OF SHIT!
NO! I'M SORRY! NO!
WHILE HE WAS FINISHING UP HIS WORK AND HEADING FOR THE WOODSHOP, JOSEP BUMPED INTO BACHMAYER BY ACCIDENT.
WOOF WOOF!
5234
HOW DARE YOU TOUCH ME, RED SCUM!
NO, I'M SORRY. IT... IT WAS AN ACCIDENT...
WHAF
WHAF!
WORSE STILL...
...JOSEP WAS CARRYING THE NEGATIVES.

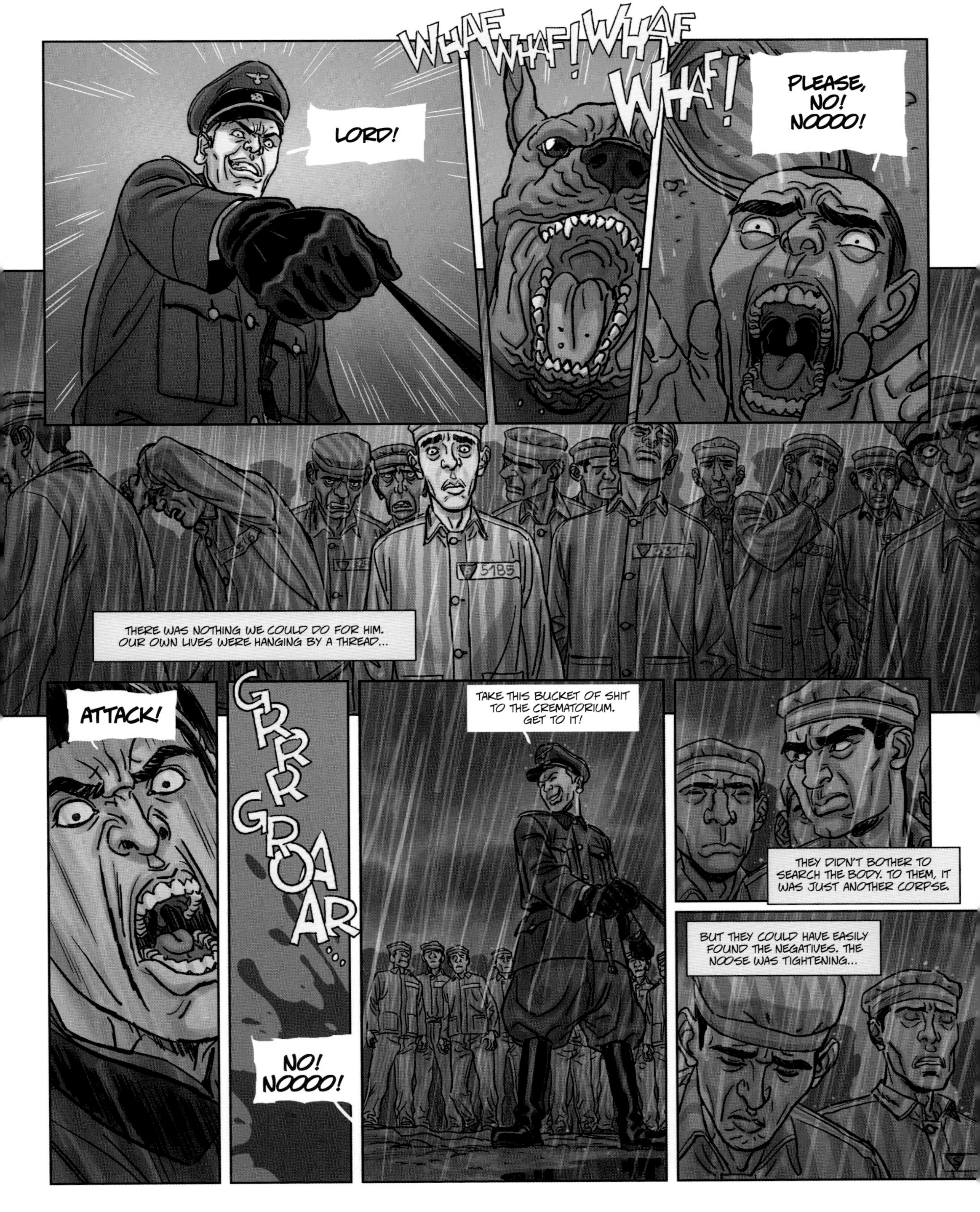
LORD!
WHAF WHAF! WHAF WHAF!
PLEASE, NO! NOOOO!
THERE WAS NOTHING WE COULD DO FOR HIM. OUR OWN LIVES WERE HANGING BY A THREAD...
ATTACK!
GRRR GROAR...
NO! NOOOO!
TAKE THIS BUCKET OF SHIT TO THE CREMATORIUM. GET TO IT!
THEY DIDN'T BOTHER TO SEARCH THE BODY. TO THEM, IT WAS JUST ANOTHER CORPSE.
BUT THEY COULD HAVE EASILY FOUND THE NEGATIVES. THE NOOSE WAS TIGHTENING...

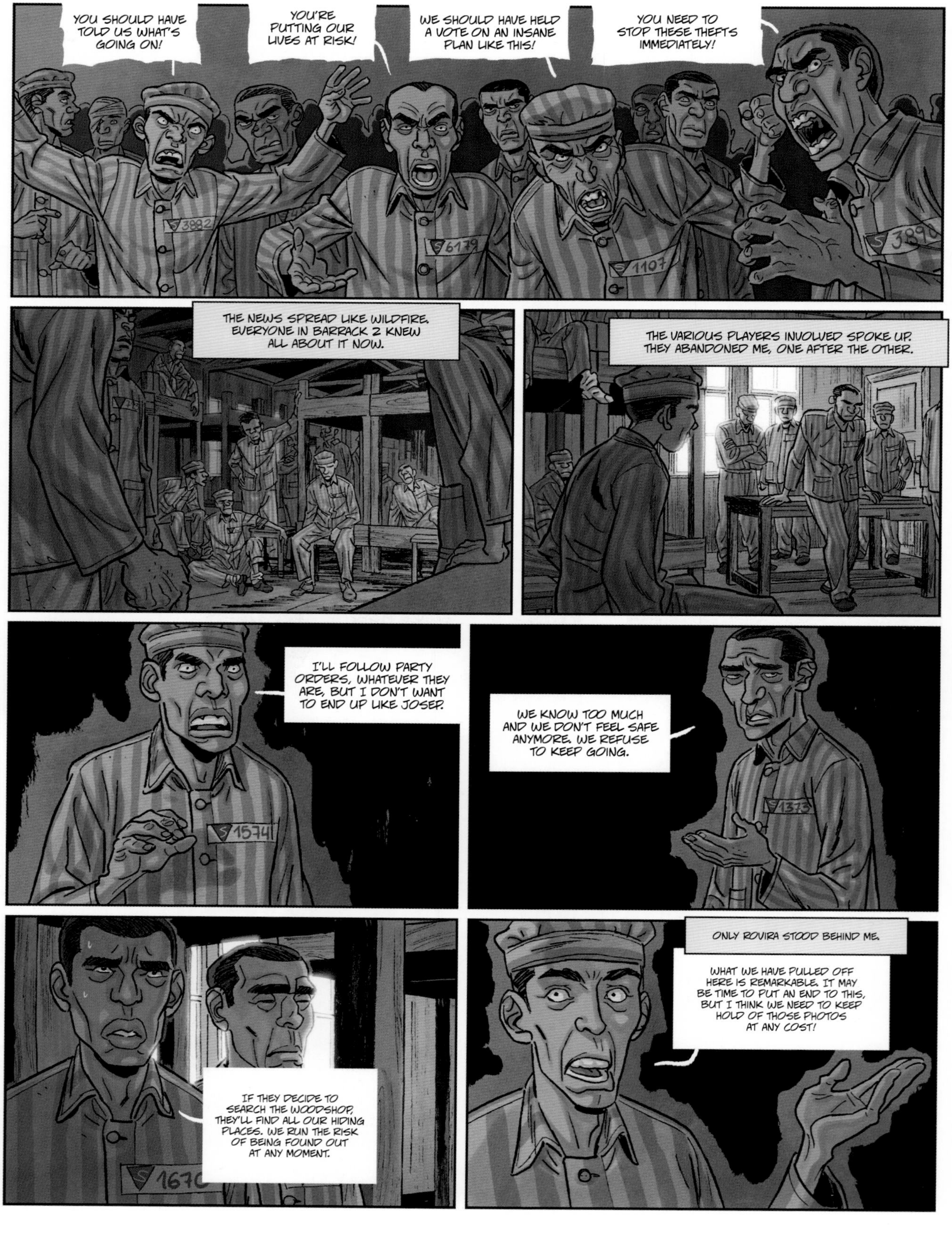
YOU SHOULD HAVE TOLD US WHAT'S GOING ON!
YOU'RE PUTTING OUR LIVES AT RISK!
WE SHOULD HAVE HELD A VOTE ON AN INSANE PLAN LIKE THIS!
YOU NEED TO STOP THESE THEFTS IMMEDIATELY!
THE NEWS SPREAD LIKE WILDFIRE. EVERYONE IN BARRACK 2 KNEW ALL ABOUT IT NOW.
THE VARIOUS PLAYERS INVOLVED SPOKE UP. THEY ABANDONED ME, ONE AFTER THE OTHER.
I'LL FOLLOW PARTY ORDERS, WHATEVER THEY ARE, BUT I DON'T WANT TO END UP LIKE JOSEP.
WE KNOW TOO MUCH AND WE DON'T FEEL SAFE ANYMORE. WE REFUSE TO KEEP GOING.
IF THEY DECIDE TO SEARCH THE WOODSHOP, THEY'LL FIND ALL OUR HIDING PLACES. WE RUN THE RISK OF BEING FOUND OUT AT ANY MOMENT.
ONLY ROVIRA STOOD BEHIND ME.
WHAT WE HAVE PULLED OFF HERE IS REMARKABLE. IT MAY BE TIME TO PUT AN END TO THIS, BUT I THINK WE NEED TO KEEP HOLD OF THOSE PHOTOS AT ANY COST!

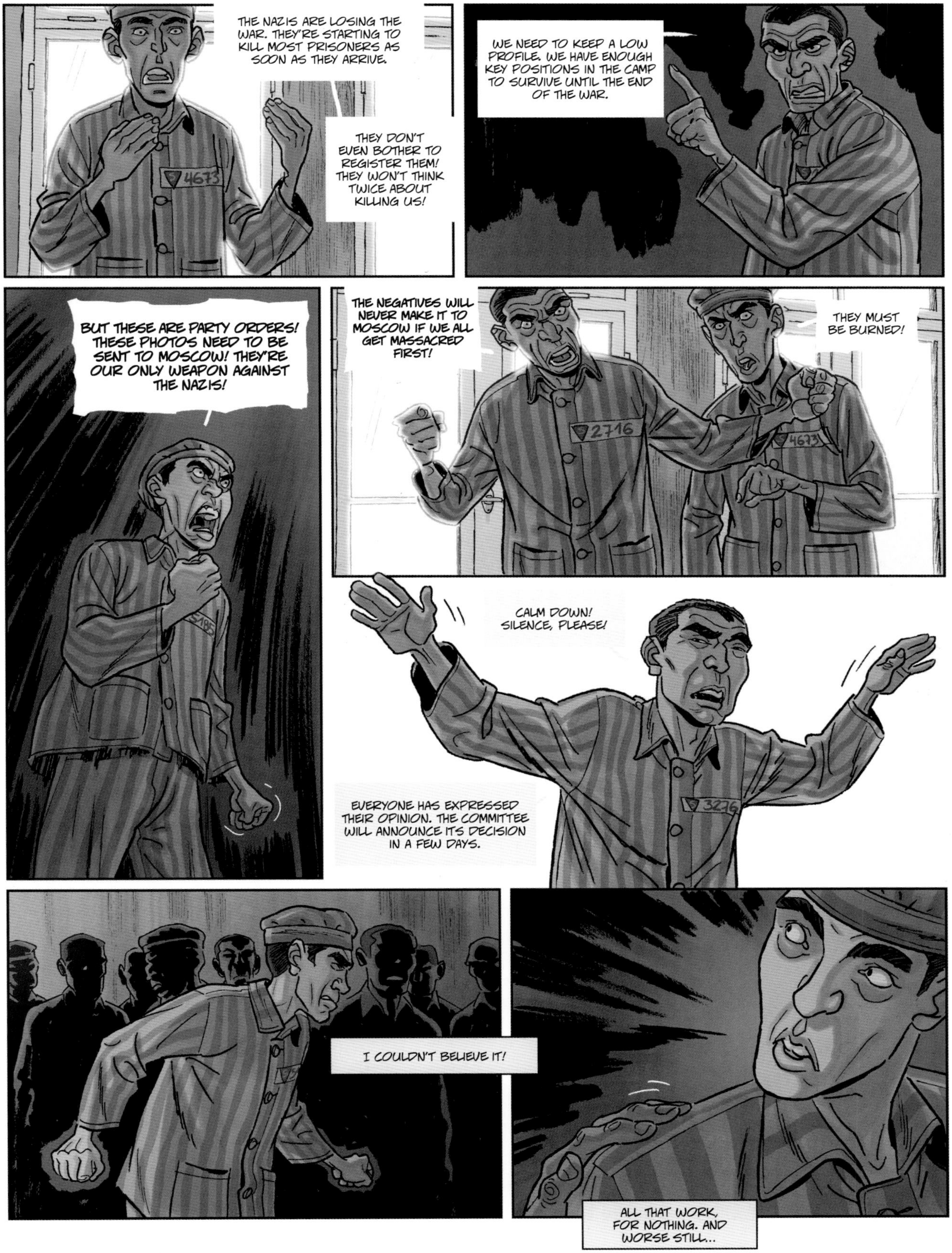
THE NAZIS ARE LOSING THE WAR. THEY'RE STARTING TO KILL MOST PRISONERS AS SOON AS THEY ARRIVE.
THEY DON'T EVEN BOTHER TO REGISTER THEM! THEY WON'T THINK TWICE ABOUT KILLING US!
WE NEED TO KEEP A LOW PROFILE. WE HAVE ENOUGH KEY POSITIONS IN THE CAMP TO SURVIVE UNTIL THE END OF THE WAR.
BUT THESE ARE PARTY ORDERS! THESE PHOTOS NEED TO BE SENT TO MOSCOW! THEY'RE OUR ONLY WEAPON AGAINST THE NAZIS!
THE NEGATIVES WILL NEVER MAKE IT TO MOSCOW IF WE ALL GET MASSACRED FIRST!
THEY MUST BE BURNED!
CALM DOWN! SILENCE, PLEASE!
EVERYONE HAS EXPRESSED THEIR OPINION. THE COMMITTEE WILL ANNOUNCE ITS DECISION IN A FEW DAYS.
I COULDN'T BELIEVE IT!
ALL THAT WORK, FOR NOTHING. AND WORSE STILL...

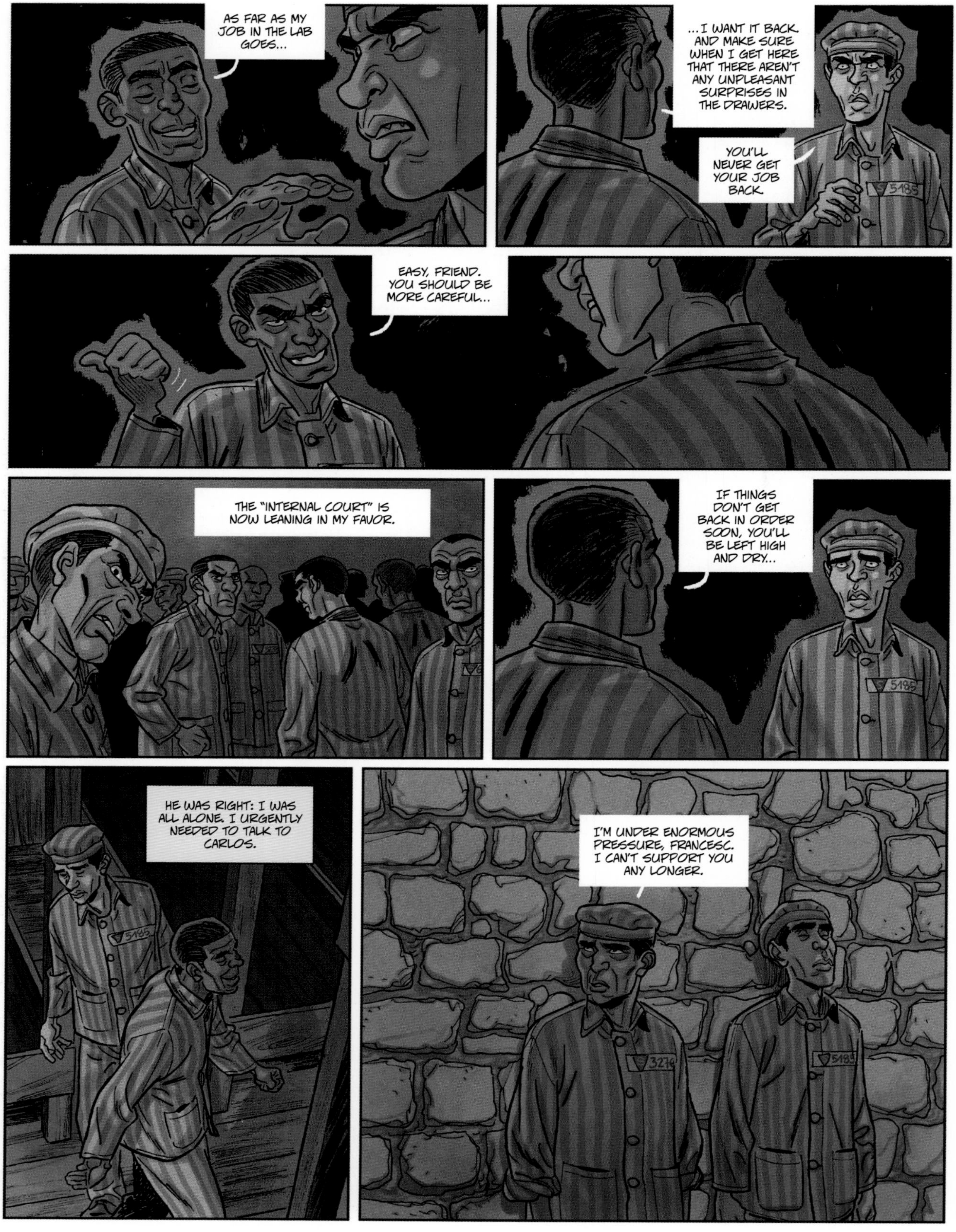
AS FAR AS MY JOB IN THE LAB GOES...
...I WANT IT BACK. AND MAKE SURE WHEN I GET HERE THAT THERE AREN'T ANY UNPLEASANT SURPRISES IN THE DRAWERS.
YOU'LL NEVER GET YOUR JOB BACK.
5185
EASY, FRIEND. YOU SHOULD BE MORE CAREFUL...
THE "INTERNAL COURT" IS NOW LEANING IN MY FAVOR.
IF THINGS DON'T GET BACK IN ORDER SOON, YOU'LL BE LEFT HIGH AND DRY...
5185
HE WAS RIGHT: I WAS ALL ALONE. I URGENTLY NEEDED TO TALK TO CARLOS.
5185
I'M UNDER ENORMOUS PRESSURE, FRANCESC. I CAN'T SUPPORT YOU ANY LONGER.
3276
5185

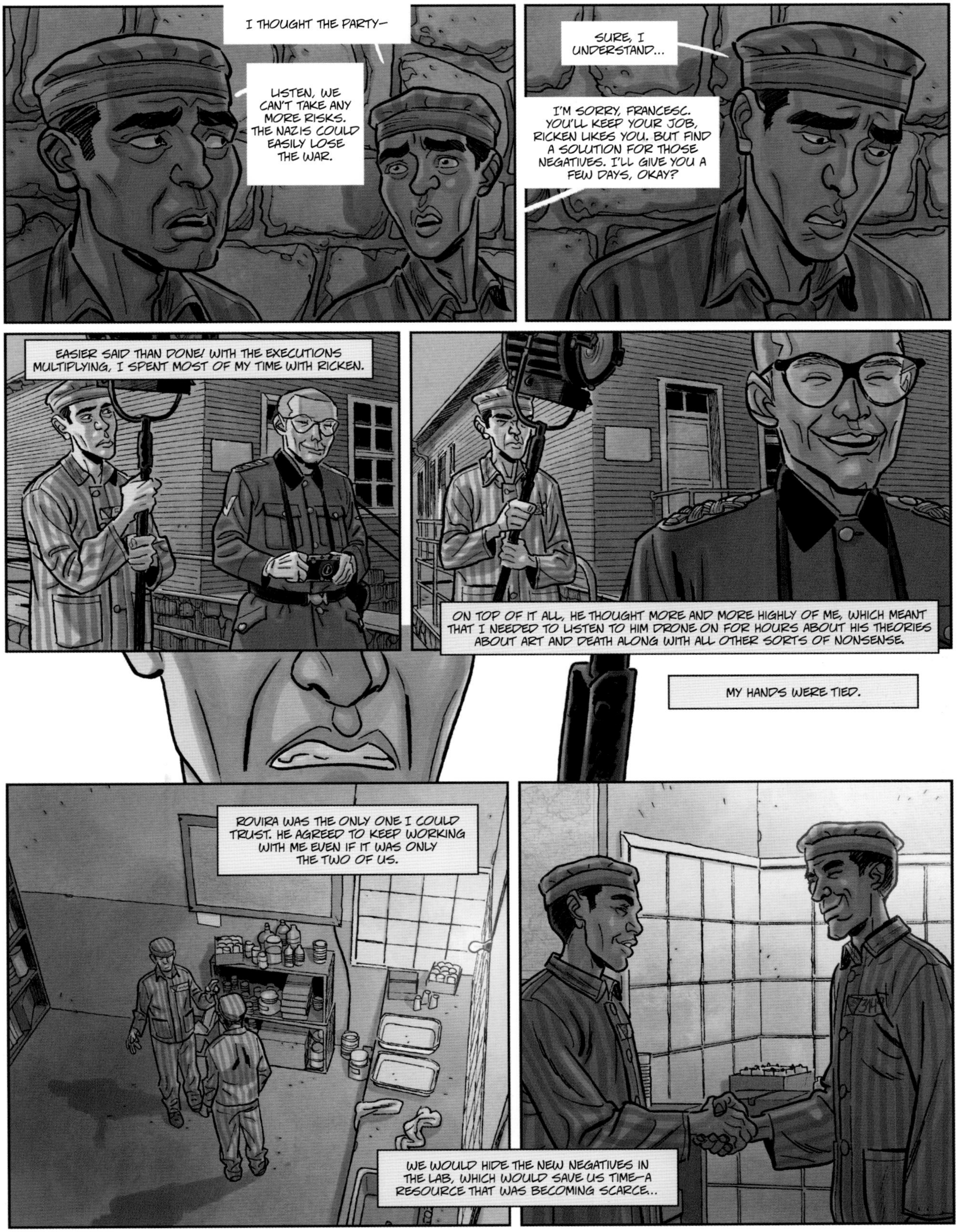
I THOUGHT THE PARTY—
LISTEN, WE CAN'T TAKE ANY MORE RISKS. THE NAZIS COULD EASILY LOSE THE WAR.
SURE, I UNDERSTAND...
I'M SORRY, FRANCESC. YOU'LL KEEP YOUR JOB, RICKEN LIKES YOU. BUT FIND A SOLUTION FOR THOSE NEGATIVES. I'LL GIVE YOU A FEW DAYS, OKAY?
EASIER SAID THAN DONE! WITH THE EXECUTIONS MULTIPLYING, I SPENT MOST OF MY TIME WITH RICKEN.
ON TOP OF IT ALL, HE THOUGHT MORE AND MORE HIGHLY OF ME, WHICH MEANT THAT I NEEDED TO LISTEN TO HIM DRONE ON FOR HOURS ABOUT HIS THEORIES ABOUT ART AND DEATH ALONG WITH ALL OTHER SORTS OF NONSENSE.
MY HANDS WERE TIED.
ROVIRA WAS THE ONLY ONE I COULD TRUST. HE AGREED TO KEEP WORKING WITH ME EVEN IF IT WAS ONLY THE TWO OF US.
WE WOULD HIDE THE NEW NEGATIVES IN THE LAB, WHICH WOULD SAVE US TIME—A RESOURCE THAT WAS BECOMING SCARCE...

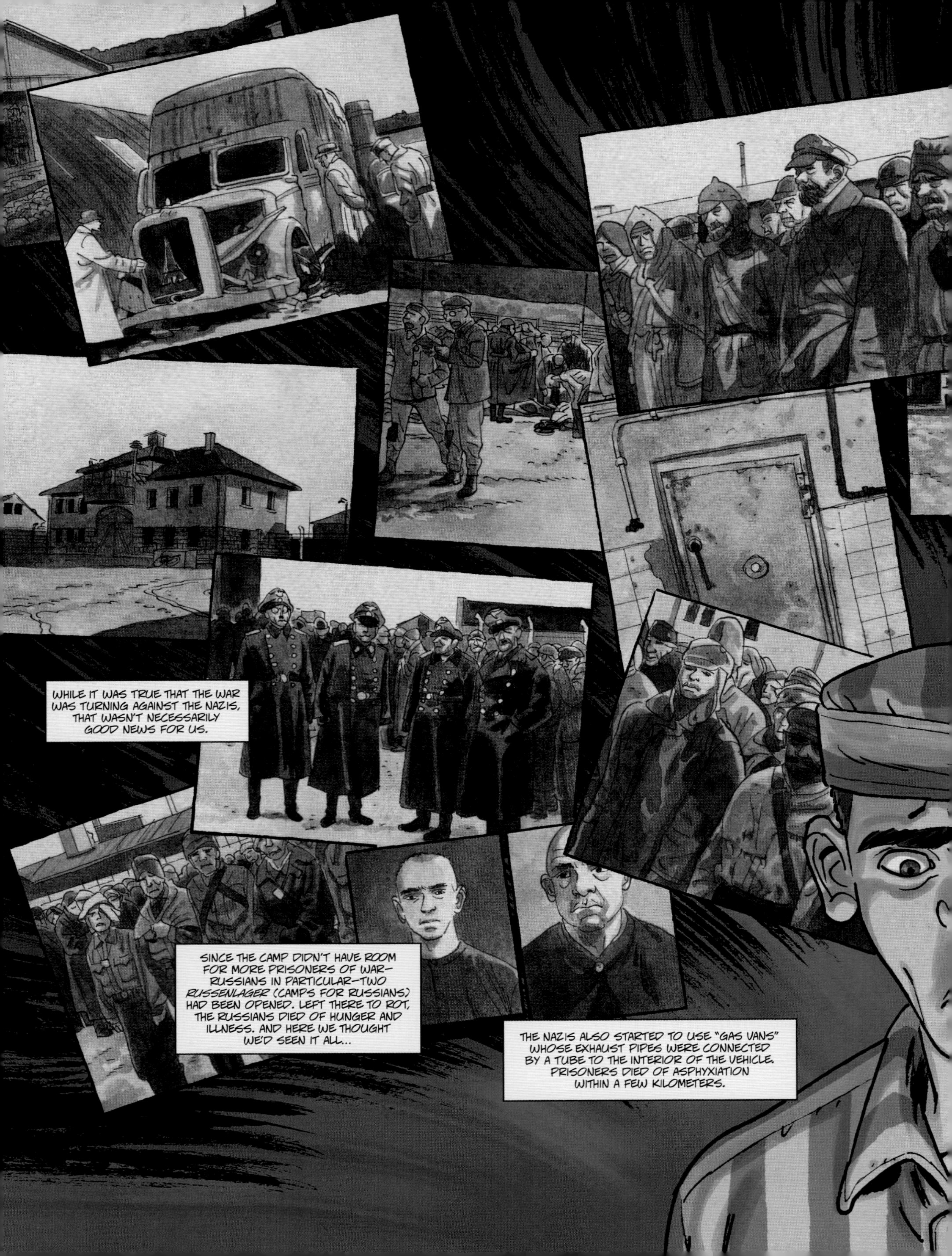
WHILE IT WAS TRUE THAT THE WAR WAS TURNING AGAINST THE NAZIS, THAT WASN'T NECESSARILY GOOD NEWS FOR US.
SINCE THE CAMP DIDN'T HAVE ROOM FOR MORE PRISONERS OF WAR—RUSSIANS IN PARTICULAR—TWO *RUSSENLAGER* (CAMPS FOR RUSSIANS) HAD BEEN OPENED. LEFT THERE TO ROT, THE RUSSIANS DIED OF HUNGER AND ILLNESS. AND HERE WE THOUGHT WE'D SEEN IT ALL...
THE NAZIS ALSO STARTED TO USE "GAS VANS" WHOSE EXHAUST PIPES WERE CONNECTED BY A TUBE TO THE INTERIOR OF THE VEHICLE. PRISONERS DIED OF ASPHYXIATION WITHIN A FEW KILOMETERS.

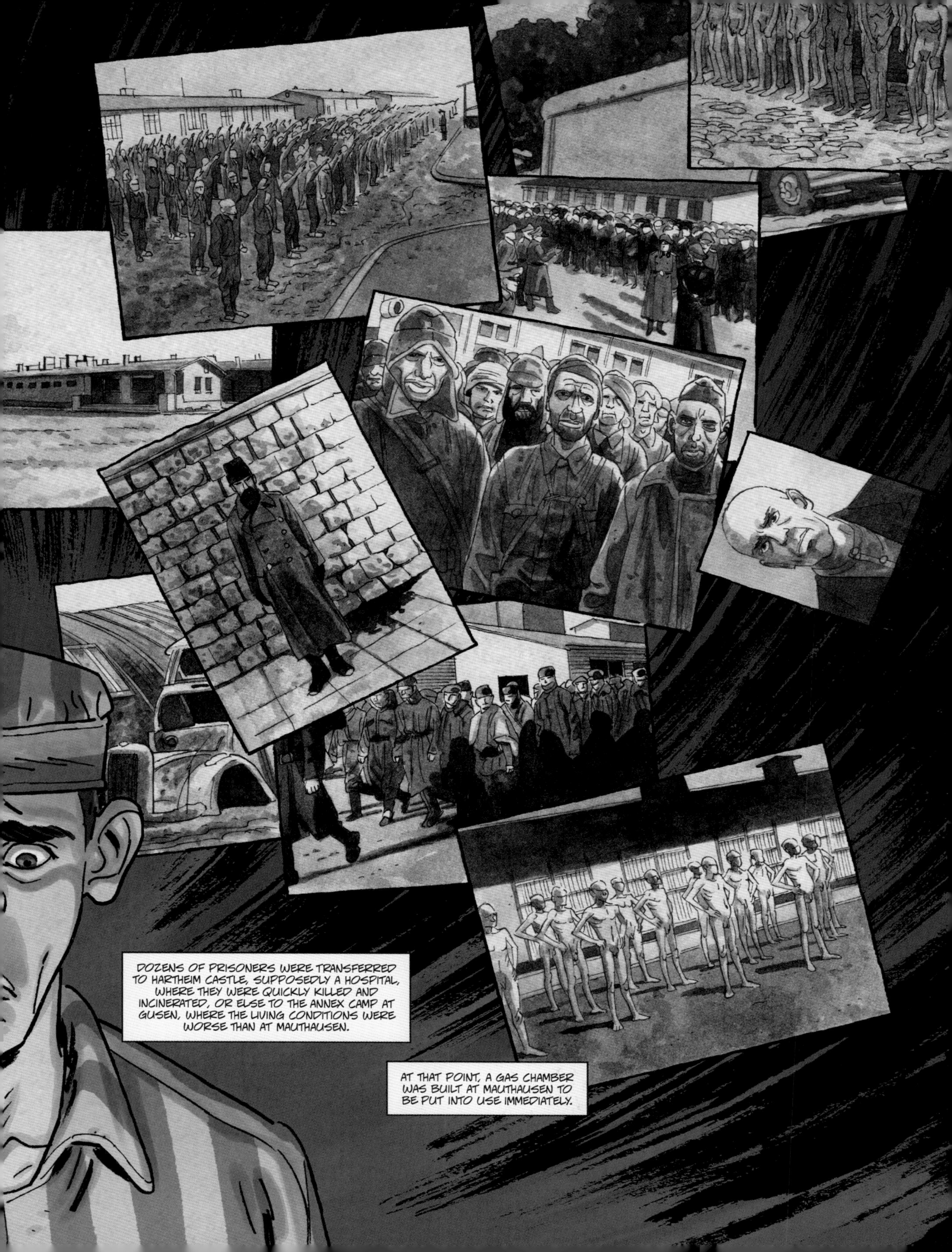
DOZENS OF PRISONERS WERE TRANSFERRED TO HARTHEIM CASTLE, SUPPOSEDLY A HOSPITAL, WHERE THEY WERE QUICKLY KILLED AND INCINERATED, OR ELSE TO THE ANNEX CAMP AT GUSEN, WHERE THE LIVING CONDITIONS WERE WORSE THAN AT MAUTHAUSEN.
AT THAT POINT, A GAS CHAMBER WAS BUILT AT MAUTHAUSEN TO BE PUT INTO USE IMMEDIATELY.

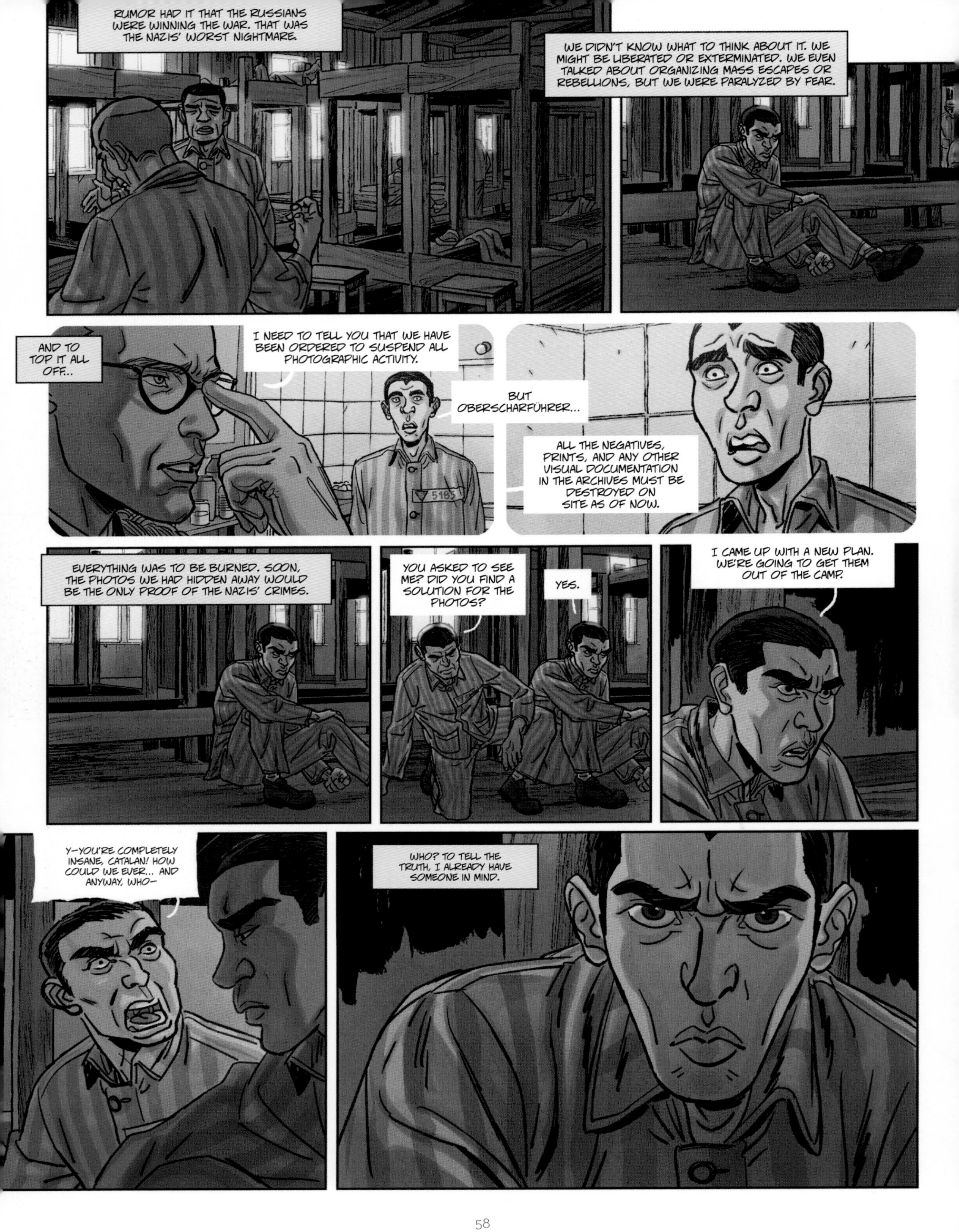

RUMOR HAD IT THAT THE RUSSIANS WERE WINNING THE WAR. THAT WAS THE NAZIS' WORST NIGHTMARE.
WE DIDN'T KNOW WHAT TO THINK ABOUT IT. WE MIGHT BE LIBERATED OR EXTERMINATED. WE EVEN TALKED ABOUT ORGANIZING MASS ESCAPES OR REBELLIONS, BUT WE WERE PARALYZED BY FEAR.
AND TO TOP IT ALL OFF...
I NEED TO TELL YOU THAT WE HAVE BEEN ORDERED TO SUSPEND ALL PHOTOGRAPHIC ACTIVITY.
5183
BUT OBERSCHARFÜHRER...
ALL THE NEGATIVES, PRINTS, AND ANY OTHER VISUAL DOCUMENTATION IN THE ARCHIVES MUST BE DESTROYED ON SITE AS OF NOW.
EVERYTHING WAS TO BE BURNED. SOON, THE PHOTOS WE HAD HIDDEN AWAY WOULD BE THE ONLY PROOF OF THE NAZIS' CRIMES.
YOU ASKED TO SEE ME? DID YOU FIND A SOLUTION FOR THE PHOTOS?
YES.
I CAME UP WITH A NEW PLAN. WE'RE GOING TO GET THEM OUT OF THE CAMP.
Y-YOU'RE COMPLETELY INSANE, CATALAN! HOW COULD WE EVER... AND ANYWAY, WHO-
WHO? TO TELL THE TRUTH, I ALREADY HAVE SOMEONE IN MIND.

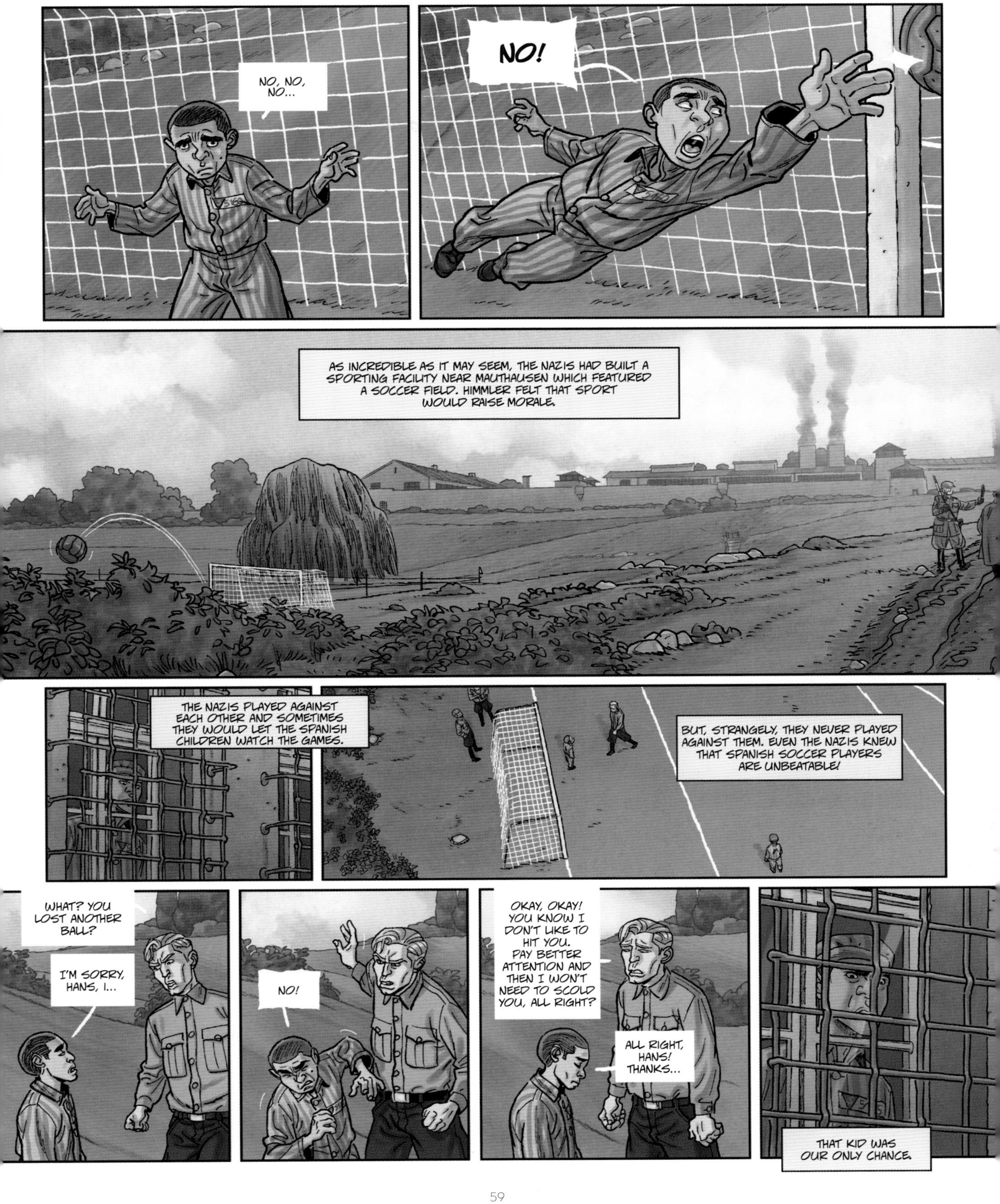
NO, NO, NO...
NO!
AS INCREDIBLE AS IT MAY SEEM, THE NAZIS HAD BUILT A SPORTING FACILITY NEAR MAUTHAUSEN WHICH FEATURED A SOCCER FIELD. HIMMLER FELT THAT SPORT WOULD RAISE MORALE.
THE NAZIS PLAYED AGAINST EACH OTHER AND SOMETIMES THEY WOULD LET THE SPANISH CHILDREN WATCH THE GAMES.
BUT, STRANGELY, THEY NEVER PLAYED AGAINST THEM. EVEN THE NAZIS KNEW THAT SPANISH SOCCER PLAYERS ARE UNBEATABLE!
WHAT? YOU LOST ANOTHER BALL?
I'M SORRY, HANS, I...
NO!
OKAY, OKAY! YOU KNOW I DON'T LIKE TO HIT YOU. PAY BETTER ATTENTION AND THEN I WON'T NEED TO SCOLD YOU, ALL RIGHT?
ALL RIGHT, HANS! THANKS...
THAT KID WAS OUR ONLY CHANCE.

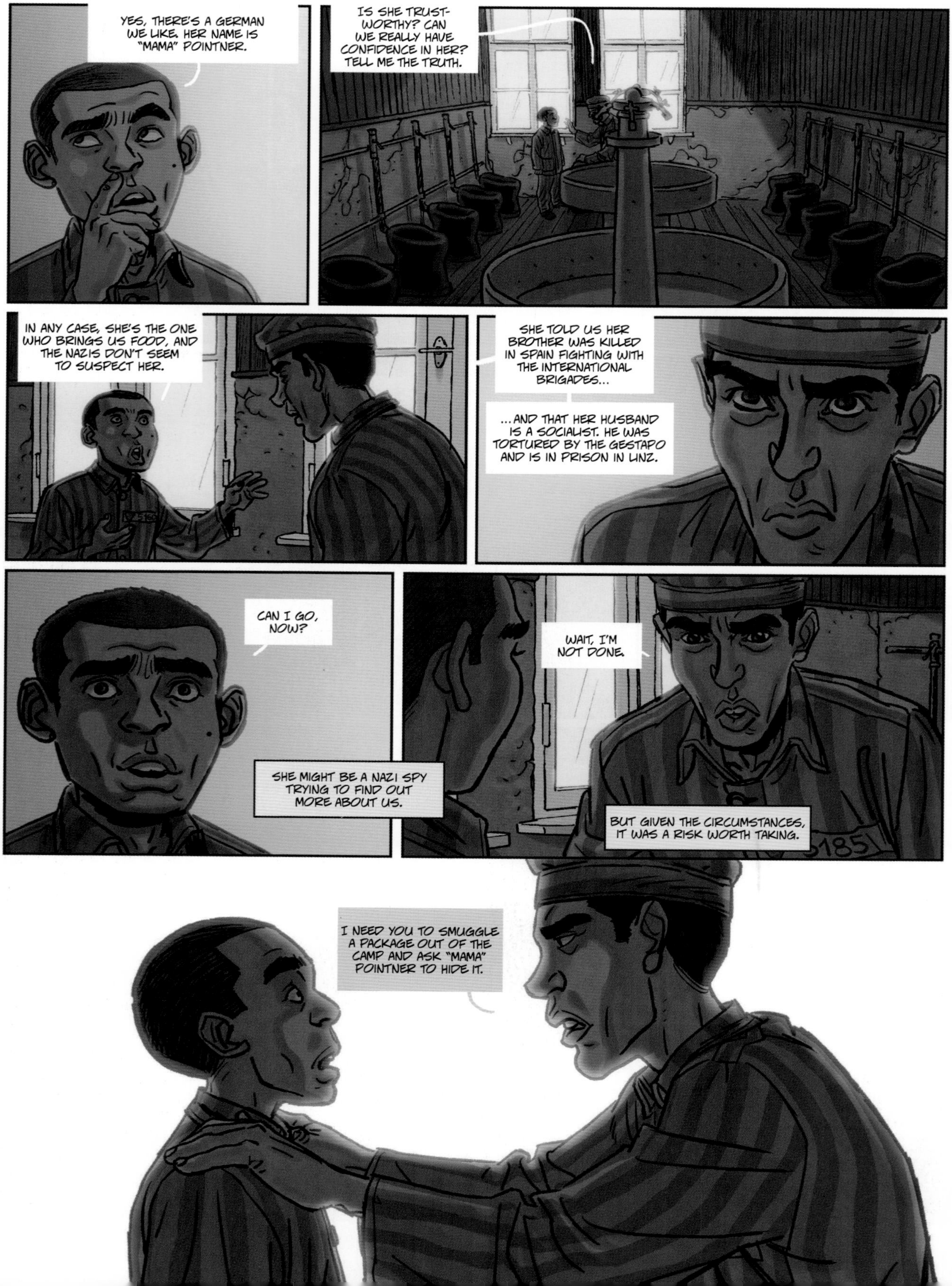
YES, THERE'S A GERMAN WE LIKE. HER NAME IS "MAMA" POINTNER.
IS SHE TRUST-WORTHY? CAN WE REALLY HAVE CONFIDENCE IN HER? TELL ME THE TRUTH.
IN ANY CASE, SHE'S THE ONE WHO BRINGS US FOOD, AND THE NAZIS DON'T SEEM TO SUSPECT HER.
SHE TOLD US HER BROTHER WAS KILLED IN SPAIN FIGHTING WITH THE INTERNATIONAL BRIGADES...
...AND THAT HER HUSBAND IS A SOCIALIST. HE WAS TORTURED BY THE GESTAPO AND IS IN PRISON IN LINZ.
CAN I GO, NOW?
SHE MIGHT BE A NAZI SPY TRYING TO FIND OUT MORE ABOUT US.
WAIT, I'M NOT DONE.
BUT GIVEN THE CIRCUMSTANCES, IT WAS A RISK WORTH TAKING.
I NEED YOU TO SMUGGLE A PACKAGE OUT OF THE CAMP AND ASK "MAMA" POINTNER TO HIDE IT.

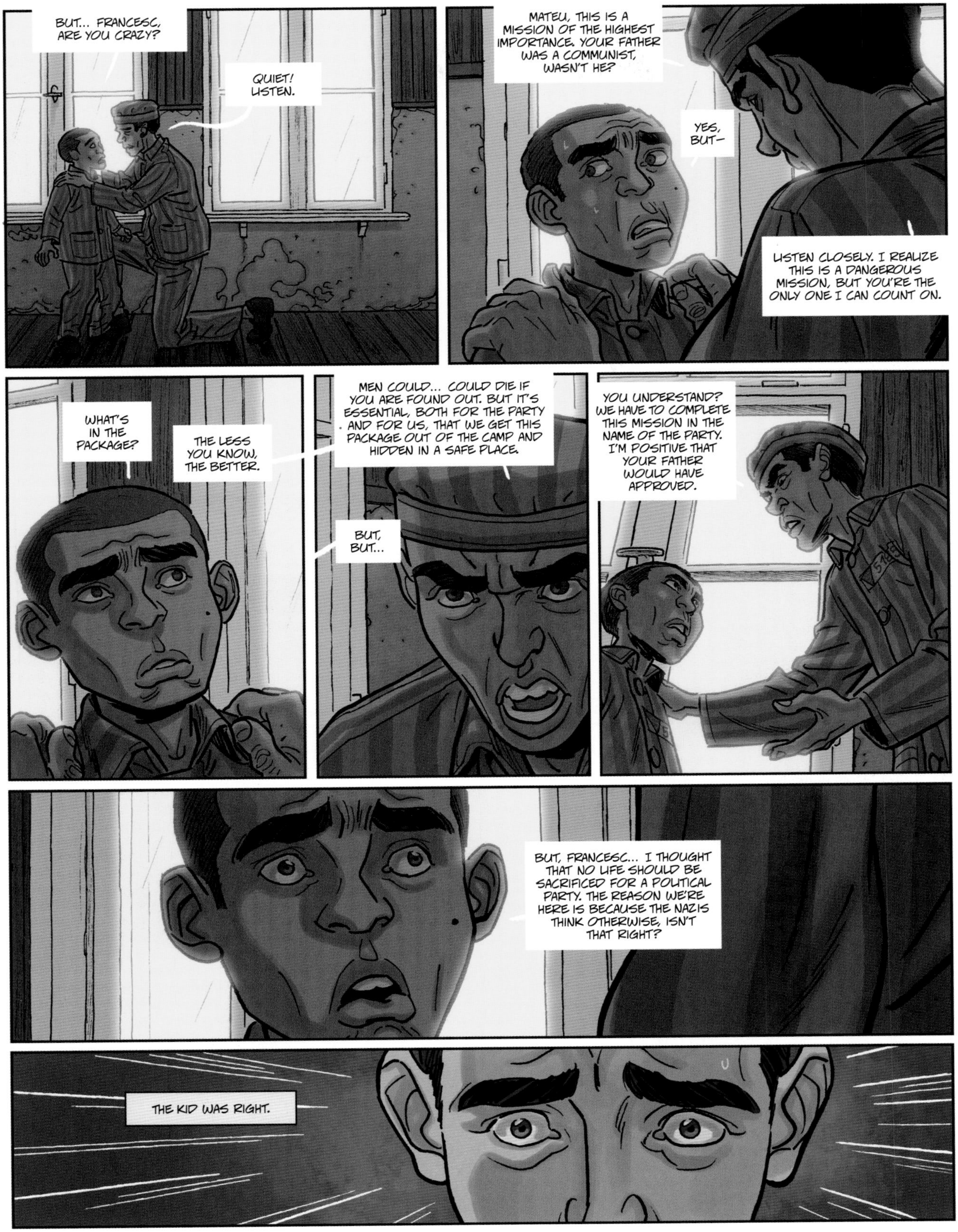
BUT... FRANCESC, ARE YOU CRAZY?
QUIET! LISTEN.
MATEU, THIS IS A MISSION OF THE HIGHEST IMPORTANCE. YOUR FATHER WAS A COMMUNIST, WASN'T HE?
YES, BUT–
LISTEN CLOSELY. I REALIZE THIS IS A DANGEROUS MISSION, BUT YOU'RE THE ONLY ONE I CAN COUNT ON.
WHAT'S IN THE PACKAGE?
THE LESS YOU KNOW, THE BETTER.
MEN COULD... COULD DIE IF YOU ARE FOUND OUT. BUT IT'S ESSENTIAL, BOTH FOR THE PARTY AND FOR US, THAT WE GET THIS PACKAGE OUT OF THE CAMP AND HIDDEN IN A SAFE PLACE.
BUT, BUT...
YOU UNDERSTAND? WE HAVE TO COMPLETE THIS MISSION IN THE NAME OF THE PARTY. I'M POSITIVE THAT YOUR FATHER WOULD HAVE APPROVED.
BUT, FRANCESC... I THOUGHT THAT NO LIFE SHOULD BE SACRIFICED FOR A POLITICAL PARTY. THE REASON WE'RE HERE IS BECAUSE THE NAZIS THINK OTHERWISE, ISN'T THAT RIGHT?
THE KID WAS RIGHT.

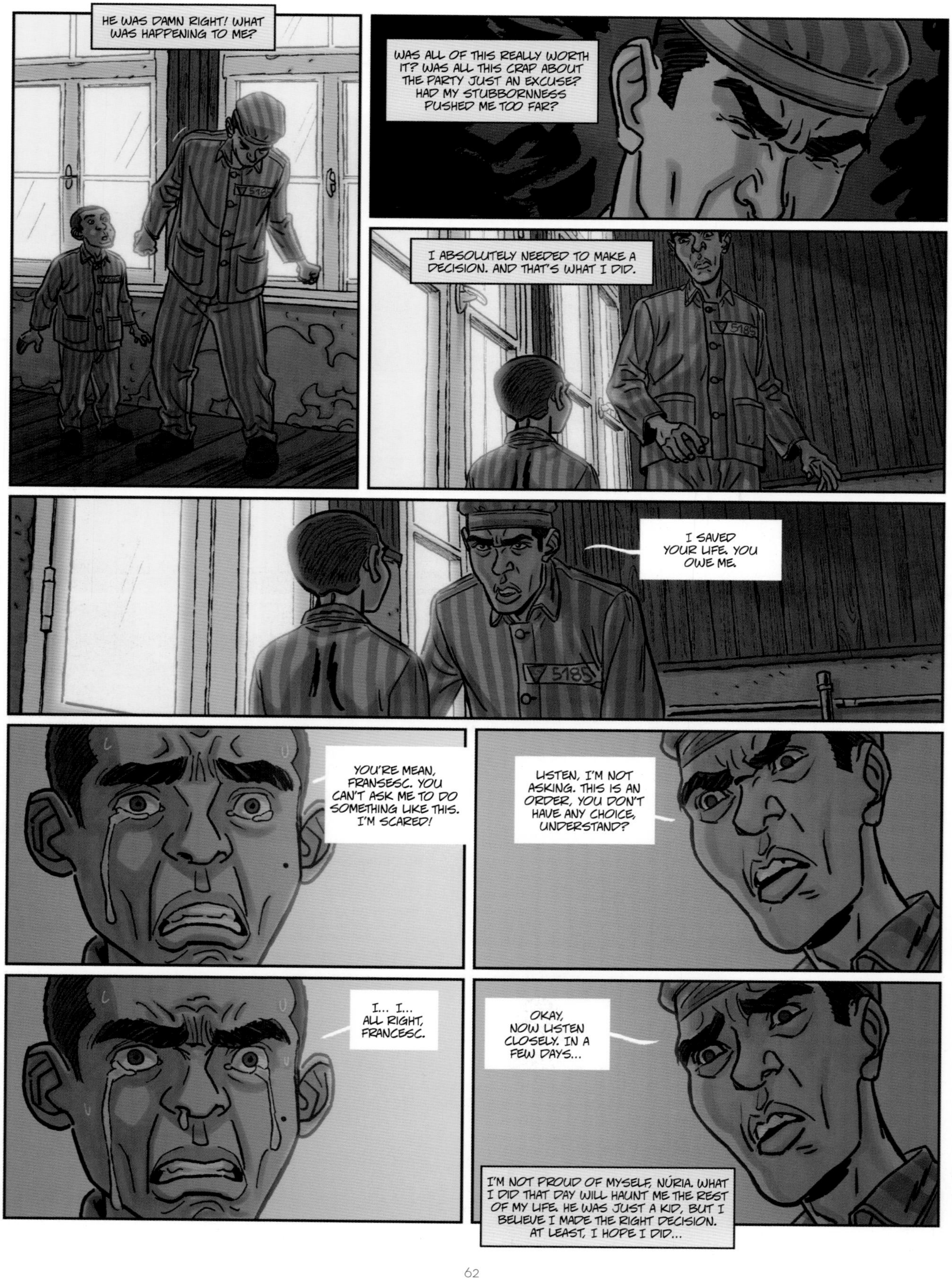
HE WAS DAMN RIGHT! WHAT WAS HAPPENING TO ME?
WAS ALL OF THIS REALLY WORTH IT? WAS ALL THIS CRAP ABOUT THE PARTY JUST AN EXCUSE? HAD MY STUBBORNNESS PUSHED ME TOO FAR?
I ABSOLUTELY NEEDED TO MAKE A DECISION. AND THAT'S WHAT I DID.
5185
I SAVED YOUR LIFE. YOU OWE ME.
5185
YOU'RE MEAN, FRANSESC. YOU CAN'T ASK ME TO DO SOMETHING LIKE THIS. I'M SCARED!
LISTEN, I'M NOT ASKING. THIS IS AN ORDER, YOU DON'T HAVE ANY CHOICE, UNDERSTAND?
I... I... ALL RIGHT, FRANCESC.
OKAY, NOW LISTEN CLOSELY. IN A FEW DAYS...
I'M NOT PROUD OF MYSELF, NÚRIA. WHAT I DID THAT DAY WILL HAUNT ME THE REST OF MY LIFE. HE WAS JUST A KID, BUT I BELIEVE I MADE THE RIGHT DECISION. AT LEAST, I HOPE I DID...

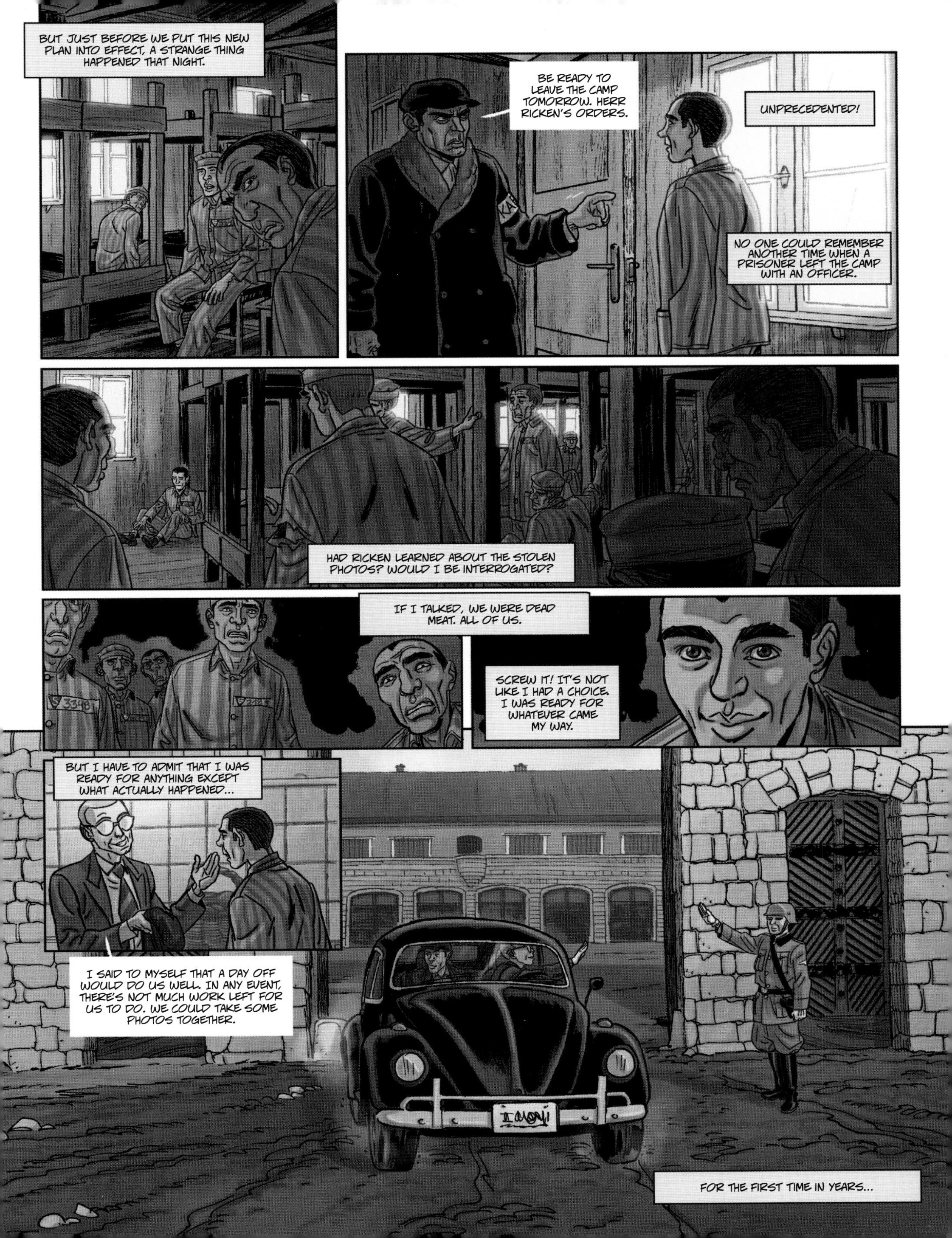
BUT JUST BEFORE WE PUT THIS NEW PLAN INTO EFFECT, A STRANGE THING HAPPENED THAT NIGHT.
BE READY TO LEAVE THE CAMP TOMORROW. HERR RICKEN'S ORDERS.
UNPRECEDENTED!
NO ONE COULD REMEMBER ANOTHER TIME WHEN A PRISONER LEFT THE CAMP WITH AN OFFICER.
HAD RICKEN LEARNED ABOUT THE STOLEN PHOTOS? WOULD I BE INTERROGATED?
IF I TALKED, WE WERE DEAD MEAT. ALL OF US.
SCREW IT! IT'S NOT LIKE I HAD A CHOICE. I WAS READY FOR WHATEVER CAME MY WAY.
BUT I HAVE TO ADMIT THAT I WAS READY FOR ANYTHING EXCEPT WHAT ACTUALLY HAPPENED...
I SAID TO MYSELF THAT A DAY OFF WOULD DO US WELL. IN ANY EVENT, THERE'S NOT MUCH WORK LEFT FOR US TO DO. WE COULD TAKE SOME PHOTOS TOGETHER.
FOR THE FIRST TIME IN YEARS...

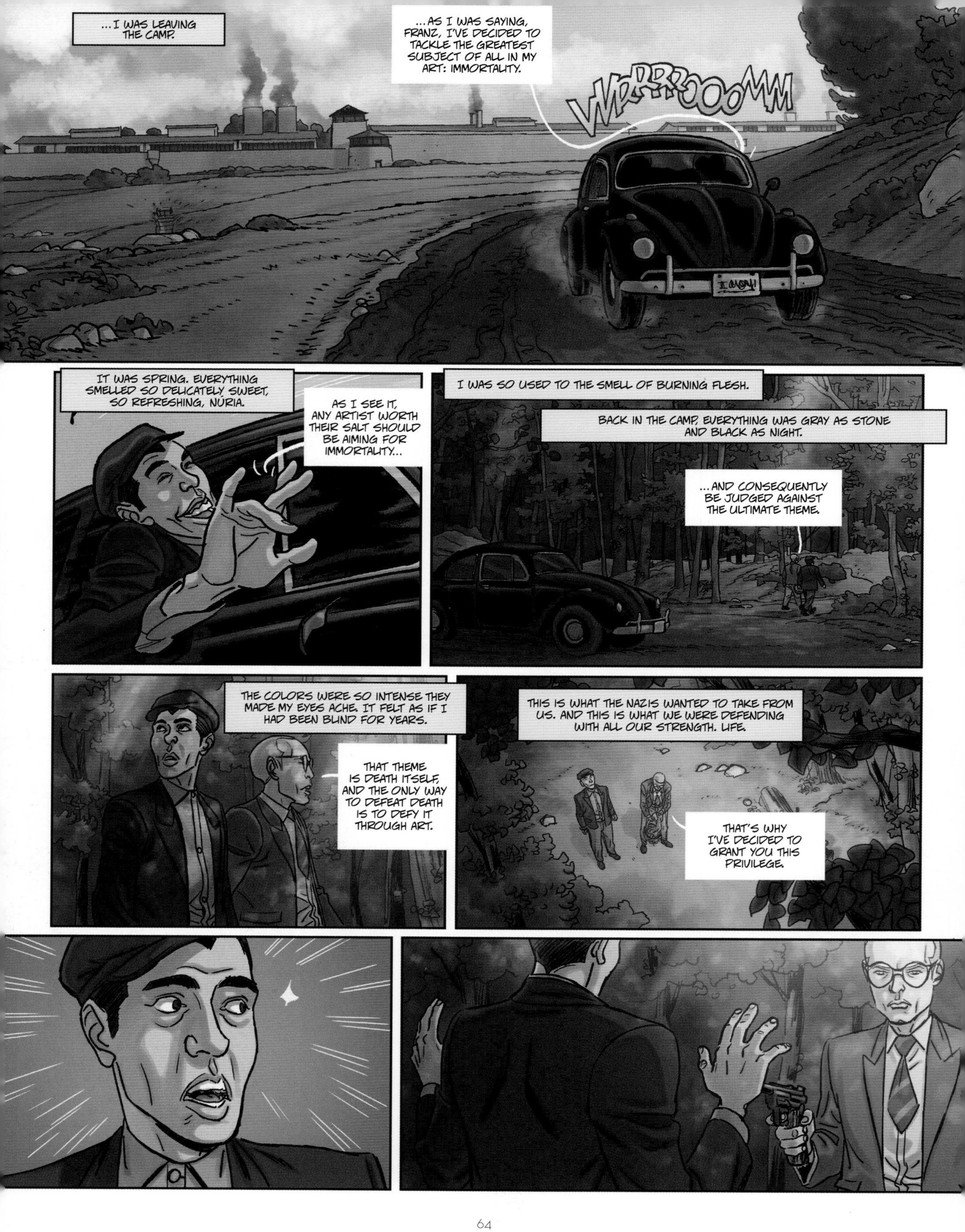

...I WAS LEAVING THE CAMP.
...AS I WAS SAYING, FRANZ, I'VE DECIDED TO TACKLE THE GREATEST SUBJECT OF ALL IN MY ART: IMMORTALITY.
WRRRROOOMM
IT WAS SPRING. EVERYTHING SMELLED SO DELICATELY SWEET, SO REFRESHING, NÚRIA.
AS I SEE IT, ANY ARTIST WORTH THEIR SALT SHOULD BE AIMING FOR IMMORTALITY...
I WAS SO USED TO THE SMELL OF BURNING FLESH.
BACK IN THE CAMP, EVERYTHING WAS GRAY AS STONE AND BLACK AS NIGHT.
...AND CONSEQUENTLY BE JUDGED AGAINST THE ULTIMATE THEME.
THE COLORS WERE SO INTENSE THEY MADE MY EYES ACHE. IT FELT AS IF I HAD BEEN BLIND FOR YEARS.
THAT THEME IS DEATH ITSELF, AND THE ONLY WAY TO DEFEAT DEATH IS TO DEFY IT THROUGH ART.
THIS IS WHAT THE NAZIS WANTED TO TAKE FROM US. AND THIS IS WHAT WE WERE DEFENDING WITH ALL OUR STRENGTH. LIFE.
THAT'S WHY I'VE DECIDED TO GRANT YOU THIS PRIVILEGE.

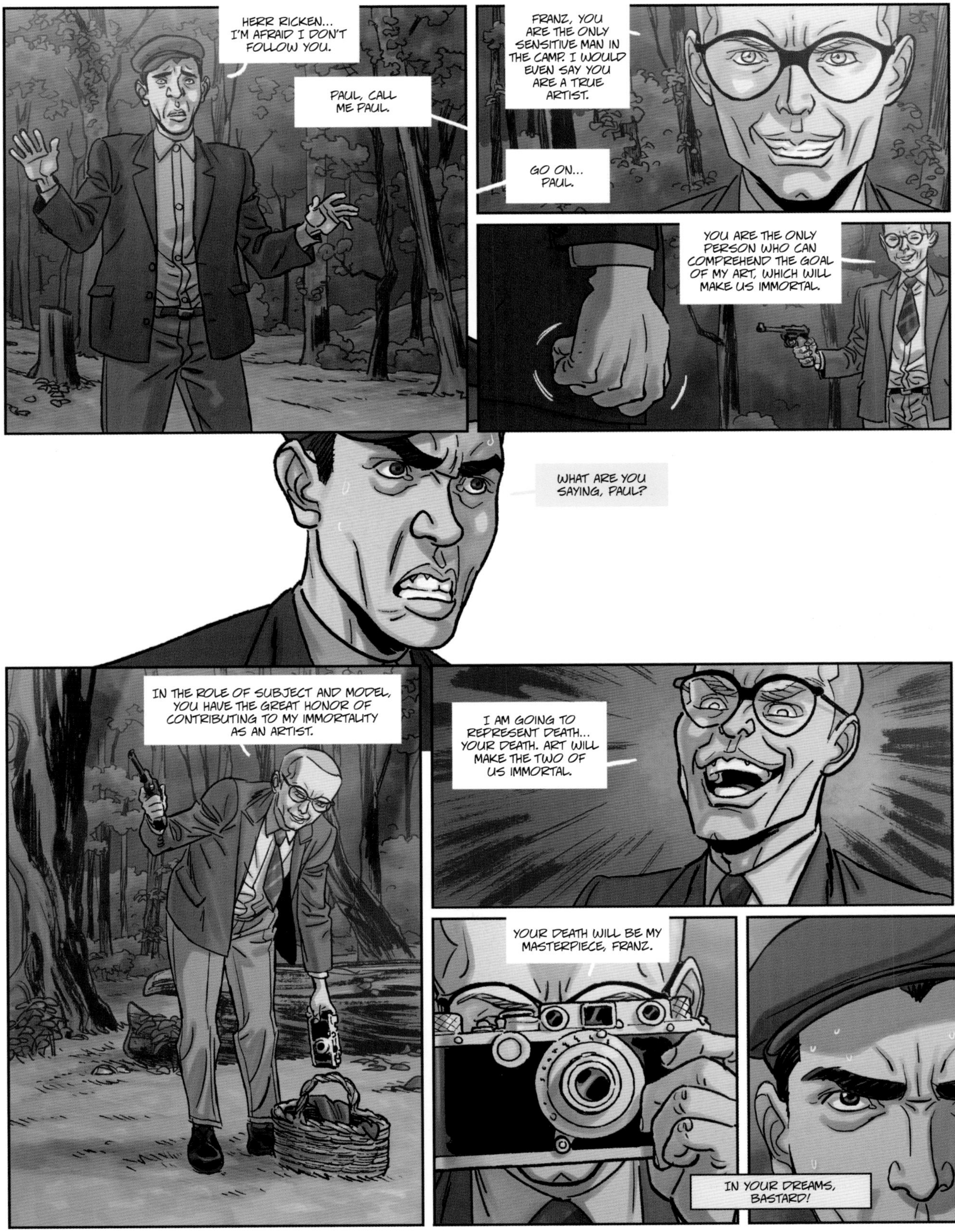
HERR RICKEN... I'M AFRAID I DON'T FOLLOW YOU.
PAUL, CALL ME PAUL.
FRANZ, YOU ARE THE ONLY SENSITIVE MAN IN THE CAMP. I WOULD EVEN SAY YOU ARE A TRUE ARTIST.
GO ON... PAUL.
YOU ARE THE ONLY PERSON WHO CAN COMPREHEND THE GOAL OF MY ART, WHICH WILL MAKE US IMMORTAL.
WHAT ARE YOU SAYING, PAUL?
IN THE ROLE OF SUBJECT AND MODEL, YOU HAVE THE GREAT HONOR OF CONTRIBUTING TO MY IMMORTALITY AS AN ARTIST.
I AM GOING TO REPRESENT DEATH... YOUR DEATH. ART WILL MAKE THE TWO OF US IMMORTAL.
YOUR DEATH WILL BE MY MASTERPIECE, FRANZ.
IN YOUR DREAMS, BASTARD!

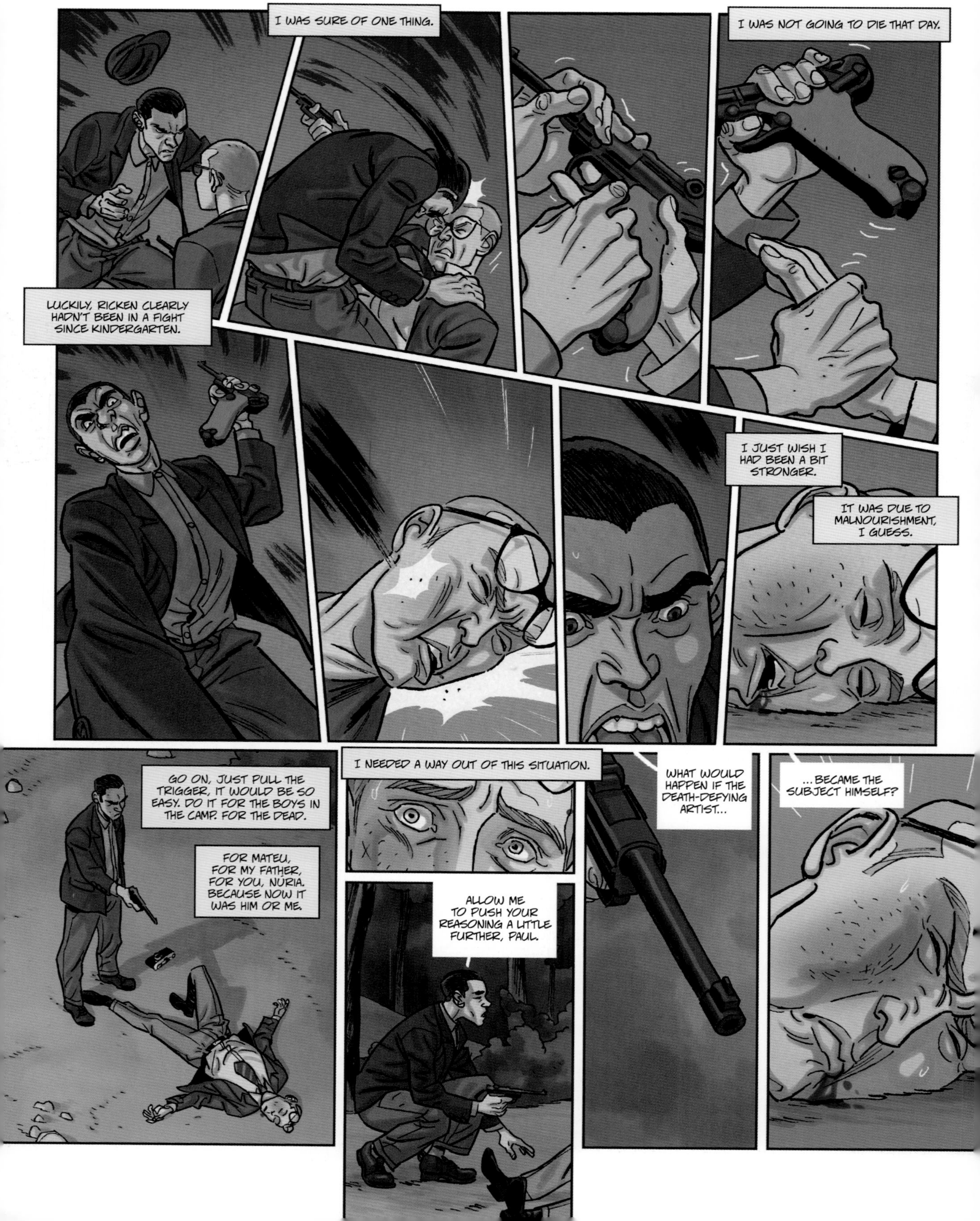
I WAS SURE OF ONE THING.
I WAS NOT GOING TO DIE THAT DAY.
LUCKILY, RICKEN CLEARLY HADN'T BEEN IN A FIGHT SINCE KINDERGARTEN.
I JUST WISH I HAD BEEN A BIT STRONGER.
IT WAS DUE TO MALNOURISHMENT, I GUESS.
GO ON, JUST PULL THE TRIGGER, IT WOULD BE SO EASY. DO IT FOR THE BOYS IN THE CAMP. FOR THE DEAD.
FOR MATEU, FOR MY FATHER, FOR YOU, NÚRIA. BECAUSE NOW IT WAS HIM OR ME.
I NEEDED A WAY OUT OF THIS SITUATION.
ALLOW ME TO PUSH YOUR REASONING A LITTLE FURTHER, PAUL.
WHAT WOULD HAPPEN IF THE DEATH-DEFYING ARTIST...
...BECAME THE SUBJECT HIMSELF?

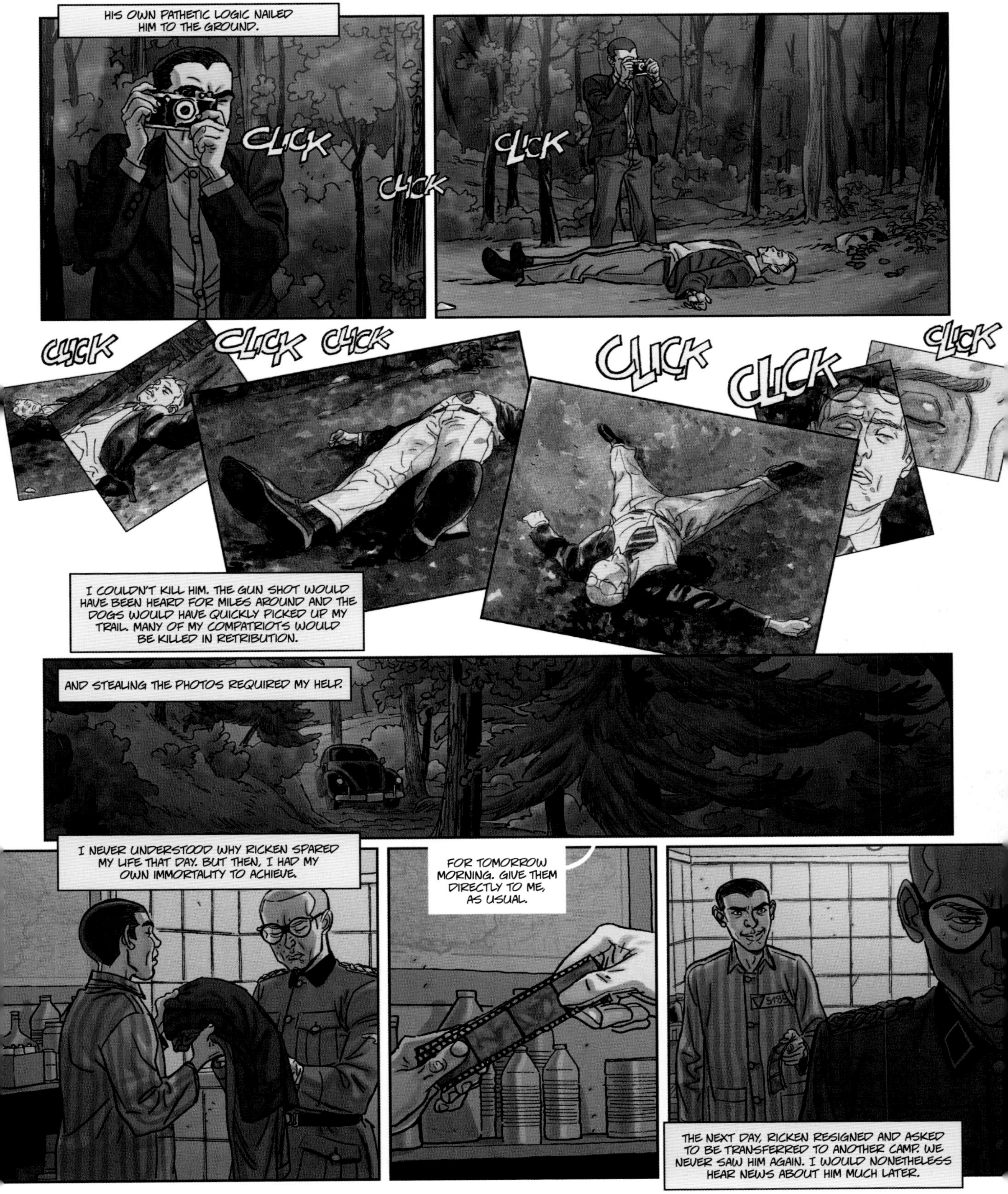
HIS OWN PATHETIC LOGIC NAILED HIM TO THE GROUND.
CLICK
CLICK
CLICK
CLICK
CLICK CLICK
CLICK
CLICK
CLICK
I COULDN'T KILL HIM. THE GUN SHOT WOULD HAVE BEEN HEARD FOR MILES AROUND AND THE DOGS WOULD HAVE QUICKLY PICKED UP MY TRAIL. MANY OF MY COMPATRIOTS WOULD BE KILLED IN RETRIBUTION.
AND STEALING THE PHOTOS REQUIRED MY HELP.
I NEVER UNDERSTOOD WHY RICKEN SPARED MY LIFE THAT DAY. BUT THEN, I HAD MY OWN IMMORTALITY TO ACHIEVE.
FOR TOMORROW MORNING. GIVE THEM DIRECTLY TO ME, AS USUAL.
5189
THE NEXT DAY, RICKEN RESIGNED AND ASKED TO BE TRANSFERRED TO ANOTHER CAMP. WE NEVER SAW HIM AGAIN. I WOULD NONETHELESS HEAR NEWS ABOUT HIM MUCH LATER.

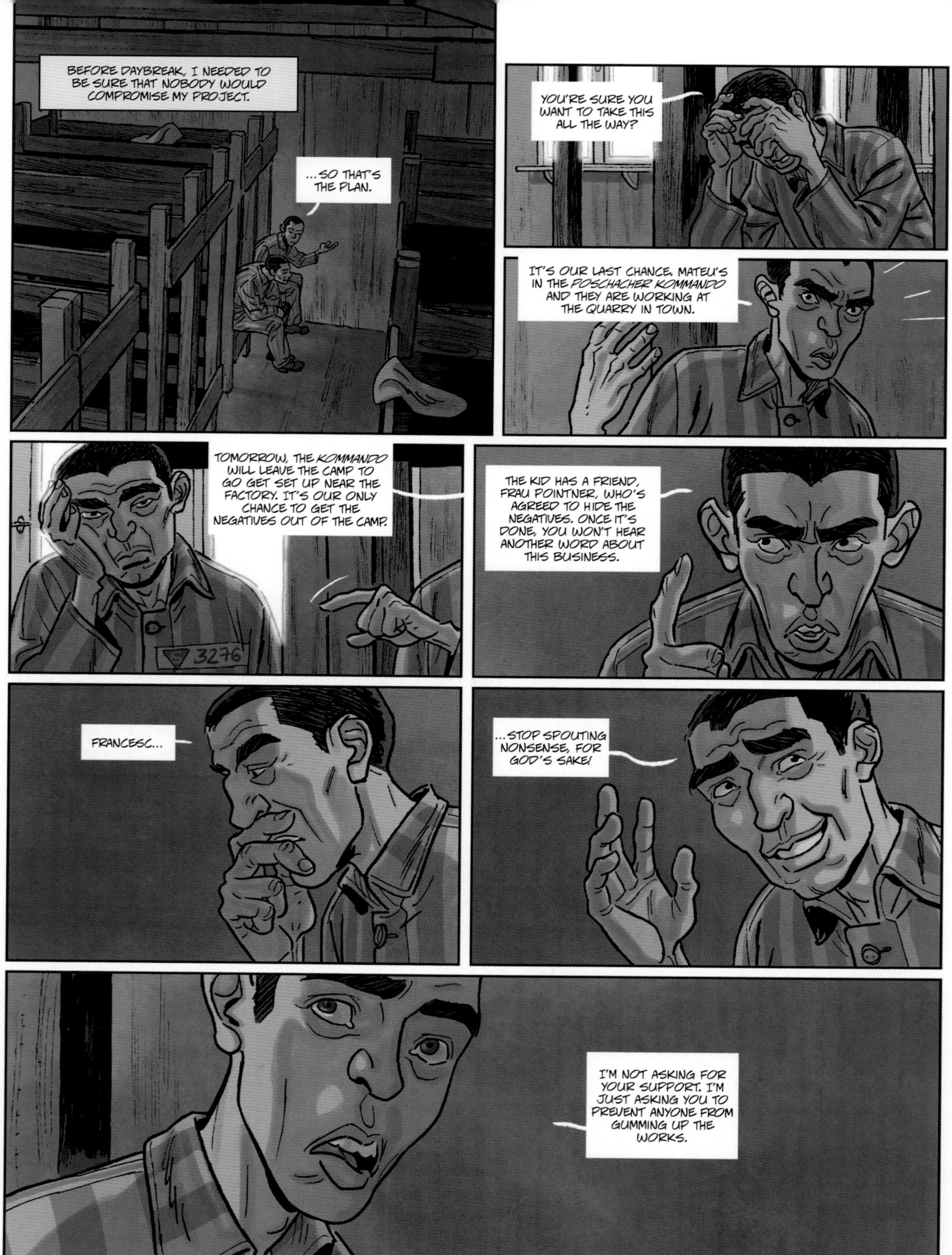
BEFORE DAYBREAK, I NEEDED TO BE SURE THAT NOBODY WOULD COMPROMISE MY PROJECT.
...SO THAT'S THE PLAN.
YOU'RE SURE YOU WANT TO TAKE THIS ALL THE WAY?
IT'S OUR LAST CHANCE. MATEU'S IN THE POSCHACHER KOMMANDO AND THEY ARE WORKING AT THE QUARRY IN TOWN.
TOMORROW, THE KOMMANDO WILL LEAVE THE CAMP TO GO GET SET UP NEAR THE FACTORY. IT'S OUR ONLY CHANCE TO GET THE NEGATIVES OUT OF THE CAMP.
3276
THE KID HAS A FRIEND, FRAU POINTNER, WHO'S AGREED TO HIDE THE NEGATIVES. ONCE IT'S DONE, YOU WON'T HEAR ANOTHER WORD ABOUT THIS BUSINESS.
FRANCESC...
...STOP SPOUTING NONSENSE, FOR GOD'S SAKE!
I'M NOT ASKING FOR YOUR SUPPORT. I'M JUST ASKING YOU TO PREVENT ANYONE FROM GUMMING UP THE WORKS.

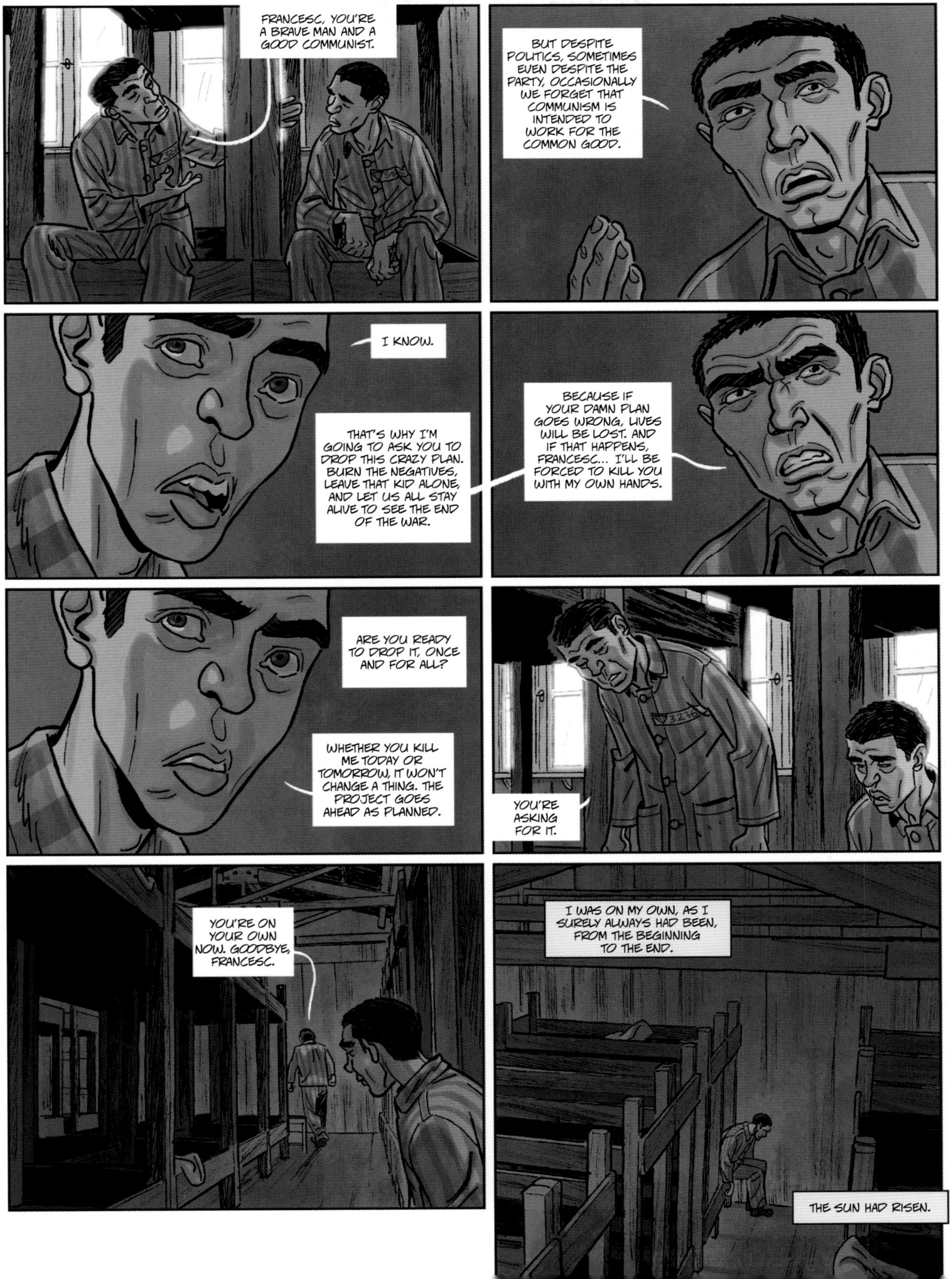
FRANCESC, YOU'RE A BRAVE MAN AND A GOOD COMMUNIST.
BUT DESPITE POLITICS, SOMETIMES EVEN DESPITE THE PARTY, OCCASIONALLY WE FORGET THAT COMMUNISM IS INTENDED TO WORK FOR THE COMMON GOOD.
I KNOW.
THAT'S WHY I'M GOING TO ASK YOU TO DROP THIS CRAZY PLAN. BURN THE NEGATIVES, LEAVE THAT KID ALONE, AND LET US ALL STAY ALIVE TO SEE THE END OF THE WAR.
BECAUSE IF YOUR DAMN PLAN GOES WRONG, LIVES WILL BE LOST. AND IF THAT HAPPENS, FRANCESC... I'LL BE FORCED TO KILL YOU WITH MY OWN HANDS.
ARE YOU READY TO DROP IT, ONCE AND FOR ALL?
WHETHER YOU KILL ME TODAY OR TOMORROW, IT WON'T CHANGE A THING. THE PROJECT GOES AHEAD AS PLANNED.
YOU'RE ASKING FOR IT.
YOU'RE ON YOUR OWN NOW. GOODBYE, FRANCESC.
I WAS ON MY OWN, AS I SURELY ALWAYS HAD BEEN, FROM THE BEGINNING TO THE END.
THE SUN HAD RISEN.

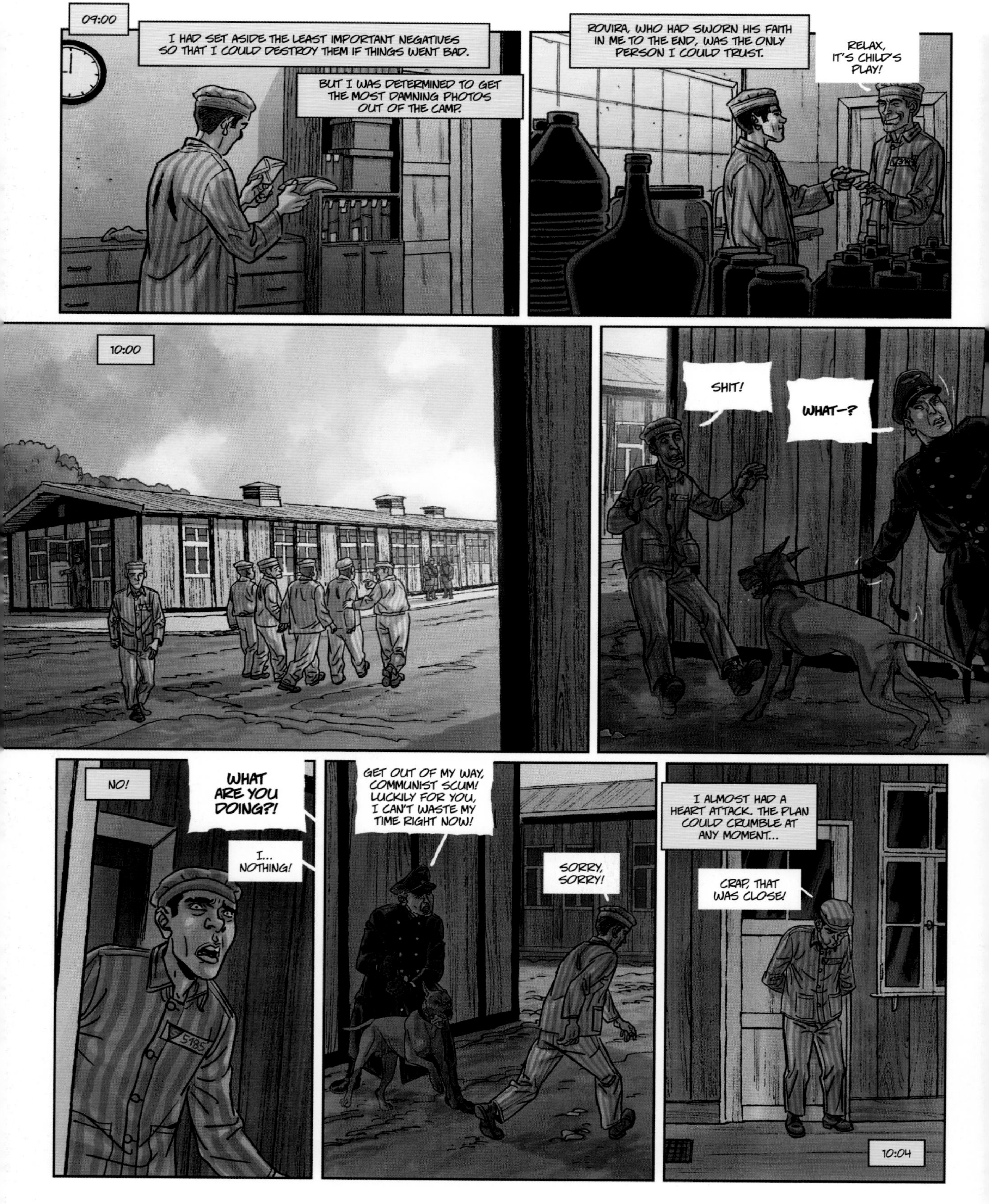

09:00
I HAD SET ASIDE THE LEAST IMPORTANT NEGATIVES SO THAT I COULD DESTROY THEM IF THINGS WENT BAD.
BUT I WAS DETERMINED TO GET THE MOST DAMNING PHOTOS OUT OF THE CAMP.
ROVIRA, WHO HAD SWORN HIS FAITH IN ME TO THE END, WAS THE ONLY PERSON I COULD TRUST.
RELAX, IT'S CHILD'S PLAY!
10:00
SHIT!
WHAT-?
NO!
WHAT ARE YOU DOING?!
I... NOTHING!
GET OUT OF MY WAY, COMMUNIST SCUM! LUCKILY FOR YOU, I CAN'T WASTE MY TIME RIGHT NOW!
SORRY, SORRY!
I ALMOST HAD A HEART ATTACK. THE PLAN COULD CRUMBLE AT ANY MOMENT...
CRAP, THAT WAS CLOSE!
10:04

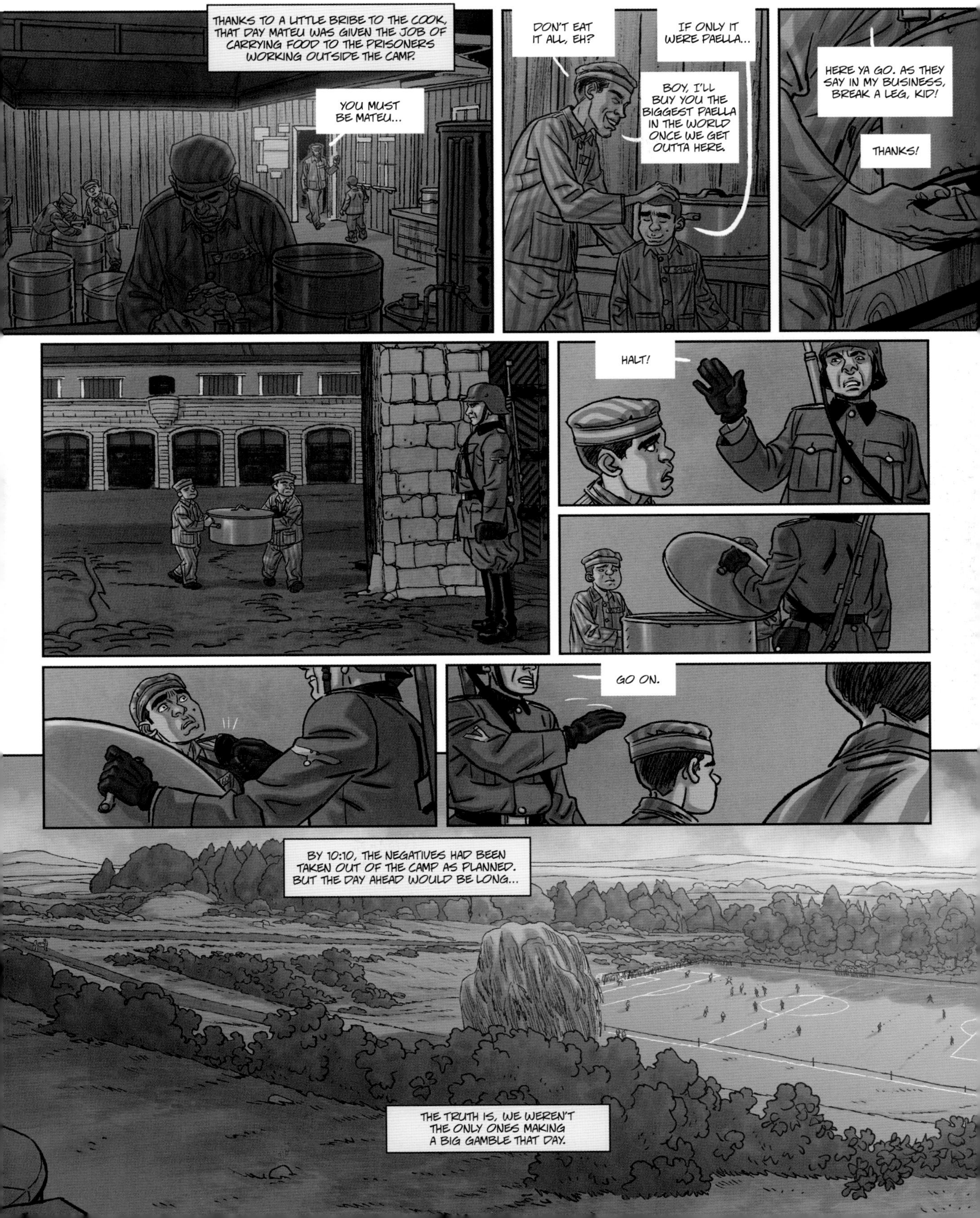
THANKS TO A LITTLE BRIBE TO THE COOK, THAT DAY MATEU WAS GIVEN THE JOB OF CARRYING FOOD TO THE PRISONERS WORKING OUTSIDE THE CAMP.
YOU MUST BE MATEU...
DON'T EAT IT ALL, EH?
IF ONLY IT WERE PAELLA...
BOY, I'LL BUY YOU THE BIGGEST PAELLA IN THE WORLD ONCE WE GET OUTTA HERE.
HERE YA GO. AS THEY SAY IN MY BUSINESS, BREAK A LEG, KID!
THANKS!
HALT!
GO ON.
BY 10:10, THE NEGATIVES HAD BEEN TAKEN OUT OF THE CAMP AS PLANNED. BUT THE DAY AHEAD WOULD BE LONG...
THE TRUTH IS, WE WEREN'T THE ONLY ONES MAKING A BIG GAMBLE THAT DAY.

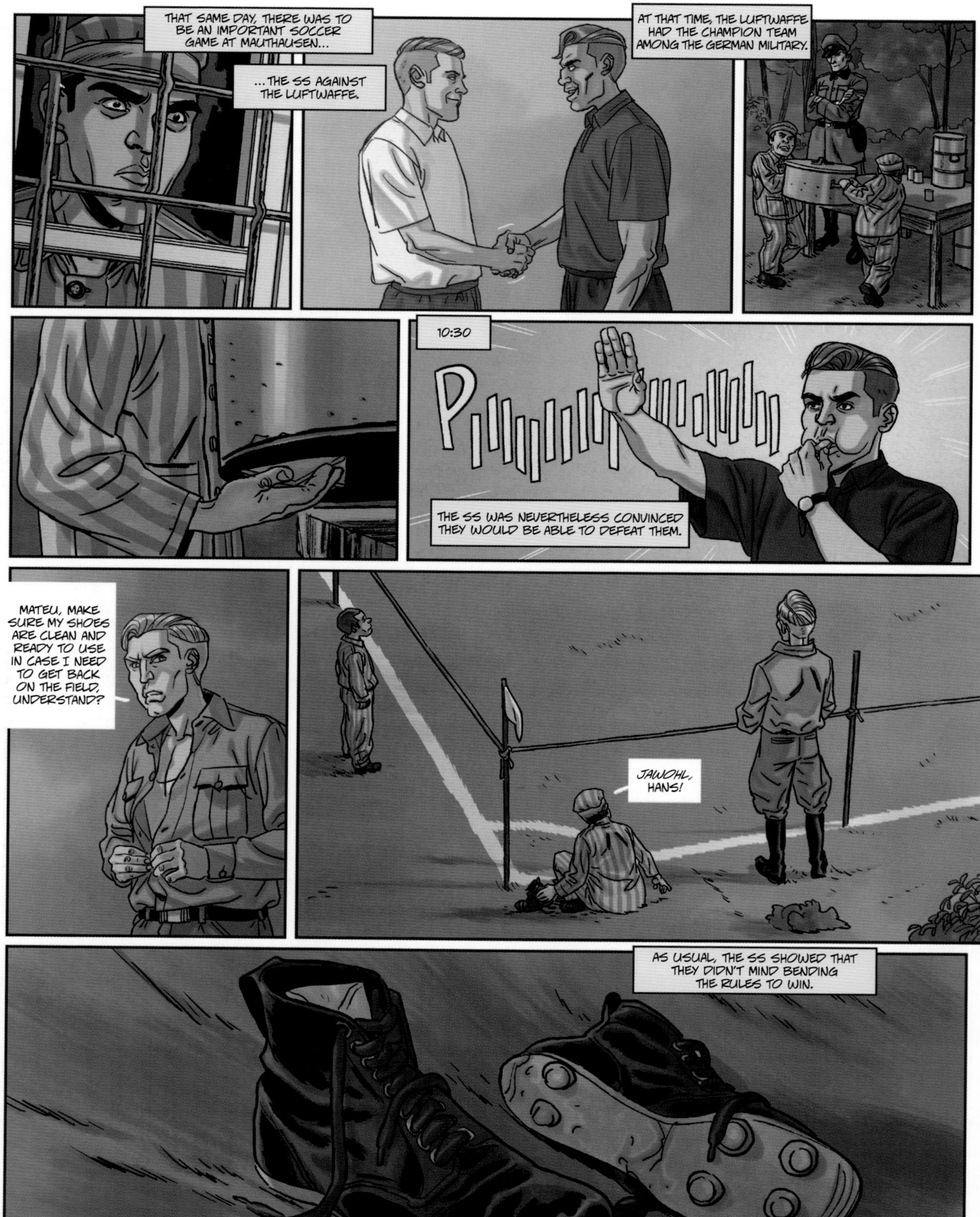
THAT SAME DAY, THERE WAS TO BE AN IMPORTANT SOCCER GAME AT MAUTHAUSEN...
...THE SS AGAINST THE LUFTWAFFE.
AT THAT TIME, THE LUFTWAFFE HAD THE CHAMPION TEAM AMONG THE GERMAN MILITARY.
10:30
PIIIIIIIIIIIIIIIIII
THE SS WAS NEVERTHELESS CONVINCED THEY WOULD BE ABLE TO DEFEAT THEM.
MATEU, MAKE SURE MY SHOES ARE CLEAN AND READY TO USE IN CASE I NEED TO GET BACK ON THE FIELD, UNDERSTAND?
JAWOHL, HANS!
AS USUAL, THE SS SHOWED THAT THEY DIDN'T MIND BENDING THE RULES TO WIN.

NOT ONLY WERE THEY BETTER FED AND RESTED THAN THE MEN OF THE LUFTWAFFE...

...BUT THEY HAD ALSO ORDERED THE CROWD TO DISTRACT THE LUFTWAFFE GOALIE AS BEST THEY COULD. THEY DID IT IN SPANISH, JUST IN CASE...

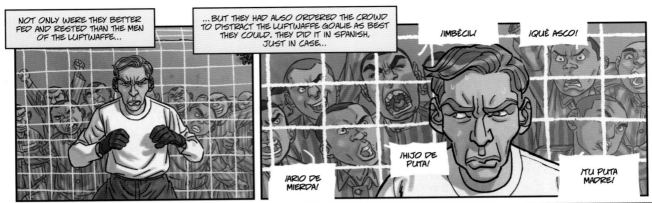

¡IMBÉCIL!

¡QUÉ ASCO!

¡HIJO DE PUTA!

¡ARIO DE MIERDA!

¡TU PUTA MADRE!

MATEU NEEDED TO MAKE IT TO THE OPPOSITE GOAL WITHOUT BEING SEEN.

THE OTHER CHILDREN HAD BEEN TOLD TO FILL UP THE LENGTH OF THE FIELD.

HE NEEDED TO MOVE DOWN THERE BIT BY BIT SO AS NOT TO ATTRACT ATTENTION.

AS LUCK WOULD HAVE IT, EVERYONE'S EYES WERE GLUED TO THE GAME.

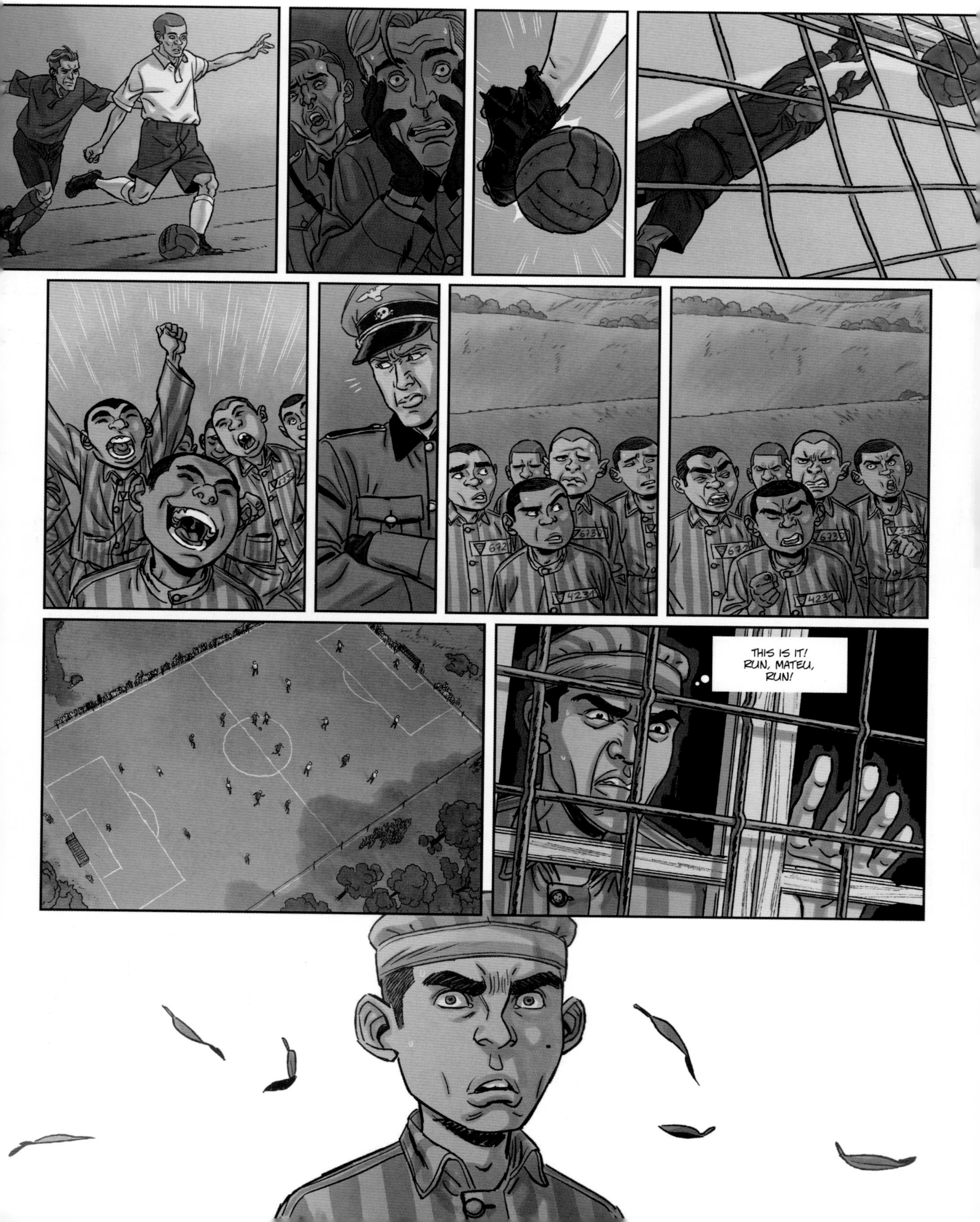
THIS IS IT!
RUN, MATEU,
RUN!

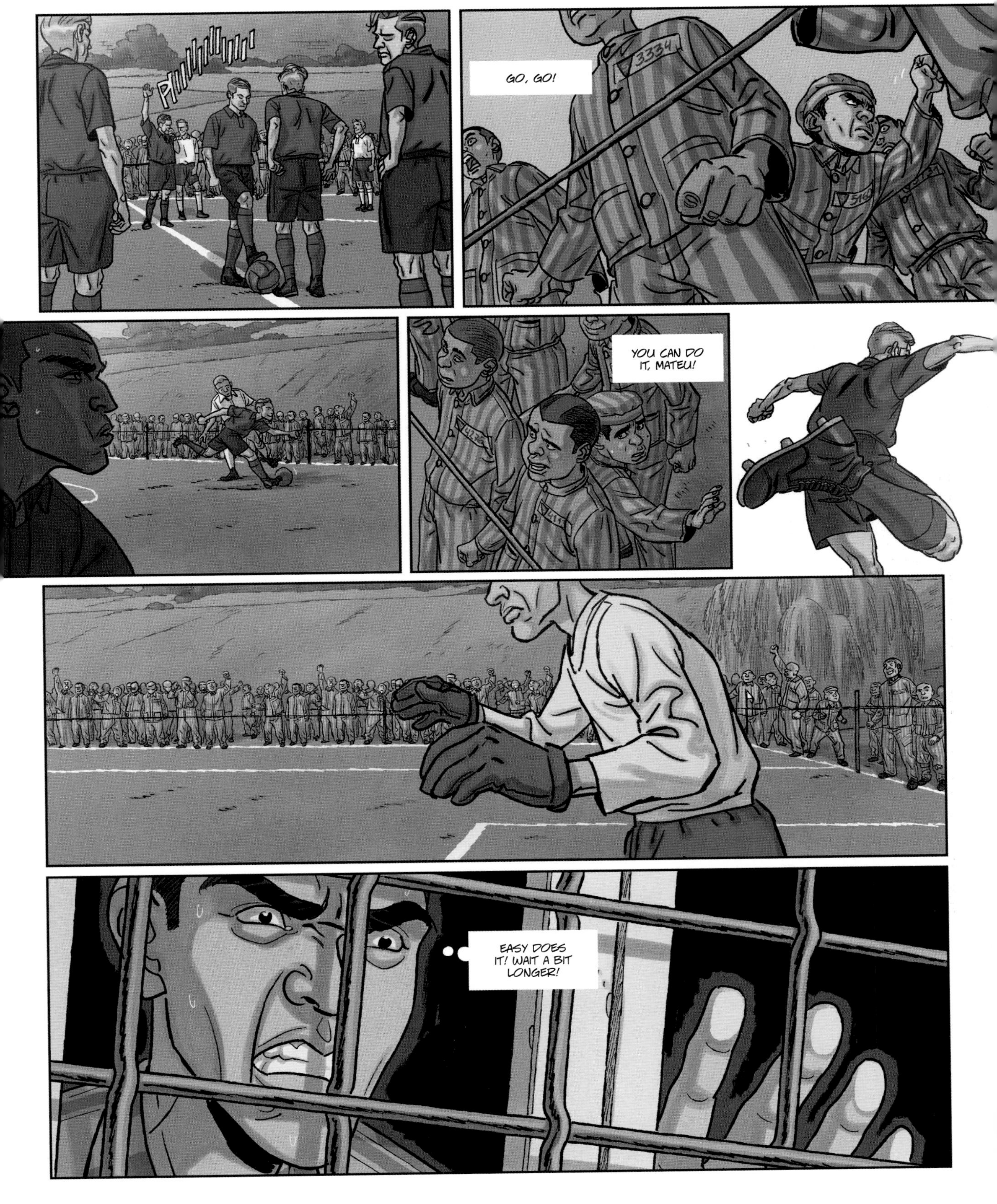
PIIIIIIIIIIIII
GO, GO!
YOU CAN DO IT, MATEU!
EASY DOES IT! WAIT A BIT LONGER!

GOAL!

NOW!

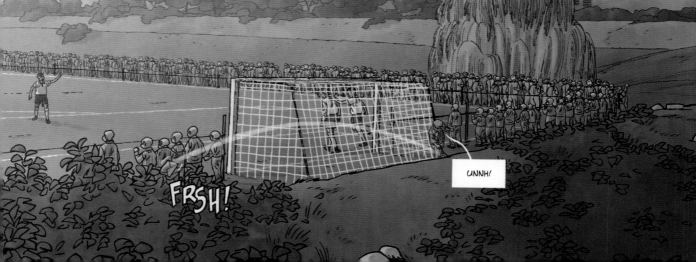

FRSH!

UNNH!

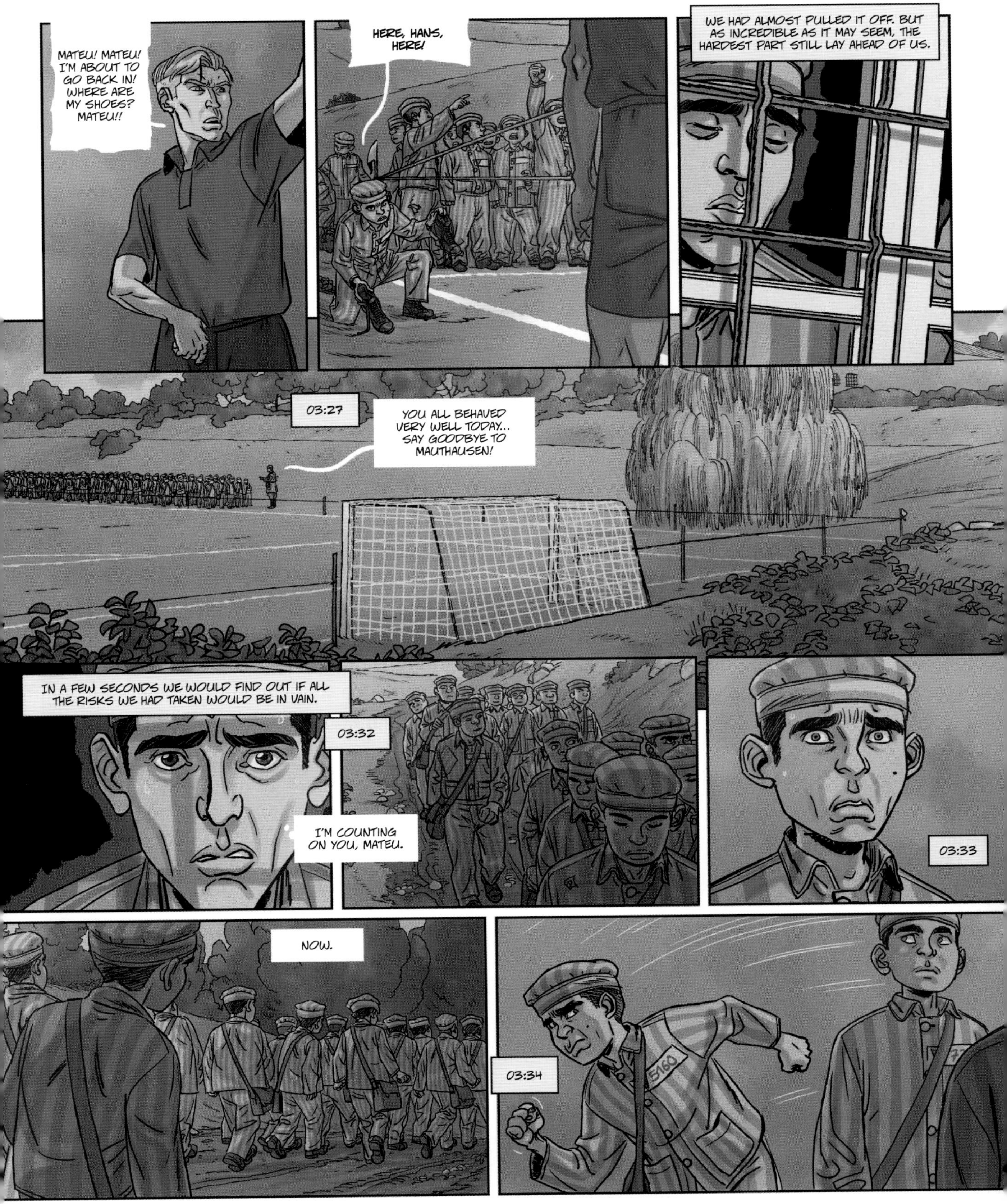
MATEU! MATEU! I'M ABOUT TO GO BACK IN! WHERE ARE MY SHOES? MATEU!!
HERE, HANS, HERE!
WE HAD ALMOST PULLED IT OFF. BUT AS INCREDIBLE AS IT MAY SEEM, THE HARDEST PART STILL LAY AHEAD OF US.
03:27
YOU ALL BEHAVED VERY WELL TODAY... SAY GOODBYE TO MAUTHAUSEN!
IN A FEW SECONDS WE WOULD FIND OUT IF ALL THE RISKS WE HAD TAKEN WOULD BE IN VAIN.
03:32
I'M COUNTING ON YOU, MATEU.
03:33
NOW.
03:34
5160

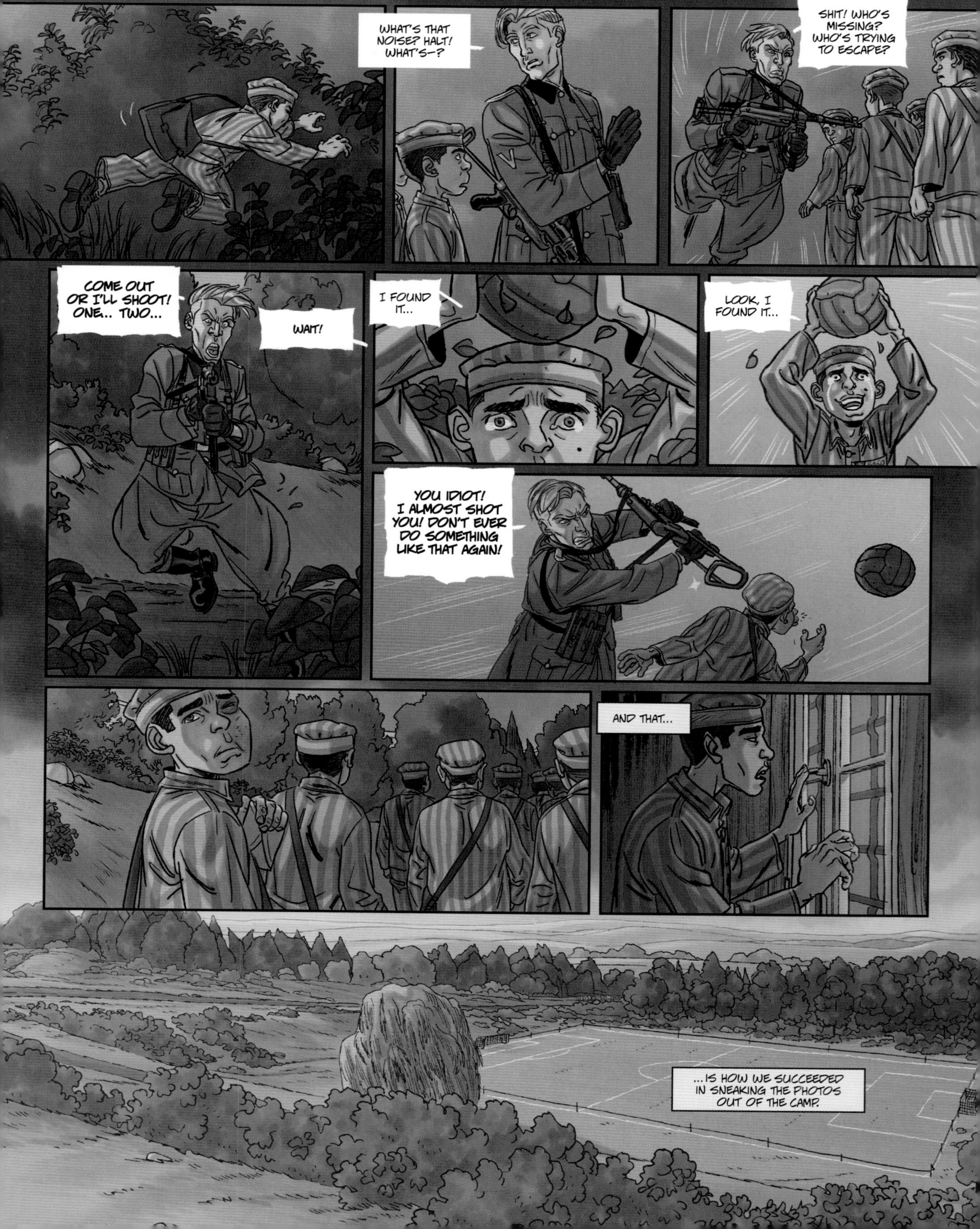
WHAT'S THAT NOISE? HALT! WHAT'S–?
SHIT! WHO'S MISSING? WHO'S TRYING TO ESCAPE?
COME OUT OR I'LL SHOOT! ONE... TWO...
WAIT!
I FOUND IT...
LOOK, I FOUND IT...
YOU IDIOT! I ALMOST SHOT YOU! DON'T EVER DO SOMETHING LIKE THAT AGAIN!
AND THAT...
...IS HOW WE SUCCEEDED IN SNEAKING THE PHOTOS OUT OF THE CAMP.

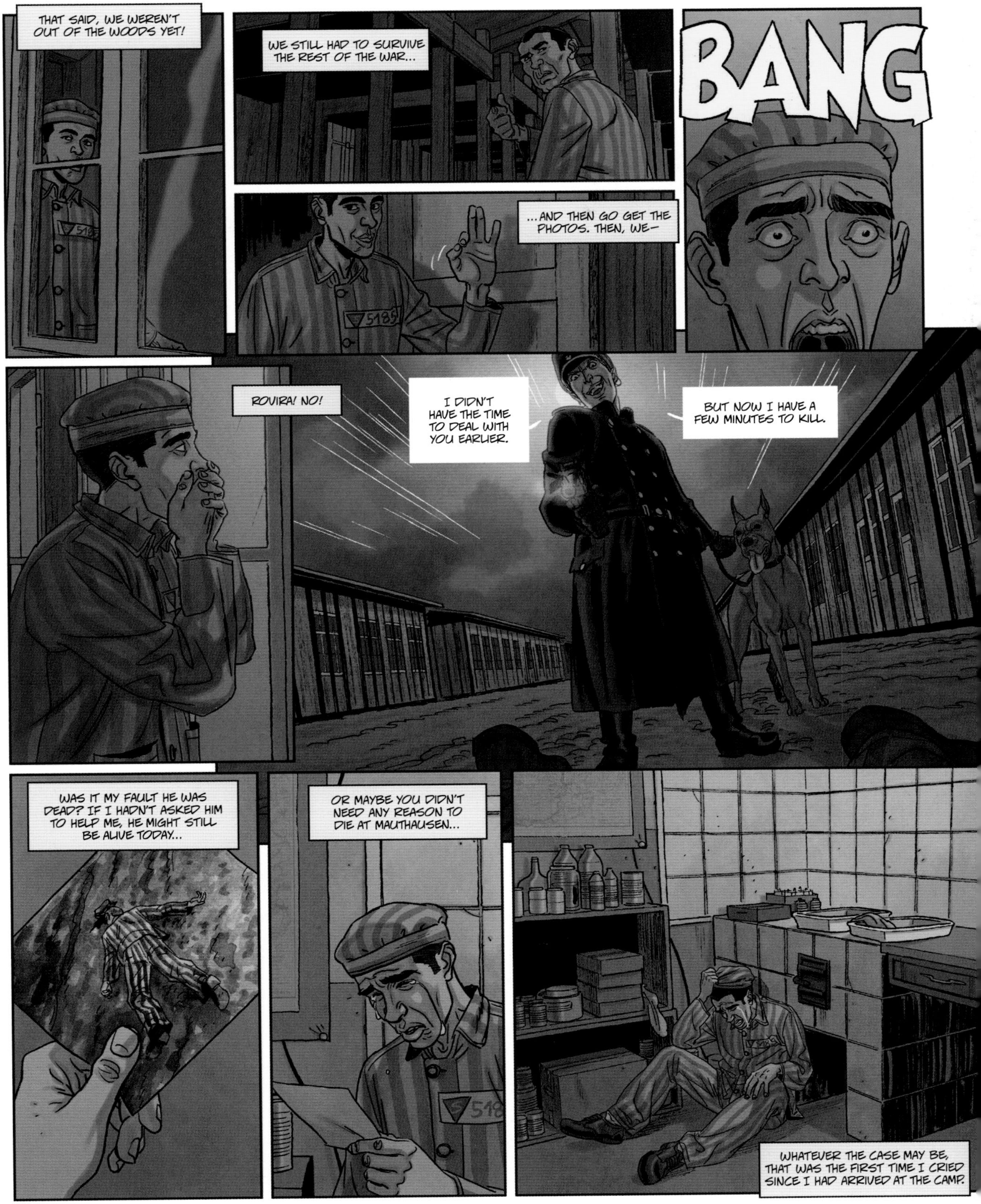
THAT SAID, WE WEREN'T OUT OF THE WOODS YET!
WE STILL HAD TO SURVIVE THE REST OF THE WAR...
...AND THEN GO GET THE PHOTOS. THEN, WE—
BANG
ROVIRA! NO!
I DIDN'T HAVE THE TIME TO DEAL WITH YOU EARLIER.
BUT NOW I HAVE A FEW MINUTES TO KILL.
WAS IT MY FAULT HE WAS DEAD? IF I HADN'T ASKED HIM TO HELP ME, HE MIGHT STILL BE ALIVE TODAY...
OR MAYBE YOU DIDN'T NEED ANY REASON TO DIE AT MAUTHAUSEN...
WHATEVER THE CASE MAY BE, THAT WAS THE FIRST TIME I CRIED SINCE I HAD ARRIVED AT THE CAMP.

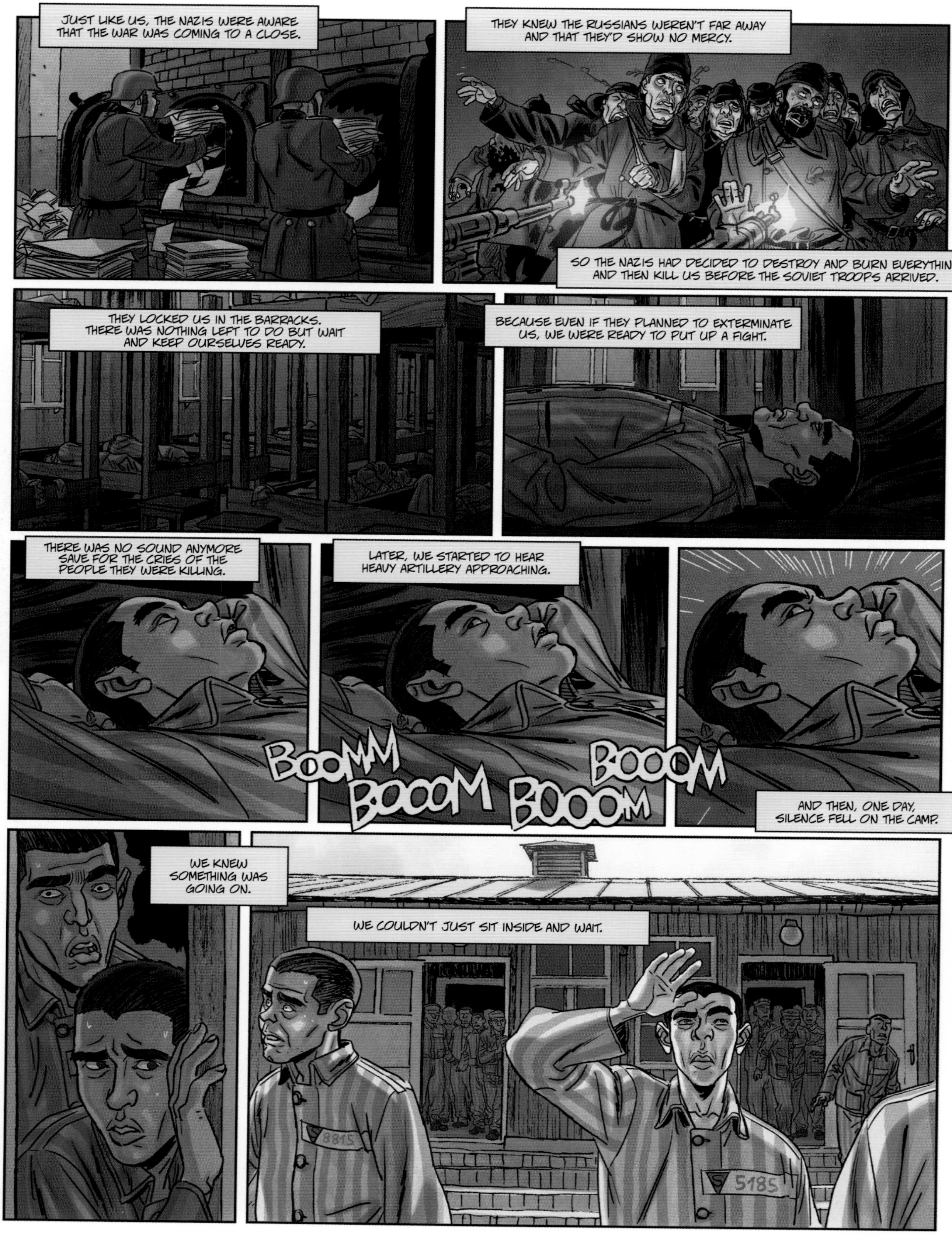
JUST LIKE US, THE NAZIS WERE AWARE THAT THE WAR WAS COMING TO A CLOSE.
THEY KNEW THE RUSSIANS WEREN'T FAR AWAY AND THAT THEY'D SHOW NO MERCY.
SO THE NAZIS HAD DECIDED TO DESTROY AND BURN EVERYTHING AND THEN KILL US BEFORE THE SOVIET TROOPS ARRIVED.
THEY LOCKED US IN THE BARRACKS. THERE WAS NOTHING LEFT TO DO BUT WAIT AND KEEP OURSELVES READY.
BECAUSE EVEN IF THEY PLANNED TO EXTERMINATE US, WE WERE READY TO PUT UP A FIGHT.
THERE WAS NO SOUND ANYMORE SAVE FOR THE CRIES OF THE PEOPLE THEY WERE KILLING.
LATER, WE STARTED TO HEAR HEAVY ARTILLERY APPROACHING.
BOOMM
BOOOM
BOOOM
BOOOM
AND THEN, ONE DAY, SILENCE FELL ON THE CAMP.
WE KNEW SOMETHING WAS GOING ON.
WE COULDN'T JUST SIT INSIDE AND WAIT.
8815
5185

BUT, UNSURPRISINGLY...

...THE SS HAD FLED, LEAVING BEHIND A HANDFUL OF OLD FIREMEN FROM THE *VOLKSSTURM*, WHO PUT UP LITTLE RESISTANCE.

NOW THAT WE WERE ARMED, WE COULD DEFEND OURSELVES IF THE SS RETURNED.

AS FOR ME...

...I HAD MY CAMERA! I WAS A PHOTOGRAPHER AGAIN.

TANKS! TANKS!

THINGS WERE GOING TO START HAPPENING FAST.

HURRY UP AND FINISH THAT BANNER! WHICH ARMY IS IT?

I NEEDED TO BE READY!

AS I HAD NEVER BEEN BEFORE...

I THINK IT'S...

AN A LAS FUERZAS.LIBERAD
нские антифашисты
приветству нотиосвосоаителеŭ
RÀ

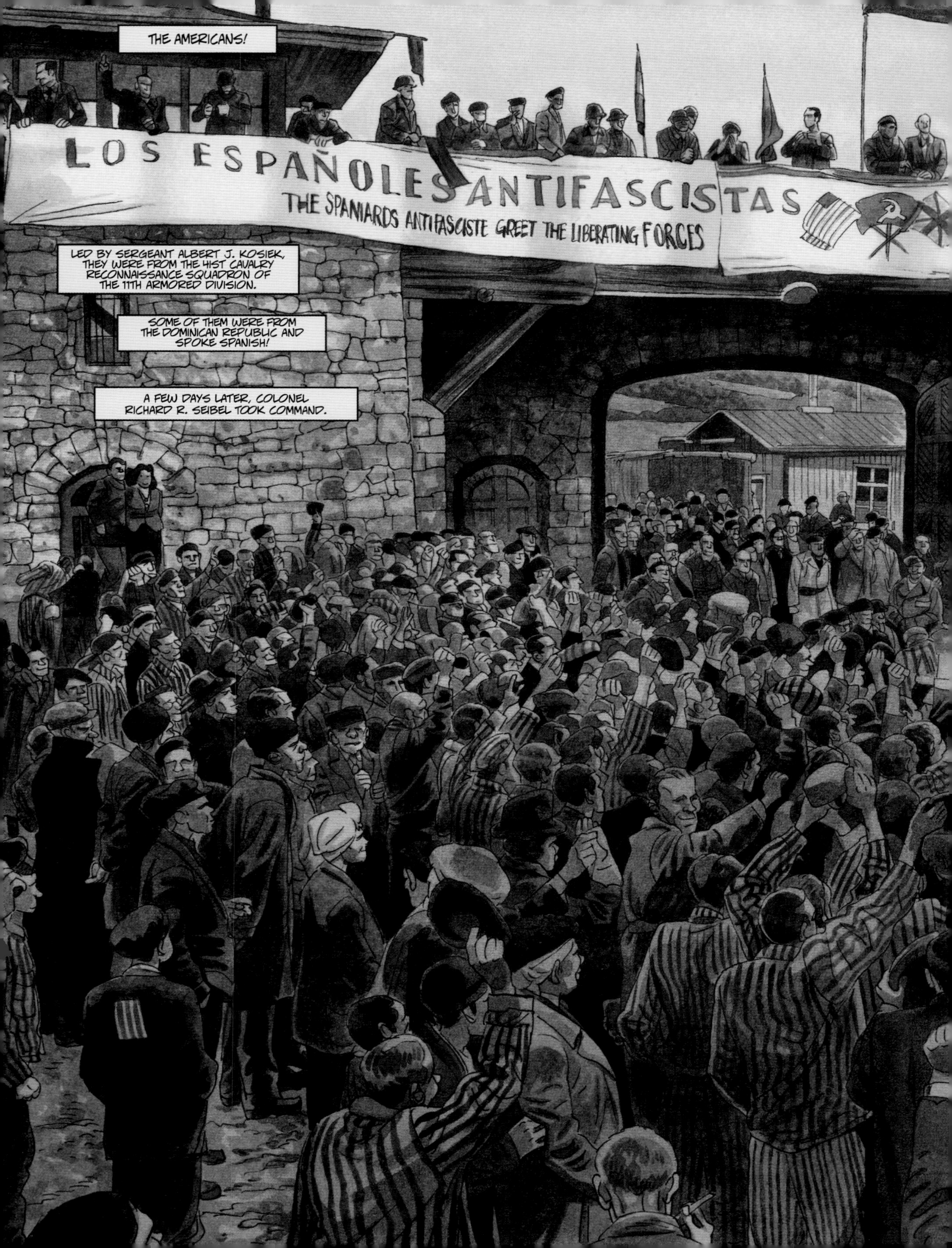
THE AMERICANS!
LOS ESPAÑOLES ANTIFASCISTAS
THE SPANIARDS ANTIFASCISTE GREET THE LIBERATING FORCES
LED BY SERGEANT ALBERT J. KOSIEK, THEY WERE FROM THE 41ST CAVALRY RECONNAISSANCE SQUADRON OF THE 11TH ARMORED DIVISION.
SOME OF THEM WERE FROM THE DOMINICAN REPUBLIC AND SPOKE SPANISH!
A FEW DAYS LATER, COLONEL RICHARD R. SEIBEL TOOK COMMAND.

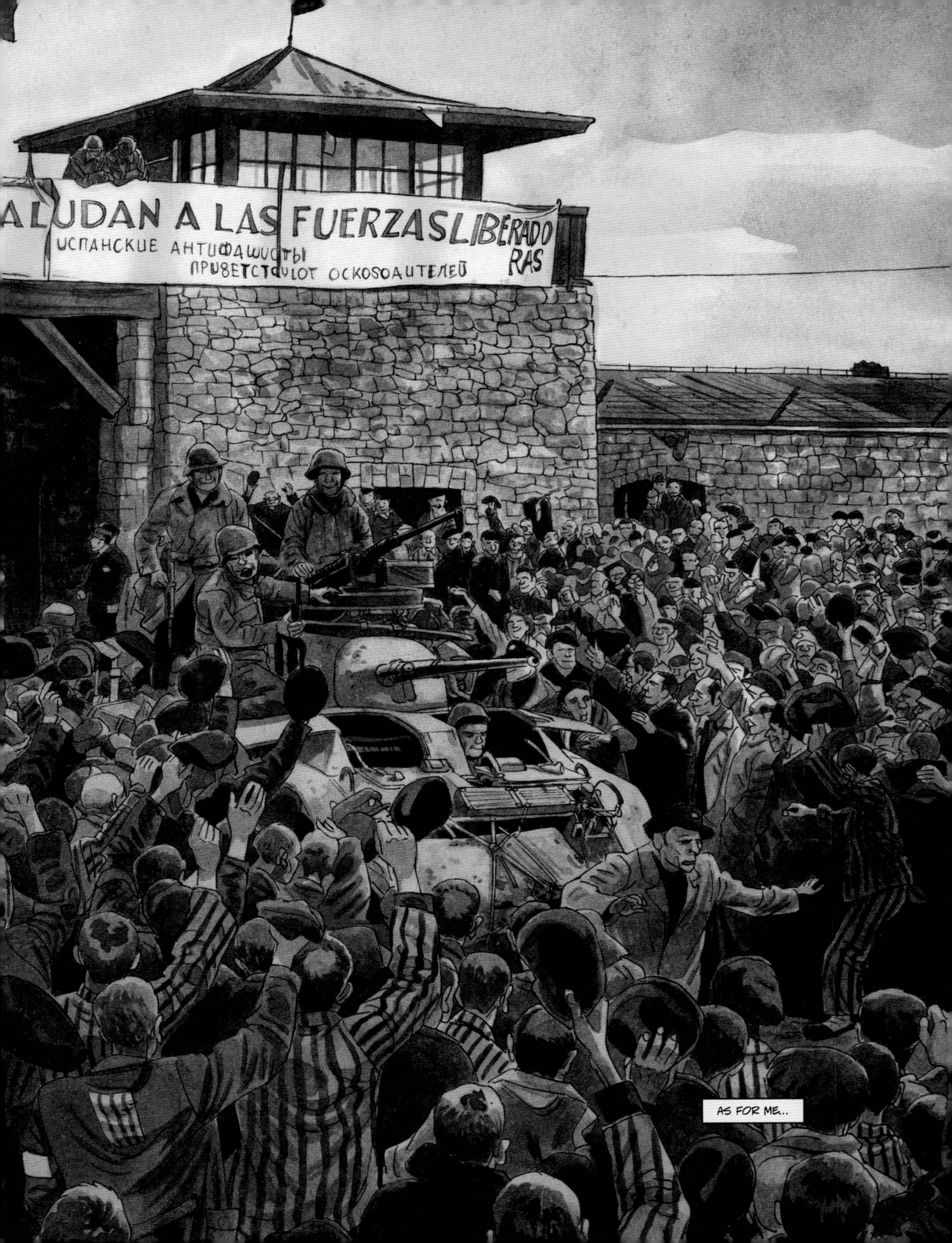
ALUDAN A LAS FUERZAS LIBERADO RAS
ИСПАНСКИЕ АНТИФАШИСТЫ
AS FOR ME...

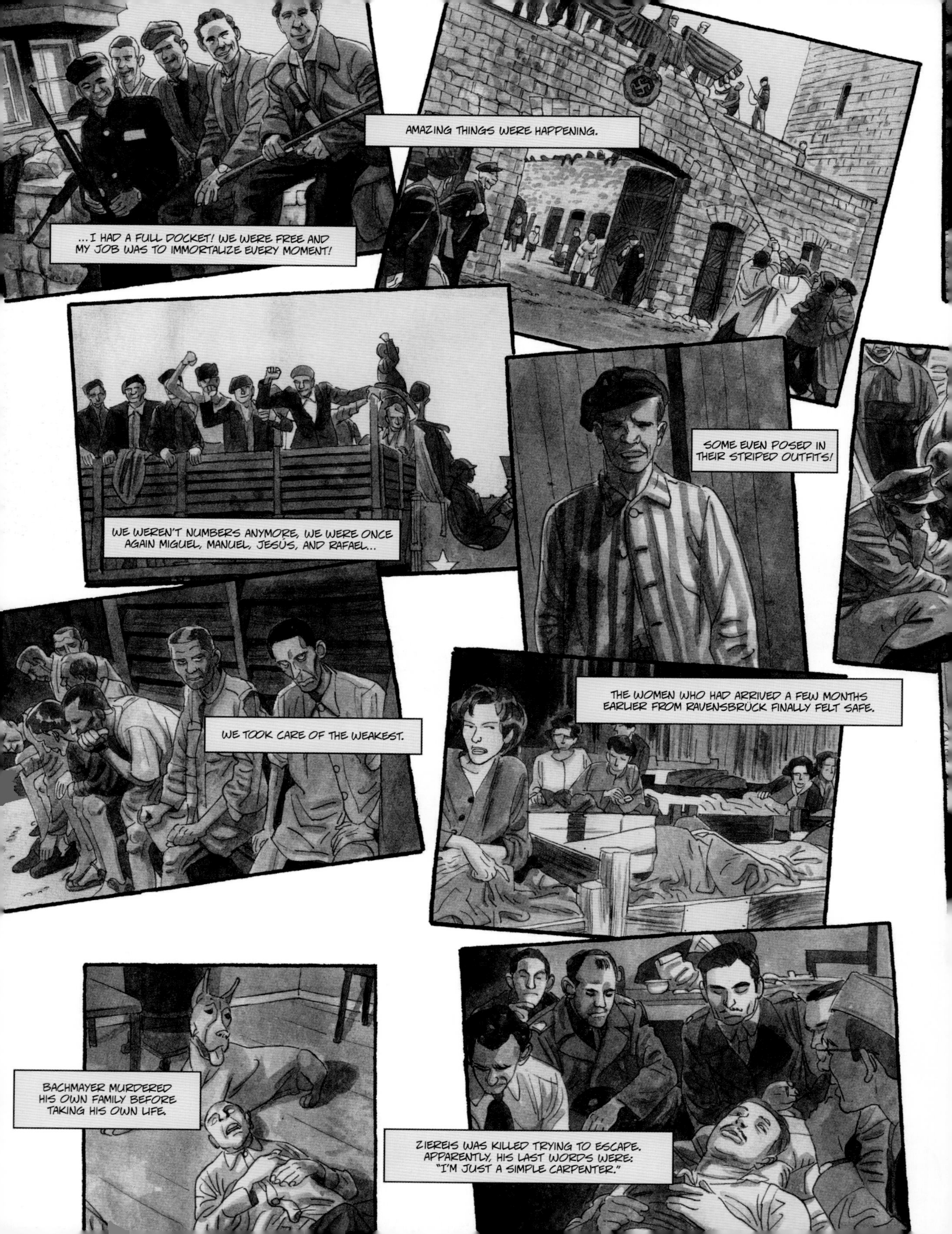
...I HAD A FULL DOCKET! WE WERE FREE AND MY JOB WAS TO IMMORTALIZE EVERY MOMENT!
AMAZING THINGS WERE HAPPENING.
WE WEREN'T NUMBERS ANYMORE, WE WERE ONCE AGAIN MIGUEL, MANUEL, JESÚS, AND RAFAEL...
SOME EVEN POSED IN THEIR STRIPED OUTFITS!
WE TOOK CARE OF THE WEAKEST.
THE WOMEN WHO HAD ARRIVED A FEW MONTHS EARLIER FROM RAVENSBRÜCK FINALLY FELT SAFE.
BACHMAYER MURDERED HIS OWN FAMILY BEFORE TAKING HIS OWN LIFE.
ZIEREIS WAS KILLED TRYING TO ESCAPE. APPARENTLY, HIS LAST WORDS WERE: "I'M JUST A SIMPLE CARPENTER."

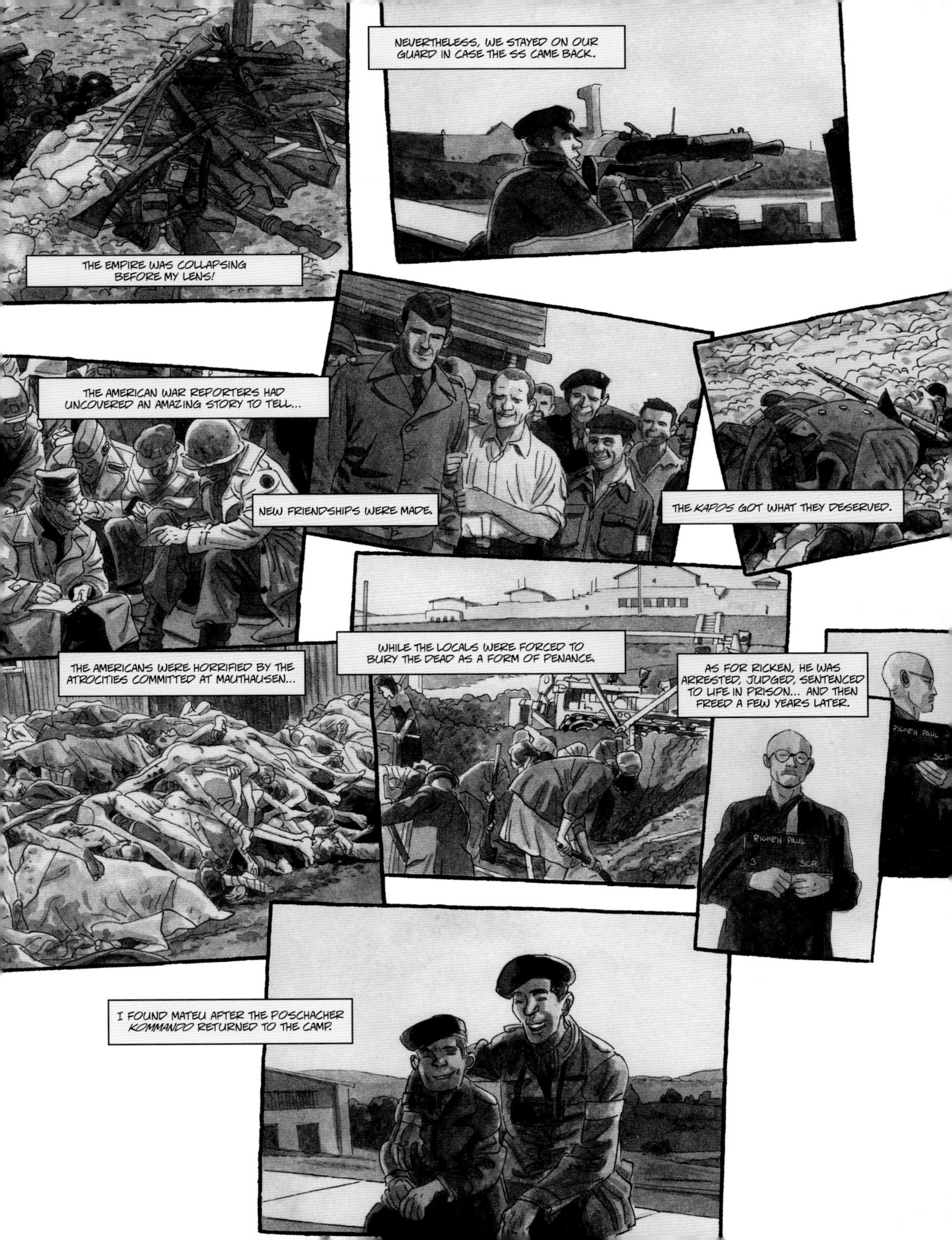
THE EMPIRE WAS COLLAPSING BEFORE MY LENS!
NEVERTHELESS, WE STAYED ON OUR GUARD IN CASE THE SS CAME BACK.
THE AMERICAN WAR REPORTERS HAD UNCOVERED AN AMAZING STORY TO TELL...
NEW FRIENDSHIPS WERE MADE.
THE *KAPOS* GOT WHAT THEY DESERVED.
THE AMERICANS WERE HORRIFIED BY THE ATROCITIES COMMITTED AT MAUTHAUSEN...
WHILE THE LOCALS WERE FORCED TO BURY THE DEAD AS A FORM OF PENANCE.
AS FOR RICKEN, HE WAS ARRESTED, JUDGED, SENTENCED TO LIFE IN PRISON... AND THEN FREED A FEW YEARS LATER.
RICKEN PAUL
3 SCR
I FOUND MATEU AFTER THE POSCHACHER *KOMMANDO* RETURNED TO THE CAMP.

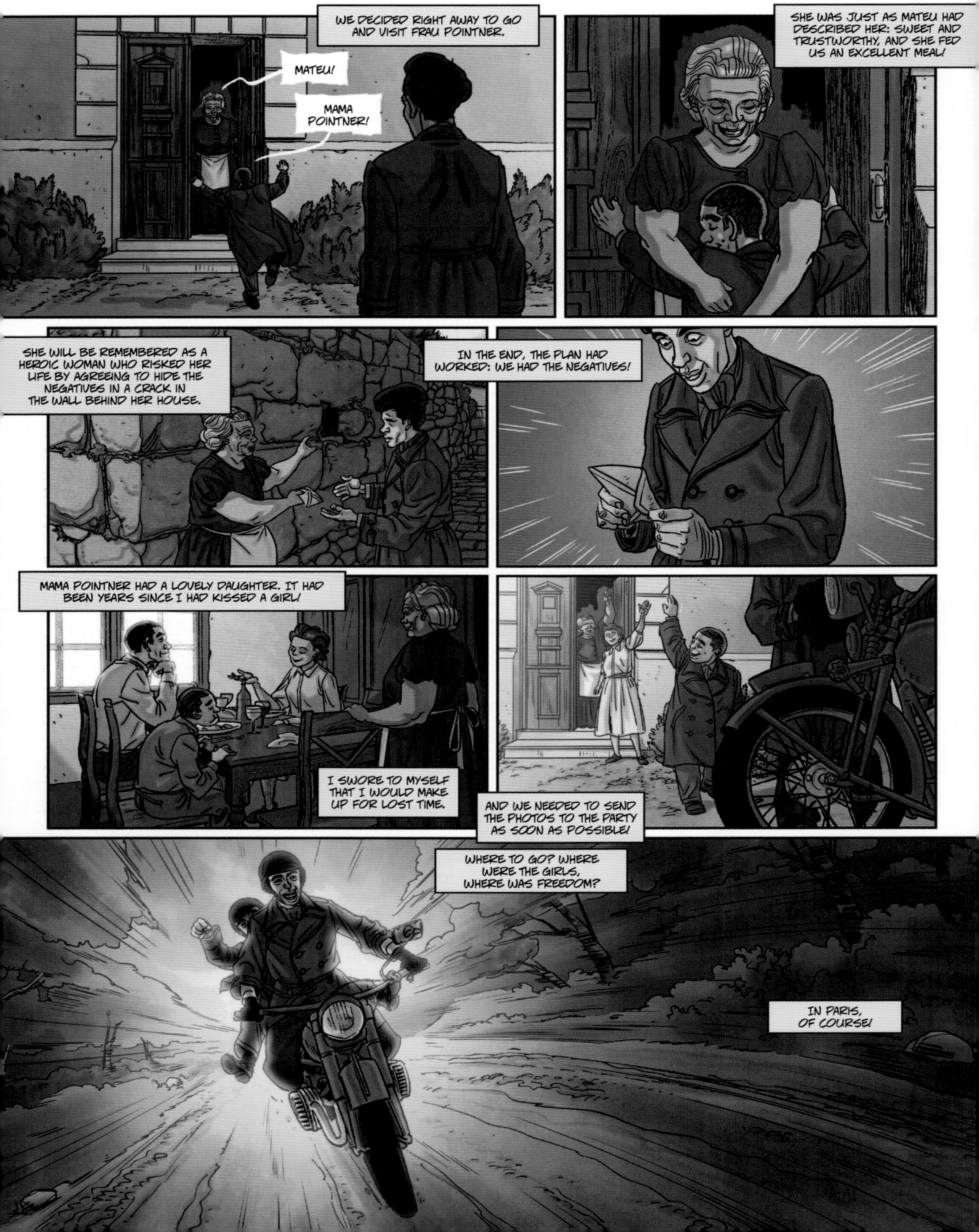

WE DECIDED RIGHT AWAY TO GO AND VISIT FRAU POINTNER.
MATEU!
MAMA POINTNER!
SHE WAS JUST AS MATEU HAD DESCRIBED HER: SWEET AND TRUSTWORTHY, AND SHE FED US AN EXCELLENT MEAL!
SHE WILL BE REMEMBERED AS A HEROIC WOMAN WHO RISKED HER LIFE BY AGREEING TO HIDE THE NEGATIVES IN A CRACK IN THE WALL BEHIND HER HOUSE.
IN THE END, THE PLAN HAD WORKED: WE HAD THE NEGATIVES!
MAMA POINTNER HAD A LOVELY DAUGHTER. IT HAD BEEN YEARS SINCE I HAD KISSED A GIRL!
I SWORE TO MYSELF THAT I WOULD MAKE UP FOR LOST TIME.
AND WE NEEDED TO SEND THE PHOTOS TO THE PARTY AS SOON AS POSSIBLE!
WHERE TO GO? WHERE WERE THE GIRLS, WHERE WAS FREEDOM?
IN PARIS, OF COURSE!

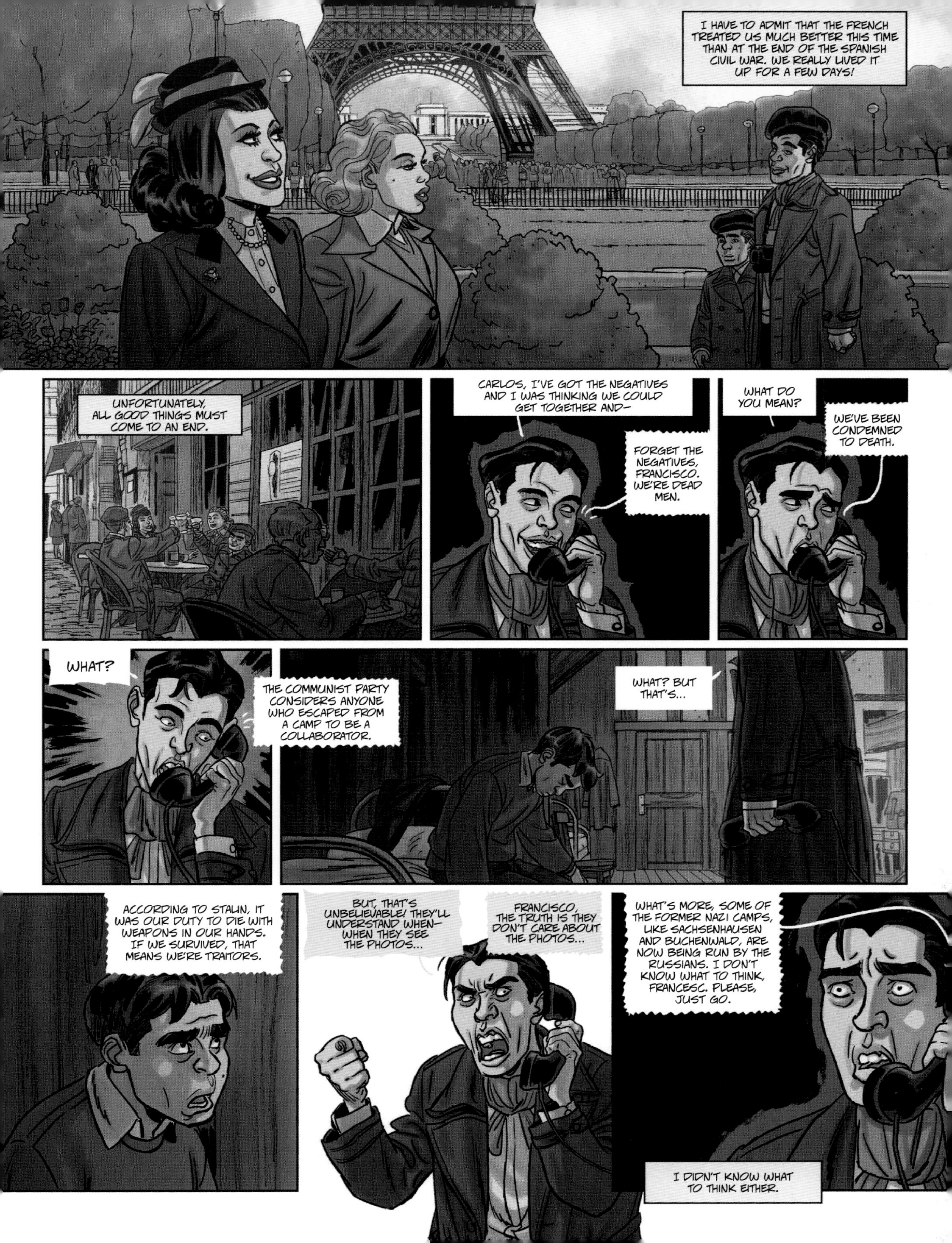
I HAVE TO ADMIT THAT THE FRENCH TREATED US MUCH BETTER THIS TIME THAN AT THE END OF THE SPANISH CIVIL WAR. WE REALLY LIVED IT UP FOR A FEW DAYS!
UNFORTUNATELY, ALL GOOD THINGS MUST COME TO AN END.
CARLOS, I'VE GOT THE NEGATIVES AND I WAS THINKING WE COULD GET TOGETHER AND—
FORGET THE NEGATIVES, FRANCISCO. WE'RE DEAD MEN.
WHAT DO YOU MEAN?
WE'VE BEEN CONDEMNED TO DEATH.
WHAT?
THE COMMUNIST PARTY CONSIDERS ANYONE WHO ESCAPED FROM A CAMP TO BE A COLLABORATOR.
WHAT? BUT THAT'S...
ACCORDING TO STALIN, IT WAS OUR DUTY TO DIE WITH WEAPONS IN OUR HANDS. IF WE SURVIVED, THAT MEANS WE'RE TRAITORS.
BUT, THAT'S UNBELIEVABLE! THEY'LL UNDERSTAND WHEN— WHEN THEY SEE THE PHOTOS...
FRANCISCO, THE TRUTH IS THEY DON'T CARE ABOUT THE PHOTOS...
WHAT'S MORE, SOME OF THE FORMER NAZI CAMPS, LIKE SACHSENHAUSEN AND BUCHENWALD, ARE NOW BEING RUN BY THE RUSSIANS. I DON'T KNOW WHAT TO THINK, FRANCESC. PLEASE, JUST GO.
I DIDN'T KNOW WHAT TO THINK EITHER.

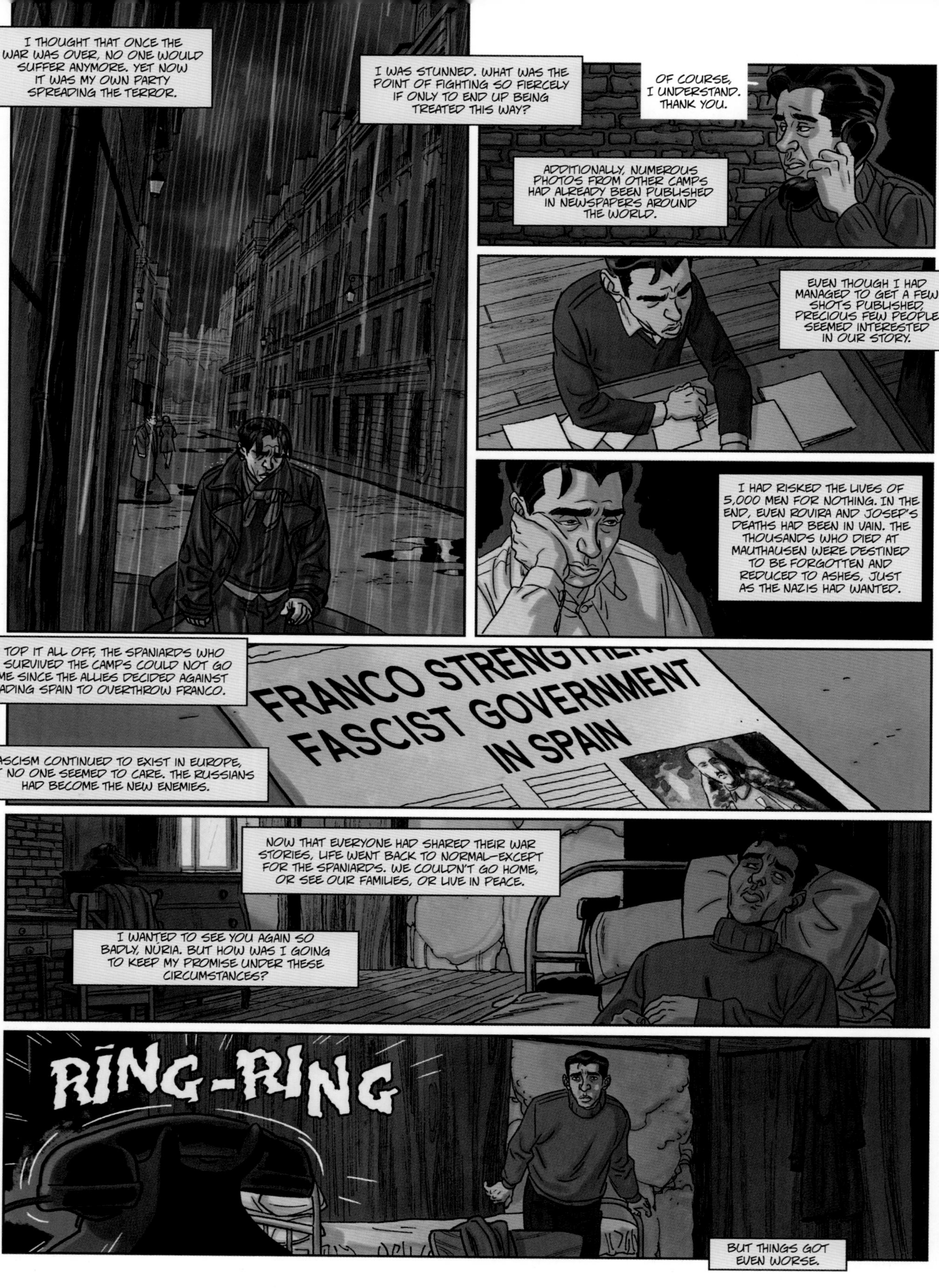
I THOUGHT THAT ONCE THE WAR WAS OVER, NO ONE WOULD SUFFER ANYMORE. YET NOW IT WAS MY OWN PARTY SPREADING THE TERROR.
I WAS STUNNED. WHAT WAS THE POINT OF FIGHTING SO FIERCELY IF ONLY TO END UP BEING TREATED THIS WAY?
OF COURSE, I UNDERSTAND. THANK YOU.
ADDITIONALLY, NUMEROUS PHOTOS FROM OTHER CAMPS HAD ALREADY BEEN PUBLISHED IN NEWSPAPERS AROUND THE WORLD.
EVEN THOUGH I HAD MANAGED TO GET A FEW SHOTS PUBLISHED, PRECIOUS FEW PEOPLE SEEMED INTERESTED IN OUR STORY.
I HAD RISKED THE LIVES OF 5,000 MEN FOR NOTHING. IN THE END, EVEN ROVIRA AND JOSEP'S DEATHS HAD BEEN IN VAIN. THE THOUSANDS WHO DIED AT MAUTHAUSEN WERE DESTINED TO BE FORGOTTEN AND REDUCED TO ASHES, JUST AS THE NAZIS HAD WANTED.
TO TOP IT ALL OFF, THE SPANIARDS WHO HAD SURVIVED THE CAMPS COULD NOT GO HOME SINCE THE ALLIES DECIDED AGAINST INVADING SPAIN TO OVERTHROW FRANCO.
FRANCO STRENGTHENS FASCIST GOVERNMENT IN SPAIN
FASCISM CONTINUED TO EXIST IN EUROPE, BUT NO ONE SEEMED TO CARE. THE RUSSIANS HAD BECOME THE NEW ENEMIES.
NOW THAT EVERYONE HAD SHARED THEIR WAR STORIES, LIFE WENT BACK TO NORMAL—EXCEPT FOR THE SPANIARDS. WE COULDN'T GO HOME, OR SEE OUR FAMILIES, OR LIVE IN PEACE.
I WANTED TO SEE YOU AGAIN SO BADLY, NÚRIA. BUT HOW WAS I GOING TO KEEP MY PROMISE UNDER THESE CIRCUMSTANCES?
RING-RING
BUT THINGS GOT EVEN WORSE.

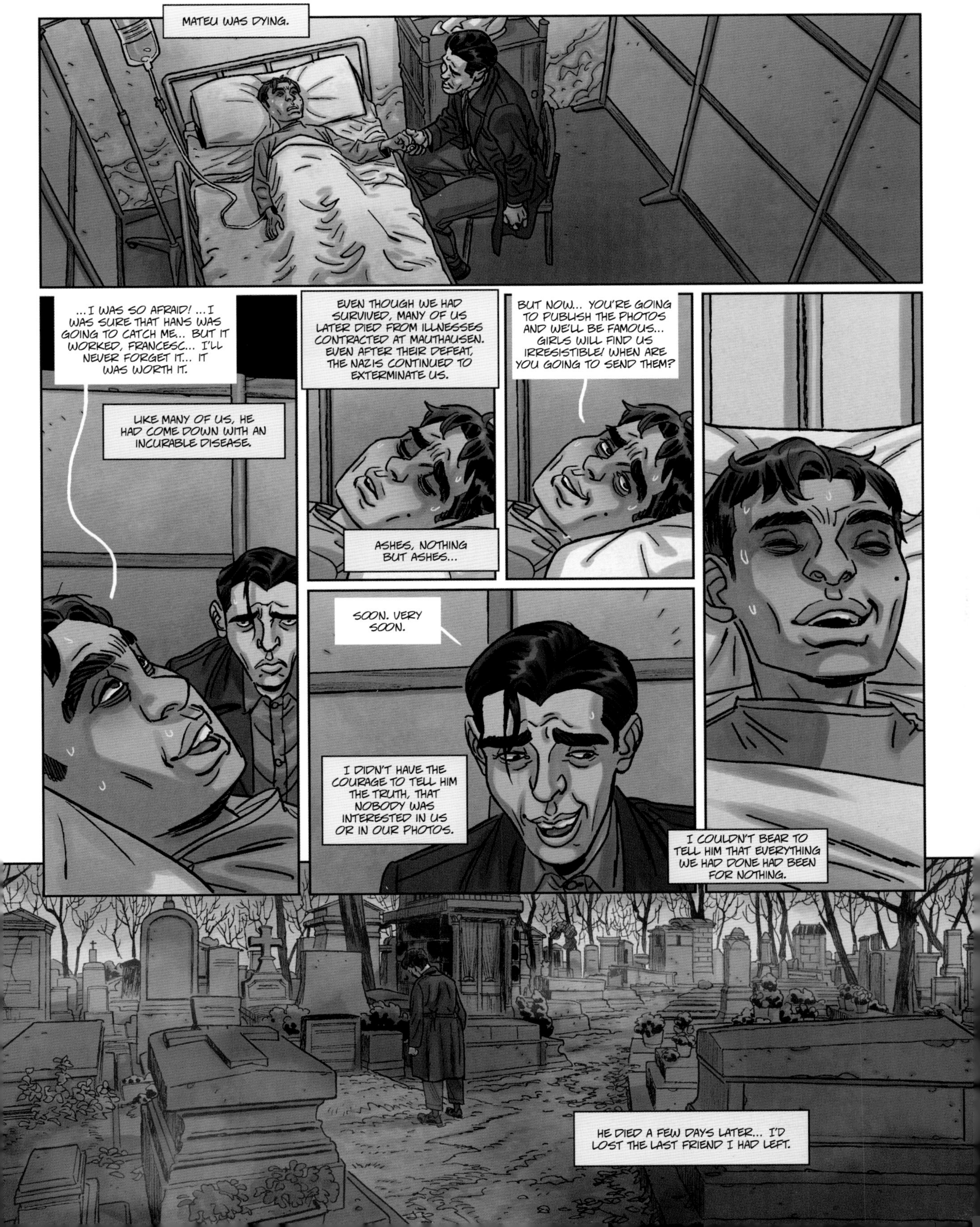
MATEU WAS DYING.
...I WAS SO AFRAID! ...I WAS SURE THAT HANS WAS GOING TO CATCH ME... BUT IT WORKED, FRANCESC... I'LL NEVER FORGET IT... IT WAS WORTH IT.
LIKE MANY OF US, HE HAD COME DOWN WITH AN INCURABLE DISEASE.
EVEN THOUGH WE HAD SURVIVED, MANY OF US LATER DIED FROM ILLNESSES CONTRACTED AT MAUTHAUSEN. EVEN AFTER THEIR DEFEAT, THE NAZIS CONTINUED TO EXTERMINATE US.
ASHES, NOTHING BUT ASHES...
BUT NOW... YOU'RE GOING TO PUBLISH THE PHOTOS AND WE'LL BE FAMOUS... GIRLS WILL FIND US IRRESISTIBLE! WHEN ARE YOU GOING TO SEND THEM?
SOON. VERY SOON.
I DIDN'T HAVE THE COURAGE TO TELL HIM THE TRUTH, THAT NOBODY WAS INTERESTED IN US OR IN OUR PHOTOS.
I COULDN'T BEAR TO TELL HIM THAT EVERYTHING WE HAD DONE HAD BEEN FOR NOTHING.
HE DIED A FEW DAYS LATER... I'D LOST THE LAST FRIEND I HAD LEFT.

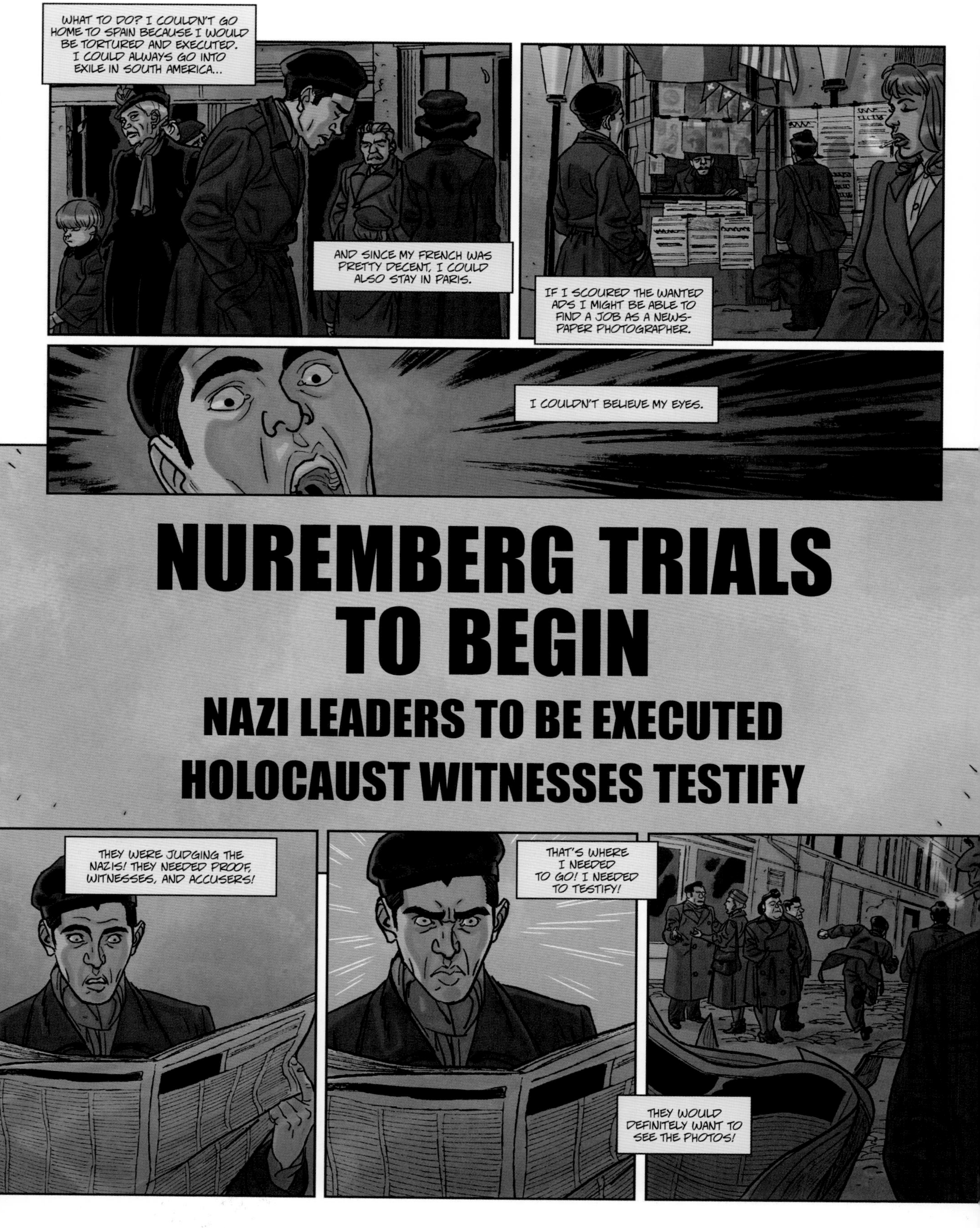
WHAT TO DO? I COULDN'T GO HOME TO SPAIN BECAUSE I WOULD BE TORTURED AND EXECUTED. I COULD ALWAYS GO INTO EXILE IN SOUTH AMERICA...
AND SINCE MY FRENCH WAS PRETTY DECENT, I COULD ALSO STAY IN PARIS.
IF I SCOURED THE WANTED ADS I MIGHT BE ABLE TO FIND A JOB AS A NEWSPAPER PHOTOGRAPHER.
I COULDN'T BELIEVE MY EYES.
NUREMBERG TRIALS TO BEGIN
NAZI LEADERS TO BE EXECUTED
HOLOCAUST WITNESSES TESTIFY
THEY WERE JUDGING THE NAZIS! THEY NEEDED PROOF, WITNESSES, AND ACCUSERS!
THAT'S WHERE I NEEDED TO GO! I NEEDED TO TESTIFY!
THEY WOULD DEFINITELY WANT TO SEE THE PHOTOS!

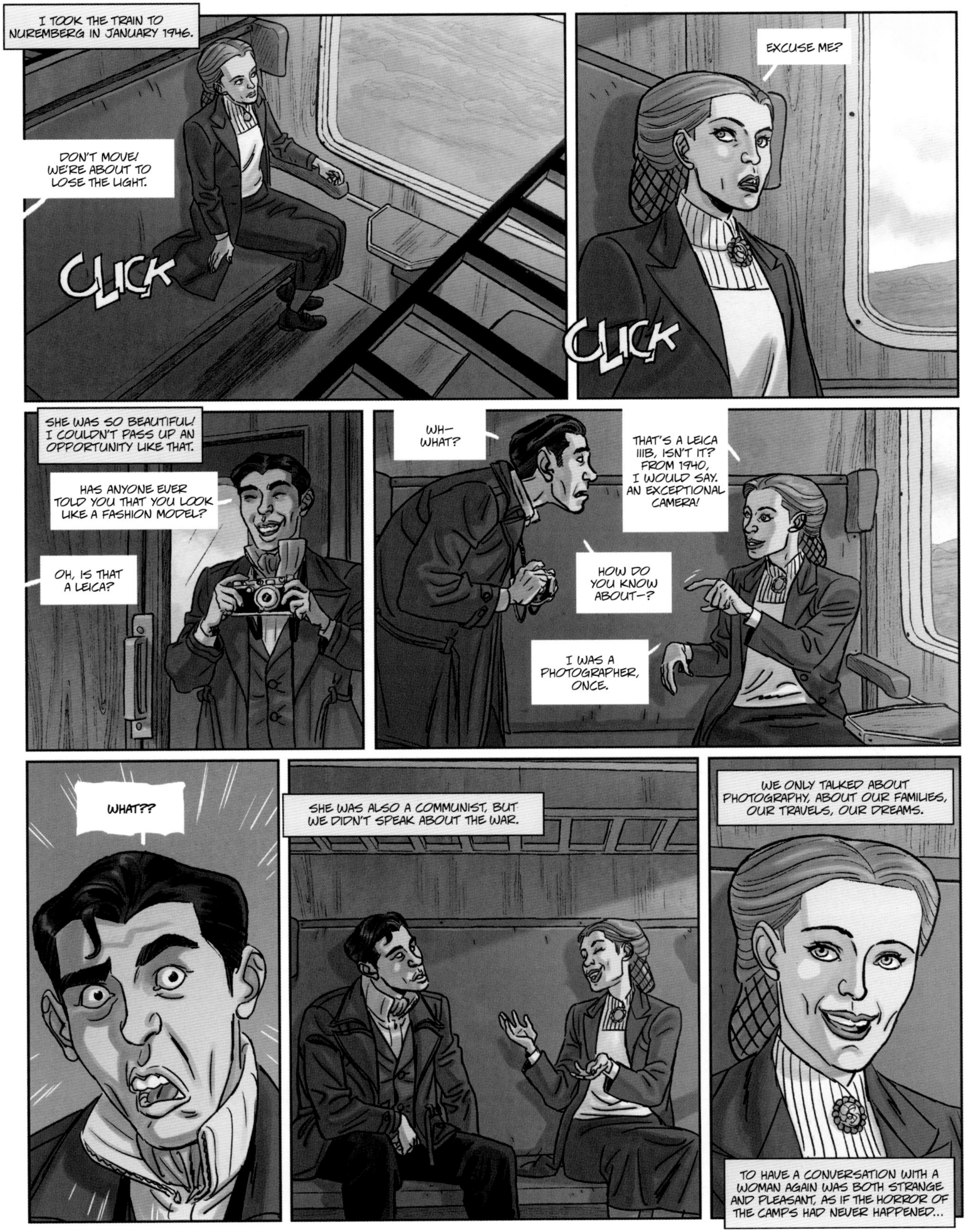
I TOOK THE TRAIN TO NUREMBERG IN JANUARY 1946.
DON'T MOVE! WE'RE ABOUT TO LOSE THE LIGHT.
CLICK
EXCUSE ME?
CLICK
SHE WAS SO BEAUTIFUL! I COULDN'T PASS UP AN OPPORTUNITY LIKE THAT.
HAS ANYONE EVER TOLD YOU THAT YOU LOOK LIKE A FASHION MODEL?
OH, IS THAT A LEICA?
WH— WHAT?
THAT'S A LEICA IIIB, ISN'T IT? FROM 1940, I WOULD SAY. AN EXCEPTIONAL CAMERA!
HOW DO YOU KNOW ABOUT—?
I WAS A PHOTOGRAPHER, ONCE.
WHAT??
SHE WAS ALSO A COMMUNIST, BUT WE DIDN'T SPEAK ABOUT THE WAR.
WE ONLY TALKED ABOUT PHOTOGRAPHY, ABOUT OUR FAMILIES, OUR TRAVELS, OUR DREAMS.
TO HAVE A CONVERSATION WITH A WOMAN AGAIN WAS BOTH STRANGE AND PLEASANT, AS IF THE HORROR OF THE CAMPS HAD NEVER HAPPENED...

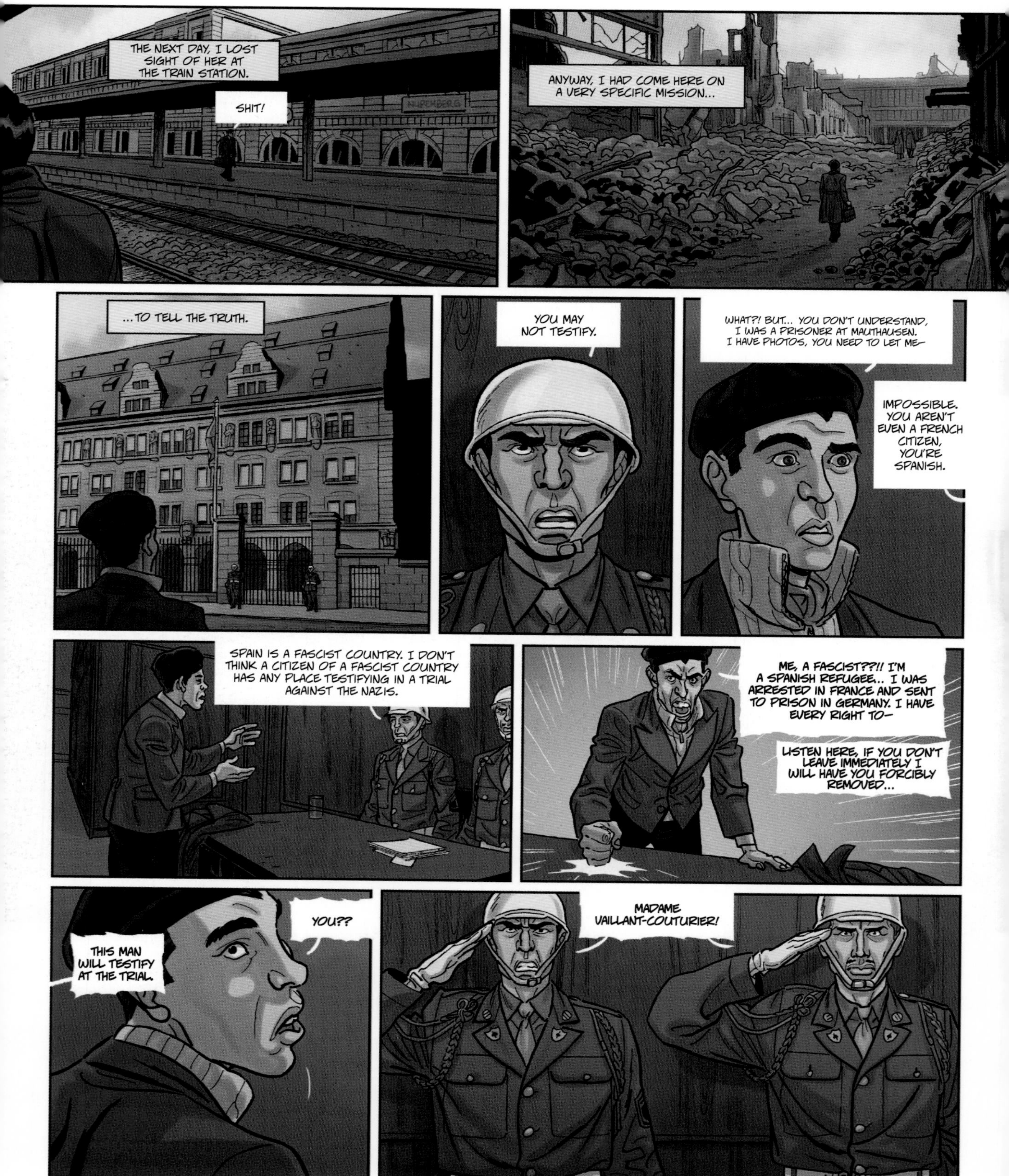
THE NEXT DAY, I LOST SIGHT OF HER AT THE TRAIN STATION.
SHIT!
NUREMBERG
ANYWAY, I HAD COME HERE ON A VERY SPECIFIC MISSION...
...TO TELL THE TRUTH.
YOU MAY NOT TESTIFY.
WHAT?! BUT... YOU DON'T UNDERSTAND, I WAS A PRISONER AT MAUTHAUSEN. I HAVE PHOTOS, YOU NEED TO LET ME–
IMPOSSIBLE. YOU AREN'T EVEN A FRENCH CITIZEN, YOU'RE SPANISH.
SPAIN IS A FASCIST COUNTRY. I DON'T THINK A CITIZEN OF A FASCIST COUNTRY HAS ANY PLACE TESTIFYING IN A TRIAL AGAINST THE NAZIS.
ME, A FASCIST??!! I'M A SPANISH REFUGEE... I WAS ARRESTED IN FRANCE AND SENT TO PRISON IN GERMANY. I HAVE EVERY RIGHT TO–
LISTEN HERE, IF YOU DON'T LEAVE IMMEDIATELY I WILL HAVE YOU FORCIBLY REMOVED...
THIS MAN WILL TESTIFY AT THE TRIAL.
YOU??
MADAME VAILLANT-COUTURIER!

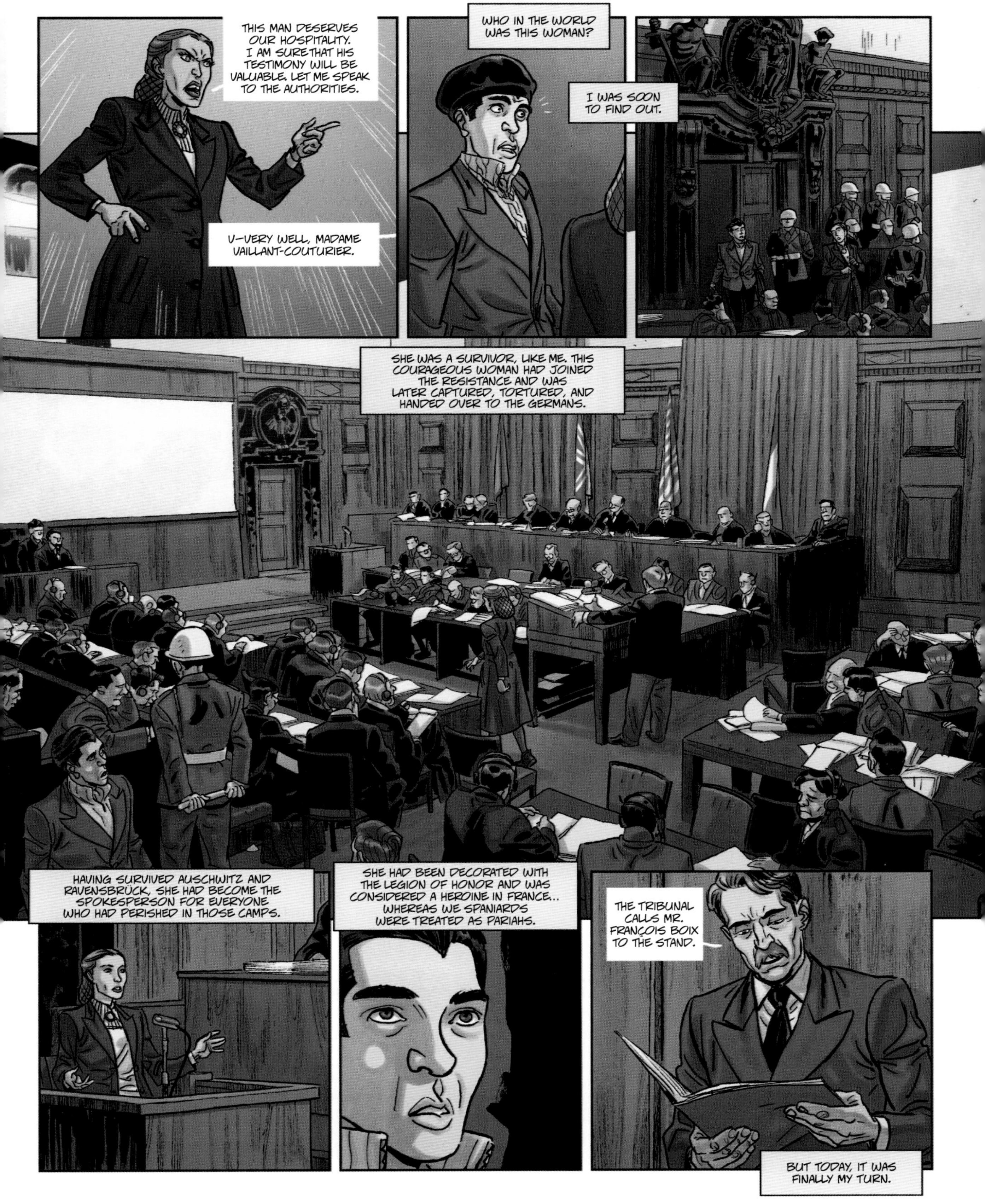

THIS MAN DESERVES OUR HOSPITALITY. I AM SURE THAT HIS TESTIMONY WILL BE VALUABLE. LET ME SPEAK TO THE AUTHORITIES.
V-VERY WELL, MADAME VAILLANT-COUTURIER.
WHO IN THE WORLD WAS THIS WOMAN?
I WAS SOON TO FIND OUT.
SHE WAS A SURVIVOR, LIKE ME. THIS COURAGEOUS WOMAN HAD JOINED THE RESISTANCE AND WAS LATER CAPTURED, TORTURED, AND HANDED OVER TO THE GERMANS.
HAVING SURVIVED AUSCHWITZ AND RAVENSBRÜCK, SHE HAD BECOME THE SPOKESPERSON FOR EVERYONE WHO HAD PERISHED IN THOSE CAMPS.
SHE HAD BEEN DECORATED WITH THE LEGION OF HONOR AND WAS CONSIDERED A HEROINE IN FRANCE... WHEREAS WE SPANIARDS WERE TREATED AS PARIAHS.
THE TRIBUNAL CALLS MR. FRANÇOIS BOIX TO THE STAND.
BUT TODAY, IT WAS FINALLY MY TURN.

THE TIME HAD COME. I WAS GOOD AND READY.

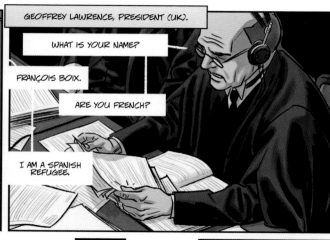

GEOFFREY LAWRENCE, PRESIDENT (UK).

WHAT IS YOUR NAME?

FRANÇOIS BOIX.

ARE YOU FRENCH?

I AM A SPANISH REFUGEE.

PLEASE REPEAT AFTER ME:

"I PROMISE TO SPEAK WITHOUT HATE OR FEAR; TO TELL THE TRUTH, THE WHOLE TRUTH, AND NOTHING BUT THE TRUTH."

YOU FOUGHT IN THE FRENCH ARMY AS A VOLUNTEER?

YES.

WERE YOU A PRISONER OF WAR OR A POLITICAL PRISONER?

PRISONER OF WAR, BUT THEY CLASSIFIED US AS "UNTERMENSCHEN" ALONG WITH THE JEWS. LATER ON, WE LEARNED THAT THE GERMANS HAD ASKED FRANCO WHAT THEY SHOULD DO WITH SPANISH PRISONERS OF WAR. HIS ANSWER WAS—

NEVER MIND THAT.

DID HE REALLY JUST SAY, "NEVER MIND THAT"?

WHAT WERE YOUR DUTIES?

I… HAD TO TRANSLATE ALL THE BARBARIC THINGS THE GERMANS WANTED TO SAY TO THE SPANISH PRISONERS. LATER, I WORKED AS A PHOTOGRAPHER: I DEVELOPED FILM SHOT ALL OVER THE CAMP SHOWING THE FULL STORY OF WHAT HAPPENED THERE.

YOU HAVE COME TO SHOW US SOME OF THESE PHOTOS. YOU WILL STATE WHEN AND WHERE THEY WERE TAKEN.

YES.

THE FLOOR GOES TO MR. DUBOST, THE FRENCH DEPUTY PUBLIC PROSECUTOR.

I CALL FOR EXHIBIT NUMBER RF-331, DOCUMENT F-321.

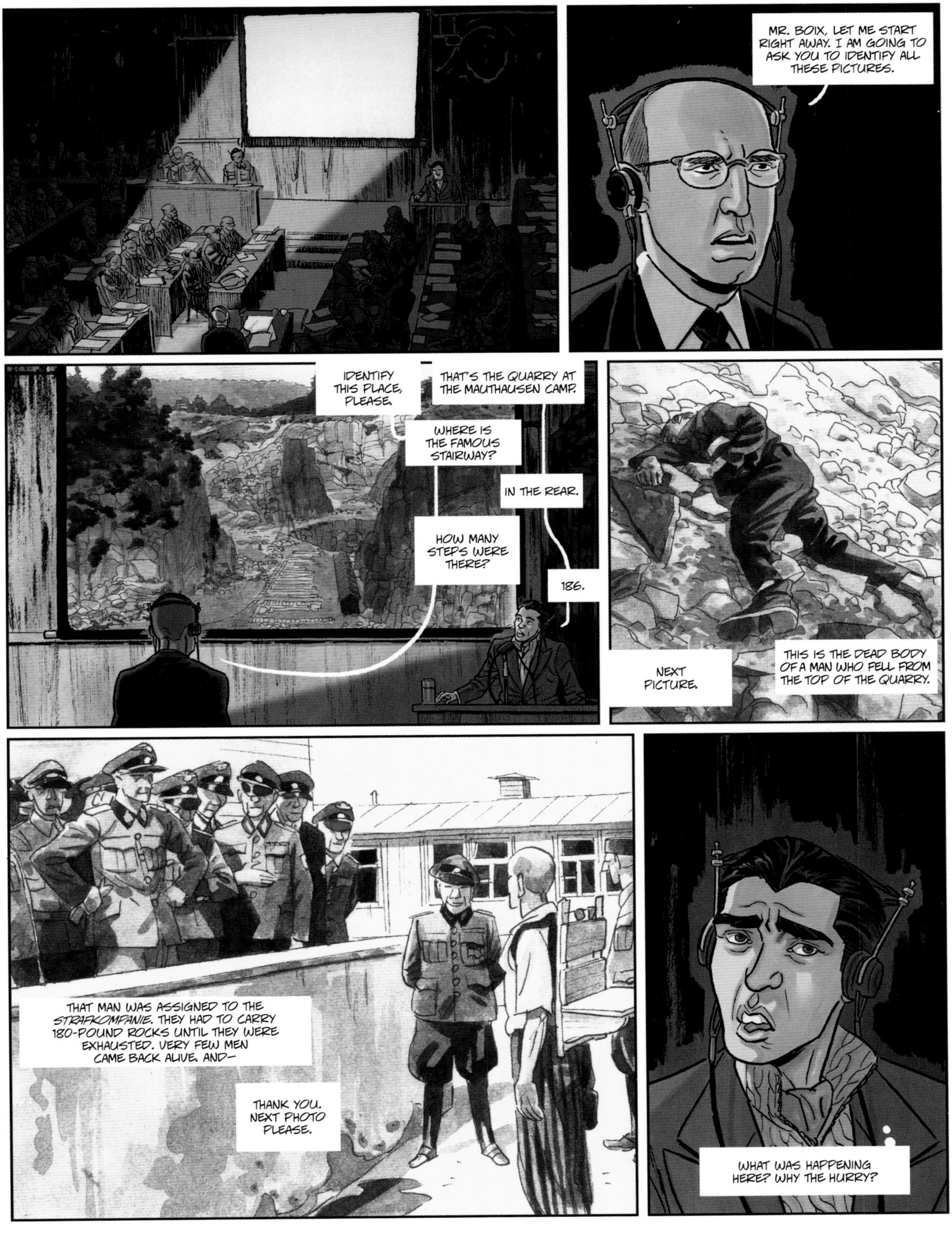
MR. BOIX, LET ME START RIGHT AWAY. I AM GOING TO ASK YOU TO IDENTIFY ALL THESE PICTURES.
IDENTIFY THIS PLACE, PLEASE.
THAT'S THE QUARRY AT THE MAUTHAUSEN CAMP.
WHERE IS THE FAMOUS STAIRWAY?
IN THE REAR.
HOW MANY STEPS WERE THERE?
186.
NEXT PICTURE.
THIS IS THE DEAD BODY OF A MAN WHO FELL FROM THE TOP OF THE QUARRY.
THAT MAN WAS ASSIGNED TO THE *STRAFKOMPANIE*. THEY HAD TO CARRY 180-POUND ROCKS UNTIL THEY WERE EXHAUSTED. VERY FEW MEN CAME BACK ALIVE. AND—
THANK YOU. NEXT PHOTO PLEASE.
WHAT WAS HAPPENING HERE? WHY THE HURRY?

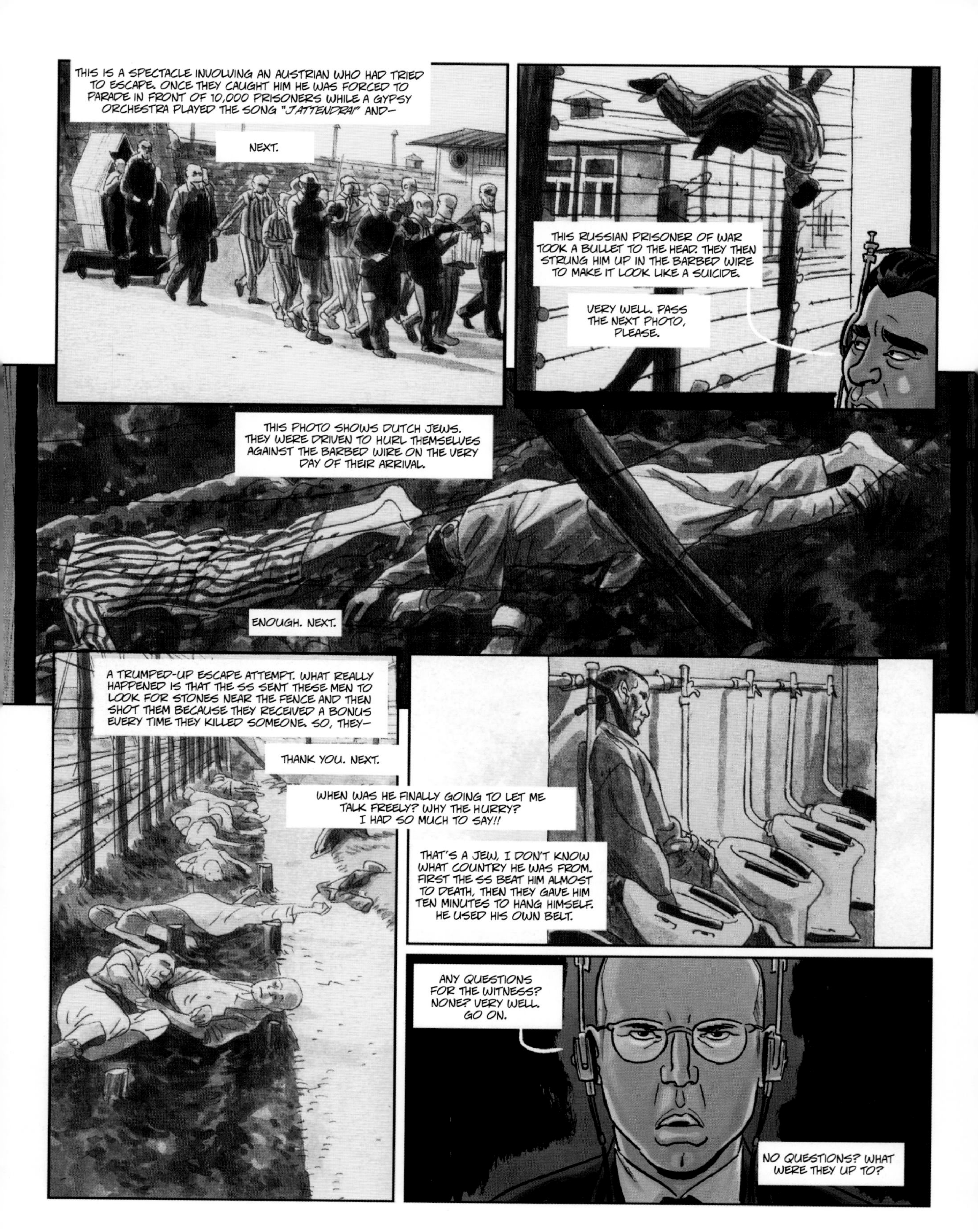
THIS IS A SPECTACLE INVOLVING AN AUSTRIAN WHO HAD TRIED TO ESCAPE. ONCE THEY CAUGHT HIM HE WAS FORCED TO PARADE IN FRONT OF 10,000 PRISONERS WHILE A GYPSY ORCHESTRA PLAYED THE SONG "J'ATTENDRAI" AND–
NEXT.
THIS RUSSIAN PRISONER OF WAR TOOK A BULLET TO THE HEAD. THEY THEN STRUNG HIM UP IN THE BARBED WIRE TO MAKE IT LOOK LIKE A SUICIDE.
VERY WELL. PASS THE NEXT PHOTO, PLEASE.
THIS PHOTO SHOWS DUTCH JEWS. THEY WERE DRIVEN TO HURL THEMSELVES AGAINST THE BARBED WIRE ON THE VERY DAY OF THEIR ARRIVAL.
ENOUGH. NEXT.
A TRUMPED-UP ESCAPE ATTEMPT. WHAT REALLY HAPPENED IS THAT THE SS SENT THESE MEN TO LOOK FOR STONES NEAR THE FENCE AND THEN SHOT THEM BECAUSE THEY RECEIVED A BONUS EVERY TIME THEY KILLED SOMEONE. SO, THEY–
THANK YOU. NEXT.
WHEN WAS HE FINALLY GOING TO LET ME TALK FREELY? WHY THE HURRY? I HAD SO MUCH TO SAY!!
THAT'S A JEW, I DON'T KNOW WHAT COUNTRY HE WAS FROM. FIRST THE SS BEAT HIM ALMOST TO DEATH, THEN THEY GAVE HIM TEN MINUTES TO HANG HIMSELF. HE USED HIS OWN BELT.
ANY QUESTIONS FOR THE WITNESS? NONE? VERY WELL. GO ON.
NO QUESTIONS? WHAT WERE THEY UP TO?

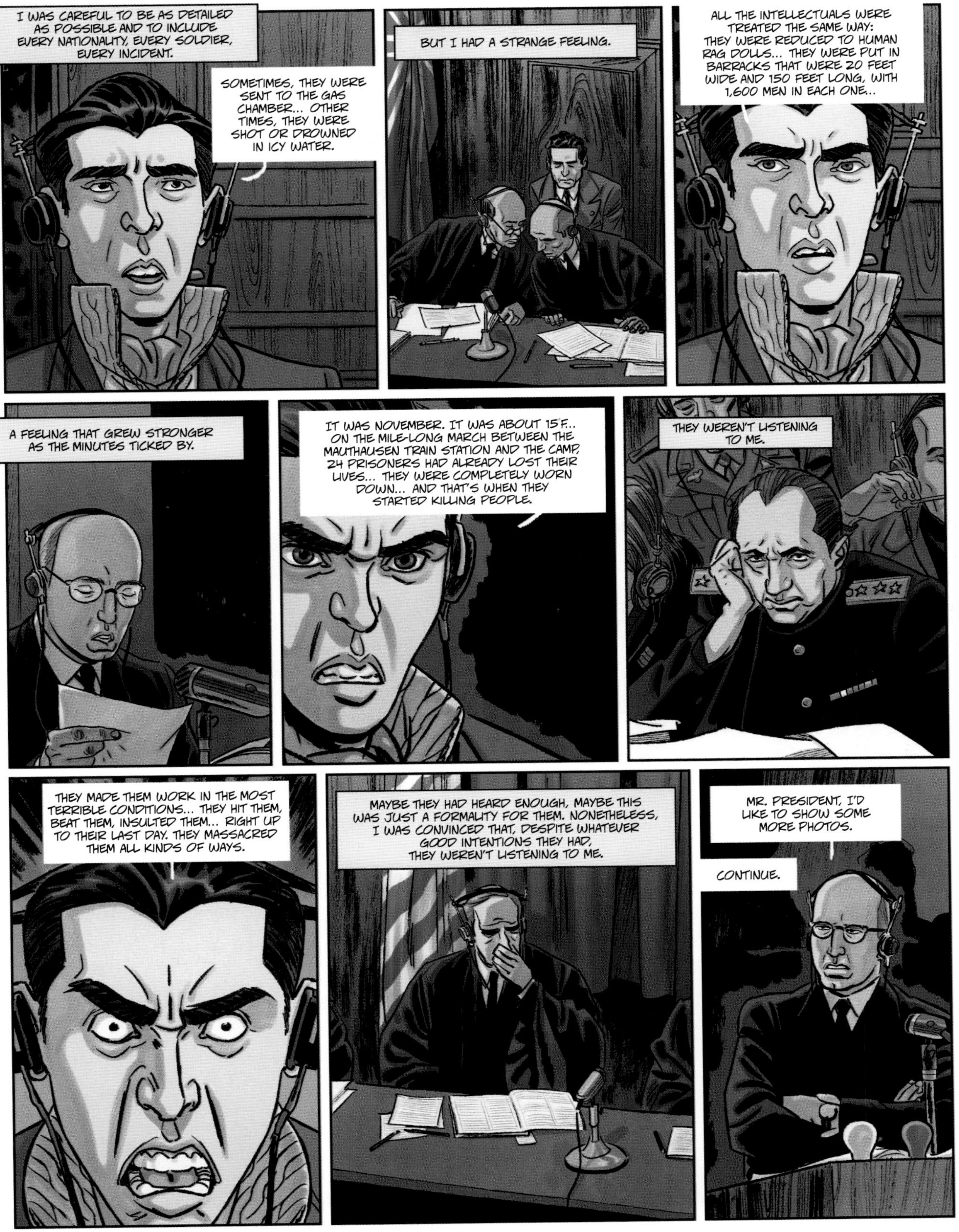
I WAS CAREFUL TO BE AS DETAILED AS POSSIBLE AND TO INCLUDE EVERY NATIONALITY, EVERY SOLDIER, EVERY INCIDENT.
SOMETIMES, THEY WERE SENT TO THE GAS CHAMBER... OTHER TIMES, THEY WERE SHOT OR DROWNED IN ICY WATER.
BUT I HAD A STRANGE FEELING.
ALL THE INTELLECTUALS WERE TREATED THE SAME WAY: THEY WERE REDUCED TO HUMAN RAG DOLLS... THEY WERE PUT IN BARRACKS THAT WERE 20 FEET WIDE AND 150 FEET LONG, WITH 1,600 MEN IN EACH ONE...
A FEELING THAT GREW STRONGER AS THE MINUTES TICKED BY.
IT WAS NOVEMBER. IT WAS ABOUT 15°F... ON THE MILE-LONG MARCH BETWEEN THE MAUTHAUSEN TRAIN STATION AND THE CAMP, 24 PRISONERS HAD ALREADY LOST THEIR LIVES... THEY WERE COMPLETELY WORN DOWN... AND THAT'S WHEN THEY STARTED KILLING PEOPLE.
THEY WEREN'T LISTENING TO ME.
THEY MADE THEM WORK IN THE MOST TERRIBLE CONDITIONS... THEY HIT THEM, BEAT THEM, INSULTED THEM... RIGHT UP TO THEIR LAST DAY. THEY MASSACRED THEM ALL KINDS OF WAYS.
MAYBE THEY HAD HEARD ENOUGH, MAYBE THIS WAS JUST A FORMALITY FOR THEM. NONETHELESS, I WAS CONVINCED THAT, DESPITE WHATEVER GOOD INTENTIONS THEY HAD, THEY WEREN'T LISTENING TO ME.
MR. PRESIDENT, I'D LIKE TO SHOW SOME MORE PHOTOS.
CONTINUE.

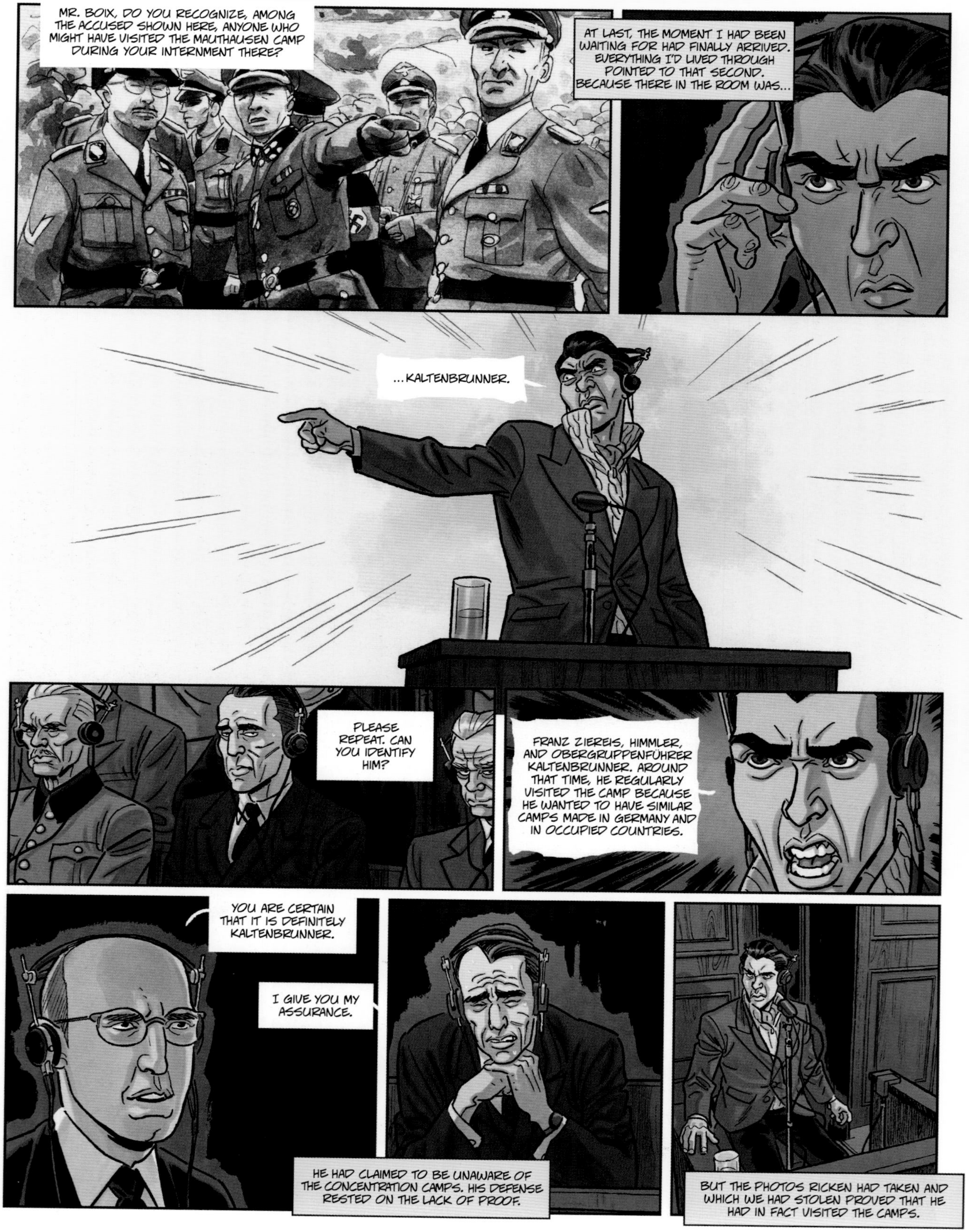
MR. BOIX, DO YOU RECOGNIZE, AMONG THE ACCUSED SHOWN HERE, ANYONE WHO MIGHT HAVE VISITED THE MAUTHAUSEN CAMP DURING YOUR INTERNMENT THERE?
AT LAST, THE MOMENT I HAD BEEN WAITING FOR HAD FINALLY ARRIVED. EVERYTHING I'D LIVED THROUGH POINTED TO THAT SECOND. BECAUSE THERE IN THE ROOM WAS...
...KALTENBRUNNER.
PLEASE REPEAT. CAN YOU IDENTIFY HIM?
FRANZ ZIEREIS, HIMMLER, AND OBERGRUPPENFÜHRER KALTENBRUNNER. AROUND THAT TIME, HE REGULARLY VISITED THE CAMP BECAUSE HE WANTED TO HAVE SIMILAR CAMPS MADE IN GERMANY AND IN OCCUPIED COUNTRIES.
YOU ARE CERTAIN THAT IT IS DEFINITELY KALTENBRUNNER.
I GIVE YOU MY ASSURANCE.
HE HAD CLAIMED TO BE UNAWARE OF THE CONCENTRATION CAMPS. HIS DEFENSE RESTED ON THE LACK OF PROOF.
BUT THE PHOTOS RICKEN HAD TAKEN AND WHICH WE HAD STOLEN PROVED THAT HE HAD IN FACT VISITED THE CAMPS.

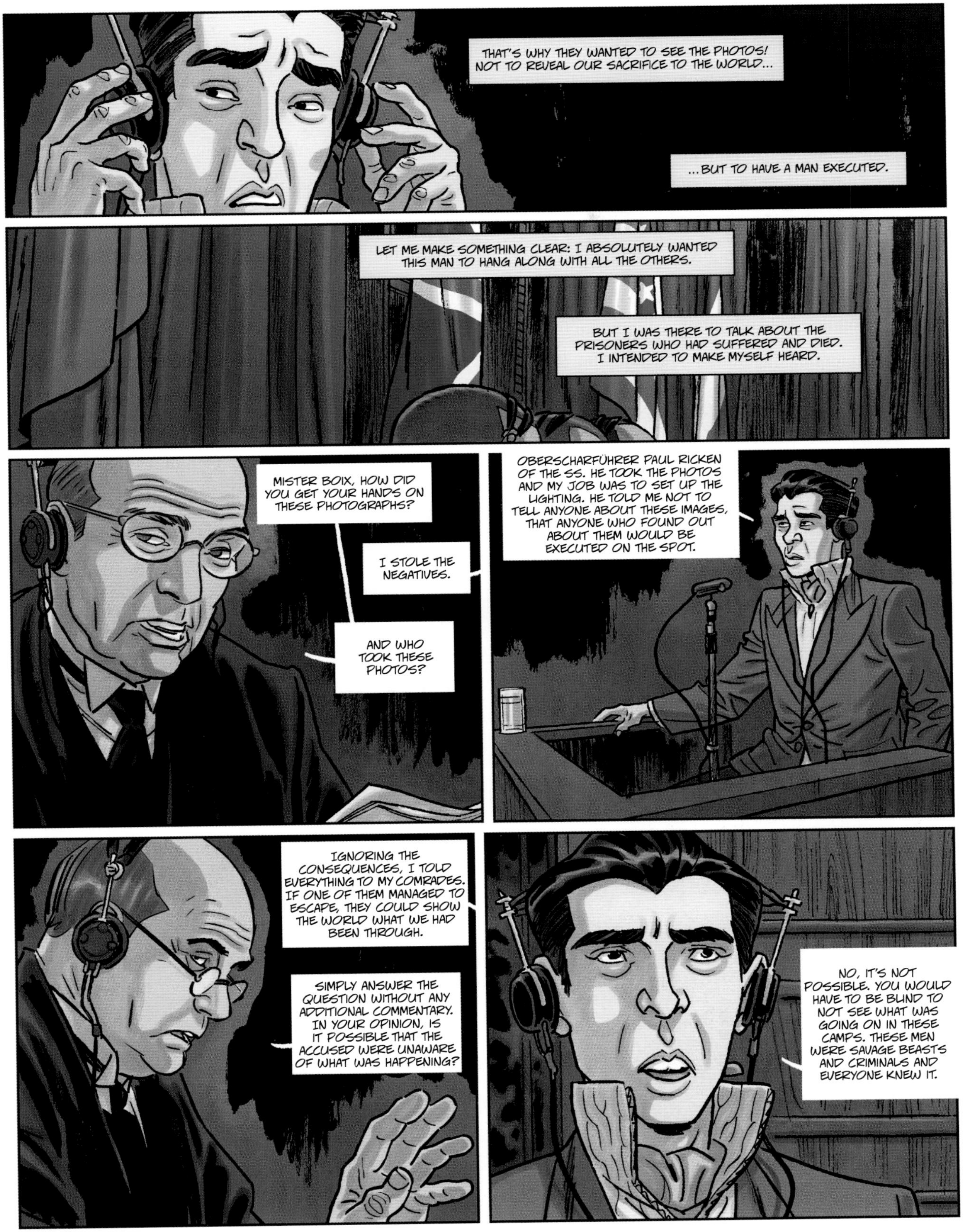
THAT'S WHY THEY WANTED TO SEE THE PHOTOS! NOT TO REVEAL OUR SACRIFICE TO THE WORLD...
...BUT TO HAVE A MAN EXECUTED.
LET ME MAKE SOMETHING CLEAR: I ABSOLUTELY WANTED THIS MAN TO HANG ALONG WITH ALL THE OTHERS.
BUT I WAS THERE TO TALK ABOUT THE PRISONERS WHO HAD SUFFERED AND DIED. I INTENDED TO MAKE MYSELF HEARD.
MISTER BOIX, HOW DID YOU GET YOUR HANDS ON THESE PHOTOGRAPHS?
I STOLE THE NEGATIVES.
AND WHO TOOK THESE PHOTOS?
OBERSCHARFÜHRER PAUL RICKEN OF THE SS. HE TOOK THE PHOTOS AND MY JOB WAS TO SET UP THE LIGHTING. HE TOLD ME NOT TO TELL ANYONE ABOUT THESE IMAGES, THAT ANYONE WHO FOUND OUT ABOUT THEM WOULD BE EXECUTED ON THE SPOT.
IGNORING THE CONSEQUENCES, I TOLD EVERYTHING TO MY COMRADES. IF ONE OF THEM MANAGED TO ESCAPE, THEY COULD SHOW THE WORLD WHAT WE HAD BEEN THROUGH.
SIMPLY ANSWER THE QUESTION WITHOUT ANY ADDITIONAL COMMENTARY. IN YOUR OPINION, IS IT POSSIBLE THAT THE ACCUSED WERE UNAWARE OF WHAT WAS HAPPENING?
NO, IT'S NOT POSSIBLE. YOU WOULD HAVE TO BE BLIND TO NOT SEE WHAT WAS GOING ON IN THESE CAMPS. THESE MEN WERE SAVAGE BEASTS AND CRIMINALS AND EVERYONE KNEW IT.

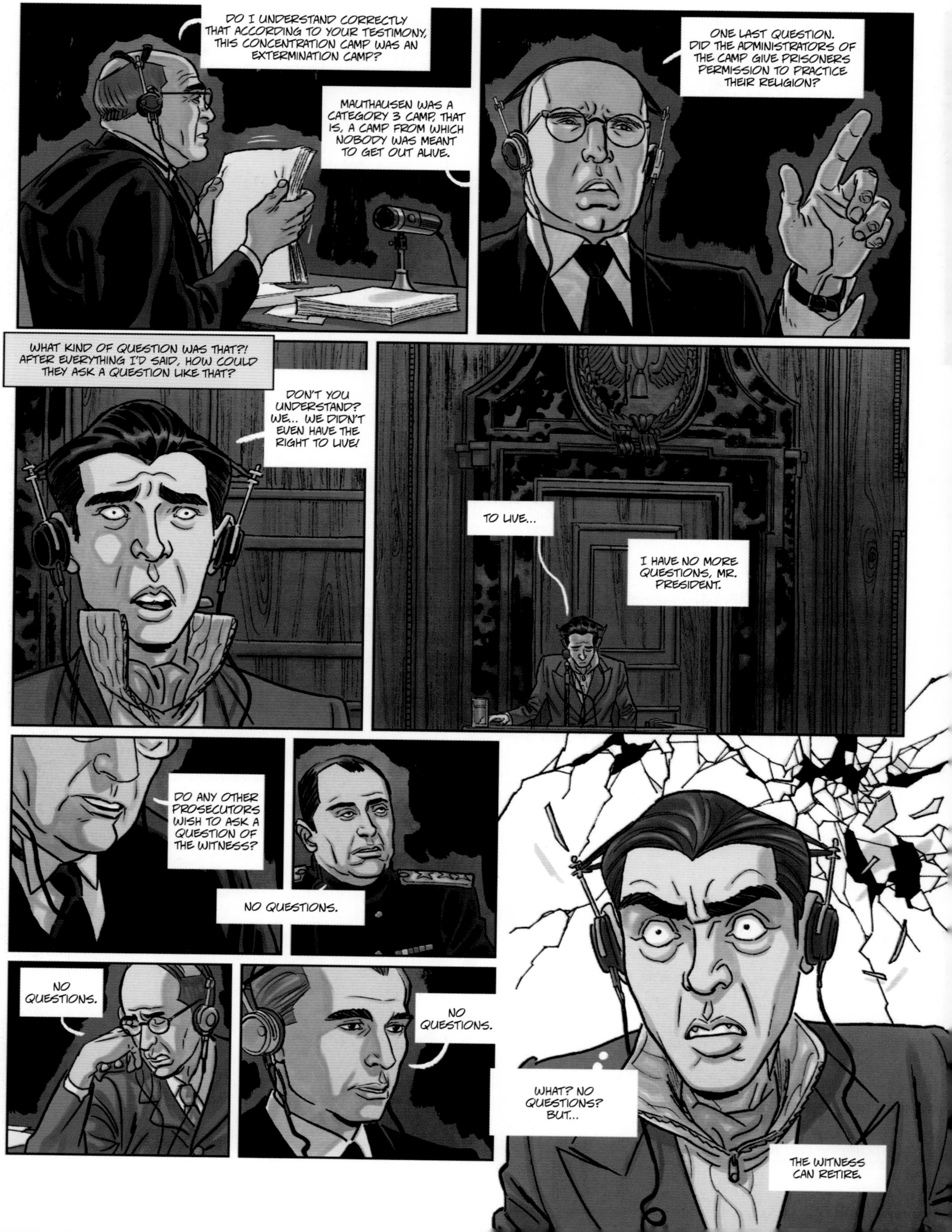
DO I UNDERSTAND CORRECTLY THAT ACCORDING TO YOUR TESTIMONY, THIS CONCENTRATION CAMP WAS AN EXTERMINATION CAMP?
MAUTHAUSEN WAS A CATEGORY 3 CAMP, THAT IS, A CAMP FROM WHICH NOBODY WAS MEANT TO GET OUT ALIVE.
ONE LAST QUESTION. DID THE ADMINISTRATORS OF THE CAMP GIVE PRISONERS PERMISSION TO PRACTICE THEIR RELIGION?
WHAT KIND OF QUESTION WAS THAT?! AFTER EVERYTHING I'D SAID, HOW COULD THEY ASK A QUESTION LIKE THAT?
DON'T YOU UNDERSTAND? WE... WE DIDN'T EVEN HAVE THE RIGHT TO LIVE!
TO LIVE...
I HAVE NO MORE QUESTIONS, MR. PRESIDENT.
DO ANY OTHER PROSECUTORS WISH TO ASK A QUESTION OF THE WITNESS?
NO QUESTIONS.
NO QUESTIONS.
NO QUESTIONS.
WHAT? NO QUESTIONS? BUT...
THE WITNESS CAN RETIRE.

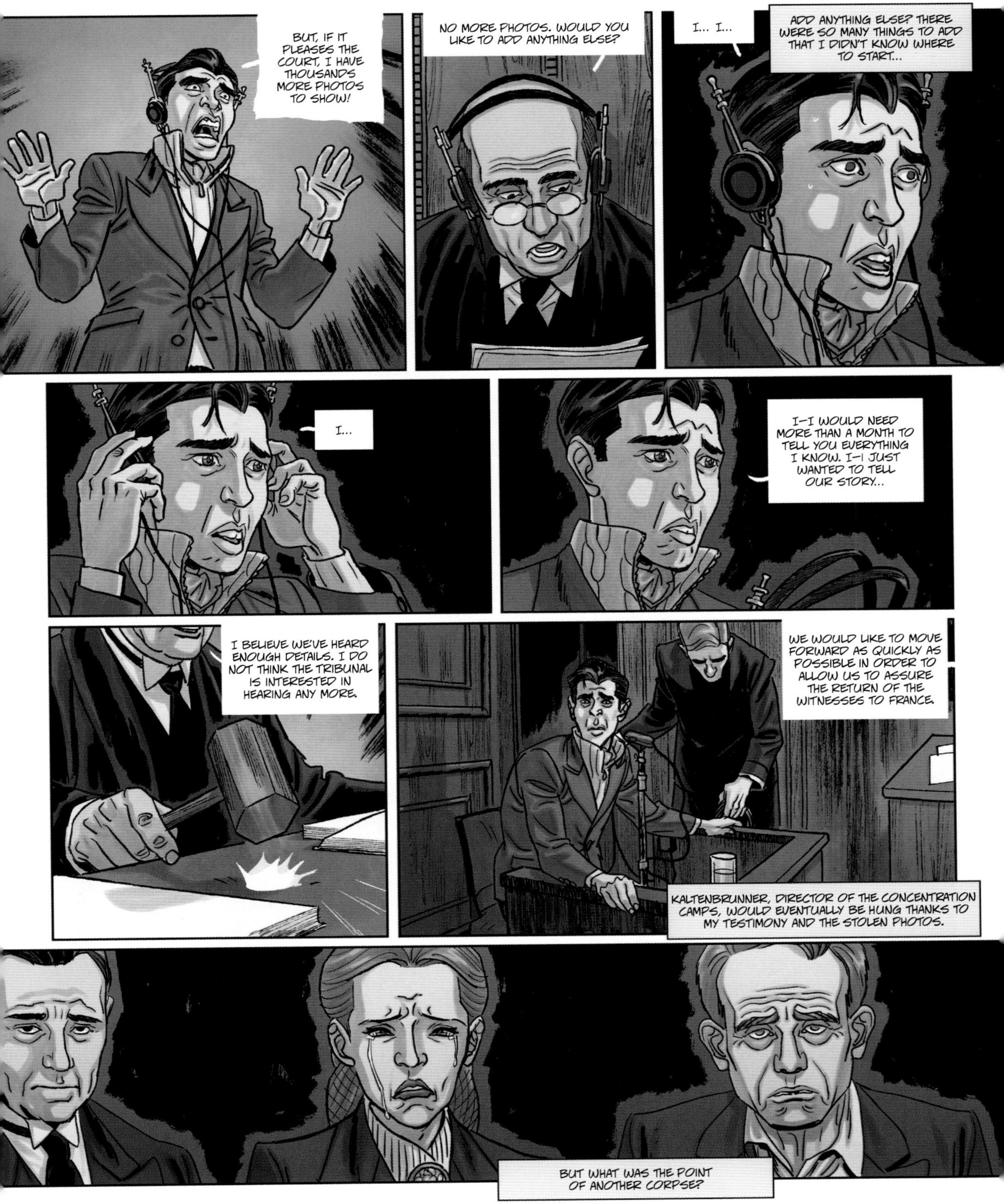

BUT, IF IT PLEASES THE COURT, I HAVE THOUSANDS MORE PHOTOS TO SHOW!
NO MORE PHOTOS. WOULD YOU LIKE TO ADD ANYTHING ELSE?
I... I...
ADD ANYTHING ELSE? THERE WERE SO MANY THINGS TO ADD THAT I DIDN'T KNOW WHERE TO START...
I...
I—I WOULD NEED MORE THAN A MONTH TO TELL YOU EVERYTHING I KNOW. I—I JUST WANTED TO TELL OUR STORY...
I BELIEVE WE'VE HEARD ENOUGH DETAILS. I DO NOT THINK THE TRIBUNAL IS INTERESTED IN HEARING ANY MORE.
WE WOULD LIKE TO MOVE FORWARD AS QUICKLY AS POSSIBLE IN ORDER TO ALLOW US TO ASSURE THE RETURN OF THE WITNESSES TO FRANCE.
KALTENBRUNNER, DIRECTOR OF THE CONCENTRATION CAMPS, WOULD EVENTUALLY BE HUNG THANKS TO MY TESTIMONY AND THE STOLEN PHOTOS.
BUT WHAT WAS THE POINT OF ANOTHER CORPSE?

GOD DAMN IT I'M SICK OF THIS! NO ONE'S LISTENING TO US!

FRANCISCO...

WHAT DO THEY WANT, ANYWAY? WHAT'S THIS TRIAL FOR? WHAT KIND OF JUSTICE IS THAT?

LISTEN TO ME, I—

DO THEY THINK WE'RE ONLY OUT FOR REVENGE? OR ARE THEY JUST OUT TO MAKE HEADLINES?

YOU'RE RIGHT, BUT—

DO THEY THINK THEY CAN WRAP UP THE AFFAIR BY HANGING A FEW OF THEM? DO THEY REALLY THINK THAT'S GOING TO MAKE US FEEL AVENGED, RELIEVED, HAPPY?

PLEASE, LISTEN TO ME—

YOU HAVE NO IDEA WHAT KIND OF HELL I'VE BEEN THROUGH TO BRING THEM THESE PHOTOS! AND THEY DON'T WANT TO LISTEN TO THE TRUTH!!

THE "TRUTH."

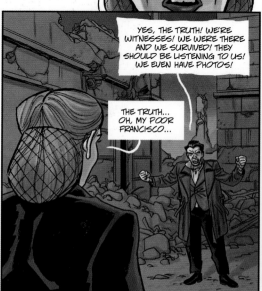

YES, THE TRUTH! WE'RE WITNESSES! WE WERE THERE AND WE SURVIVED! THEY SHOULD BE LISTENING TO US! WE EVEN HAVE PHOTOS!

THE TRUTH... OH, MY POOR FRANCISCO...

"MY POOR FRANCISCO"?

YOU TALK ABOUT "TRUTH," BUT WHAT IS TRUTH, FRANCISCO?

THE "TRUTH" IS WHAT HAPPENED IN THOSE CAMPS. I'M NOT TEACHING YOU ANYTHING, YOU WERE THERE!

YES, I WAS THERE AND I SAW EVERYTHING. BUT THERE'S SOMETHING YOU STILL HAVEN'T UNDERSTOOD.

AND WHAT IS THAT, MADAME VAILLANT-COUTURIER?

THEY'LL LISTEN TO US, BUT... THEY'LL PROBABLY NEVER BE ABLE TO UNDERSTAND US.

WHY NOT?

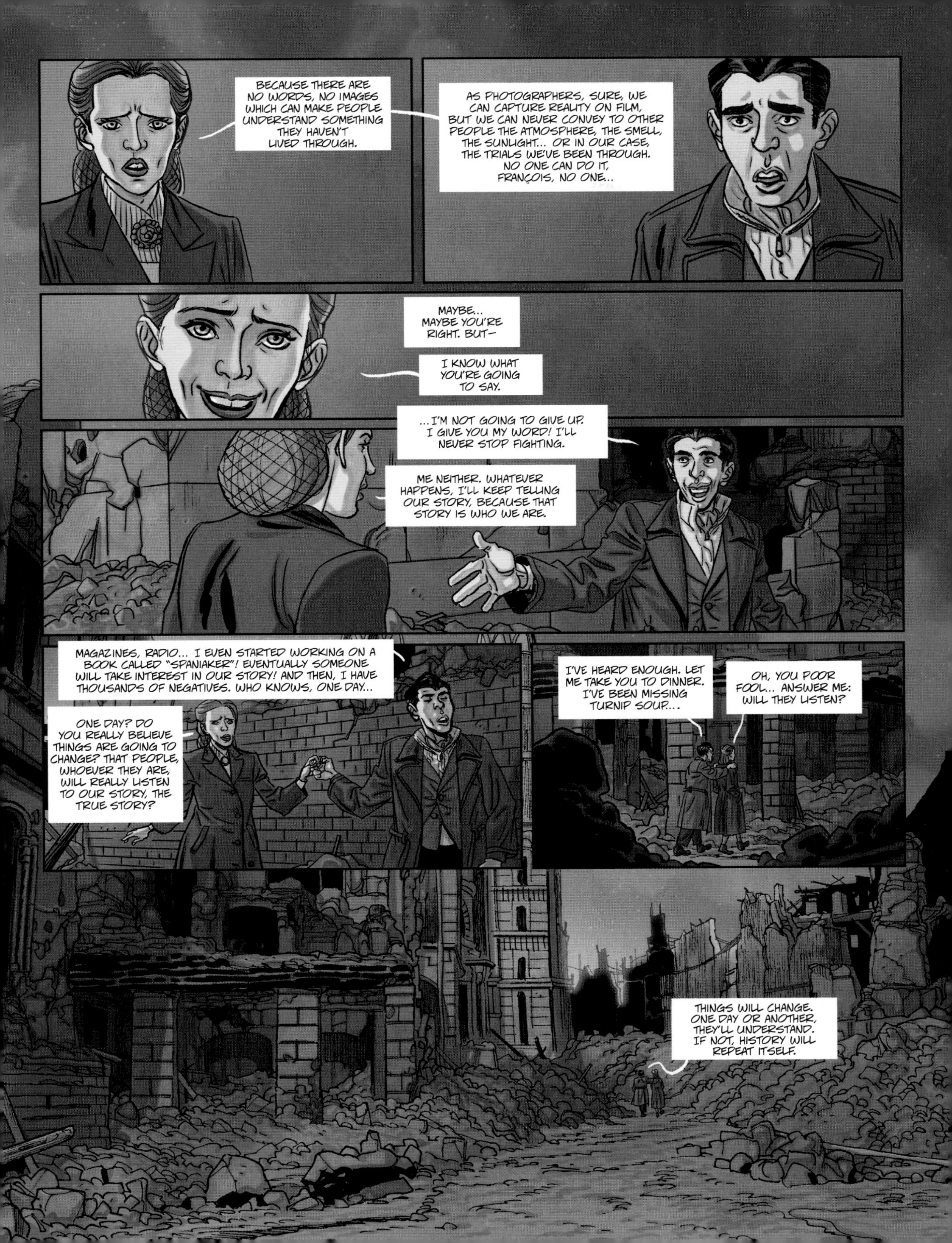
BECAUSE THERE ARE NO WORDS, NO IMAGES WHICH CAN MAKE PEOPLE UNDERSTAND SOMETHING THEY HAVEN'T LIVED THROUGH.
AS PHOTOGRAPHERS, SURE, WE CAN CAPTURE REALITY ON FILM, BUT WE CAN NEVER CONVEY TO OTHER PEOPLE THE ATMOSPHERE, THE SMELL, THE SUNLIGHT... OR IN OUR CASE, THE TRIALS WE'VE BEEN THROUGH. NO ONE CAN DO IT, FRANÇOIS, NO ONE...
MAYBE... MAYBE YOU'RE RIGHT. BUT–
I KNOW WHAT YOU'RE GOING TO SAY.
...I'M NOT GOING TO GIVE UP. I GIVE YOU MY WORD! I'LL NEVER STOP FIGHTING.
ME NEITHER. WHATEVER HAPPENS, I'LL KEEP TELLING OUR STORY, BECAUSE THAT STORY IS WHO WE ARE.
MAGAZINES, RADIO... I EVEN STARTED WORKING ON A BOOK CALLED "SPANIAKER"! EVENTUALLY SOMEONE WILL TAKE INTEREST IN OUR STORY! AND THEN, I HAVE THOUSANDS OF NEGATIVES. WHO KNOWS, ONE DAY...
ONE DAY? DO YOU REALLY BELIEVE THINGS ARE GOING TO CHANGE? THAT PEOPLE, WHOEVER THEY ARE, WILL REALLY LISTEN TO OUR STORY, THE TRUE STORY?
I'VE HEARD ENOUGH. LET ME TAKE YOU TO DINNER. I'VE BEEN MISSING TURNIP SOUP....
OH, YOU POOR FOOL... ANSWER ME: WILL THEY LISTEN?
THINGS WILL CHANGE. ONE DAY OR ANOTHER, THEY'LL UNDERSTAND. IF NOT, HISTORY WILL REPEAT ITSELF.

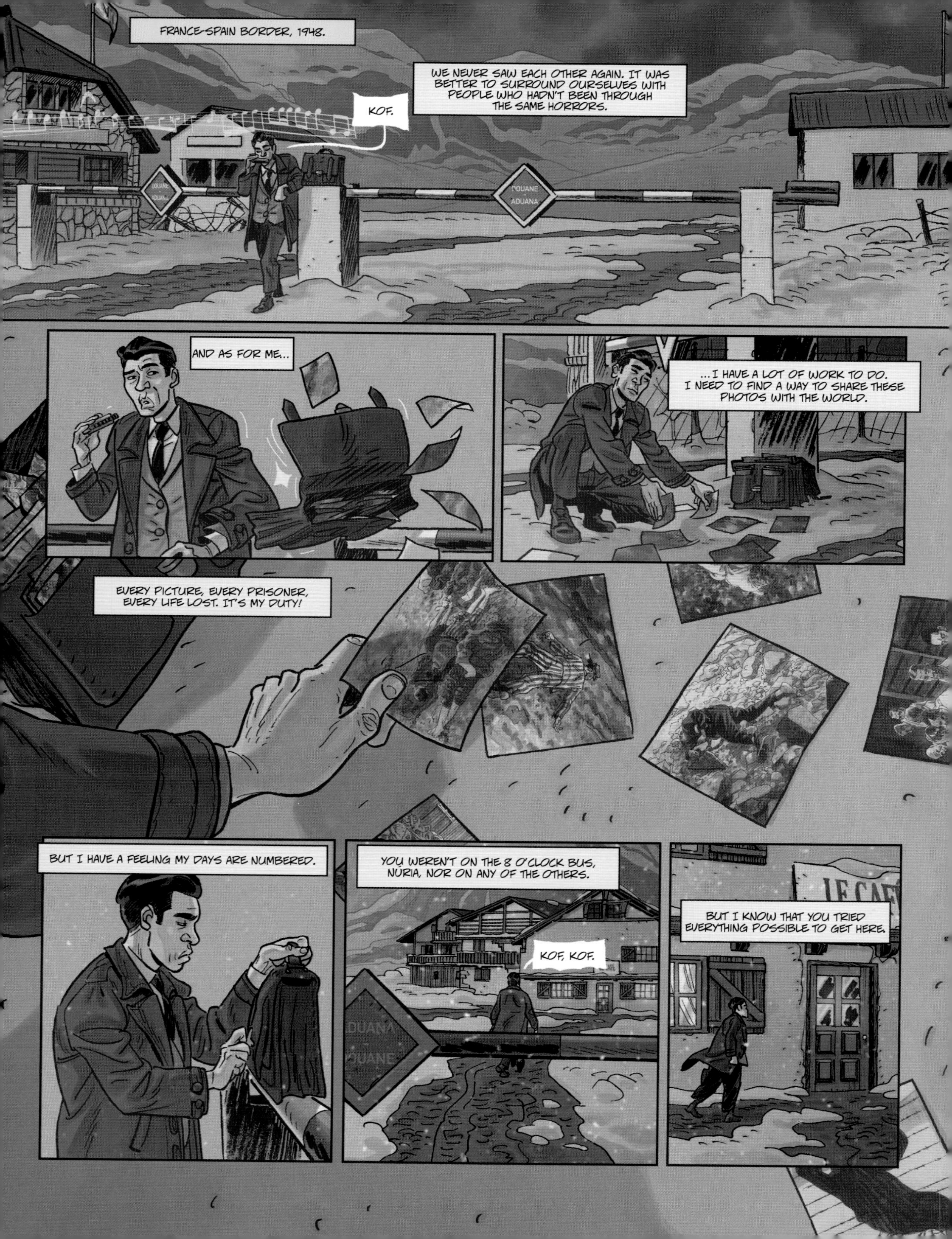
FRANCE-SPAIN BORDER, 1948.
WE NEVER SAW EACH OTHER AGAIN. IT WAS BETTER TO SURROUND OURSELVES WITH PEOPLE WHO HADN'T BEEN THROUGH THE SAME HORRORS.
KOF.
DOUANE ADUANA
AND AS FOR ME...
...I HAVE A LOT OF WORK TO DO. I NEED TO FIND A WAY TO SHARE THESE PHOTOS WITH THE WORLD.
EVERY PICTURE, EVERY PRISONER, EVERY LIFE LOST. IT'S MY DUTY!
BUT I HAVE A FEELING MY DAYS ARE NUMBERED.
YOU WEREN'T ON THE 8 O'CLOCK BUS, NÚRIA, NOR ON ANY OF THE OTHERS.
KOF, KOF.
BUT I KNOW THAT YOU TRIED EVERYTHING POSSIBLE TO GET HERE.

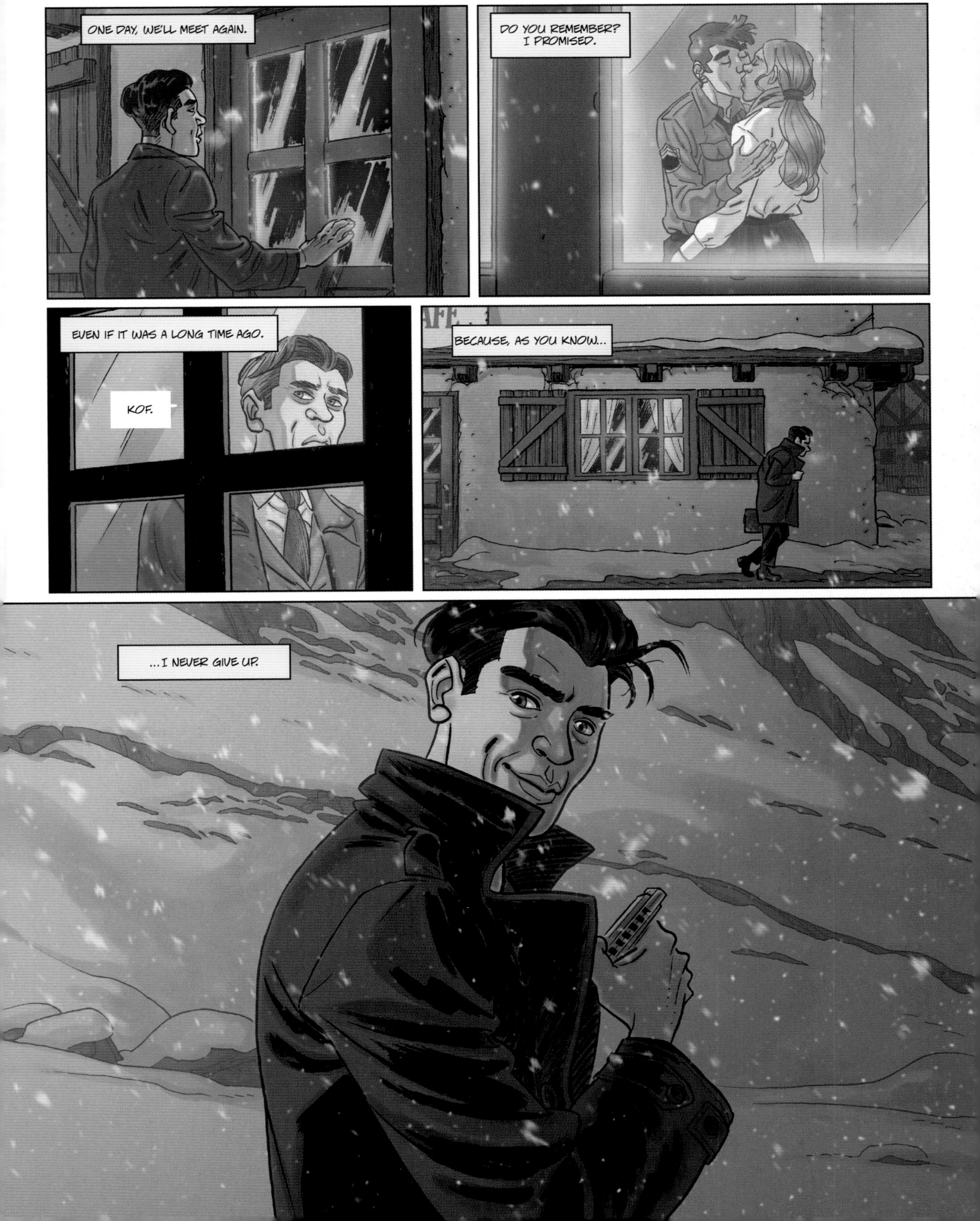
ONE DAY, WE'LL MEET AGAIN.
DO YOU REMEMBER? I PROMISED.
EVEN IF IT WAS A LONG TIME AGO.
KOF.
BECAUSE, AS YOU KNOW...
...I NEVER GIVE UP.

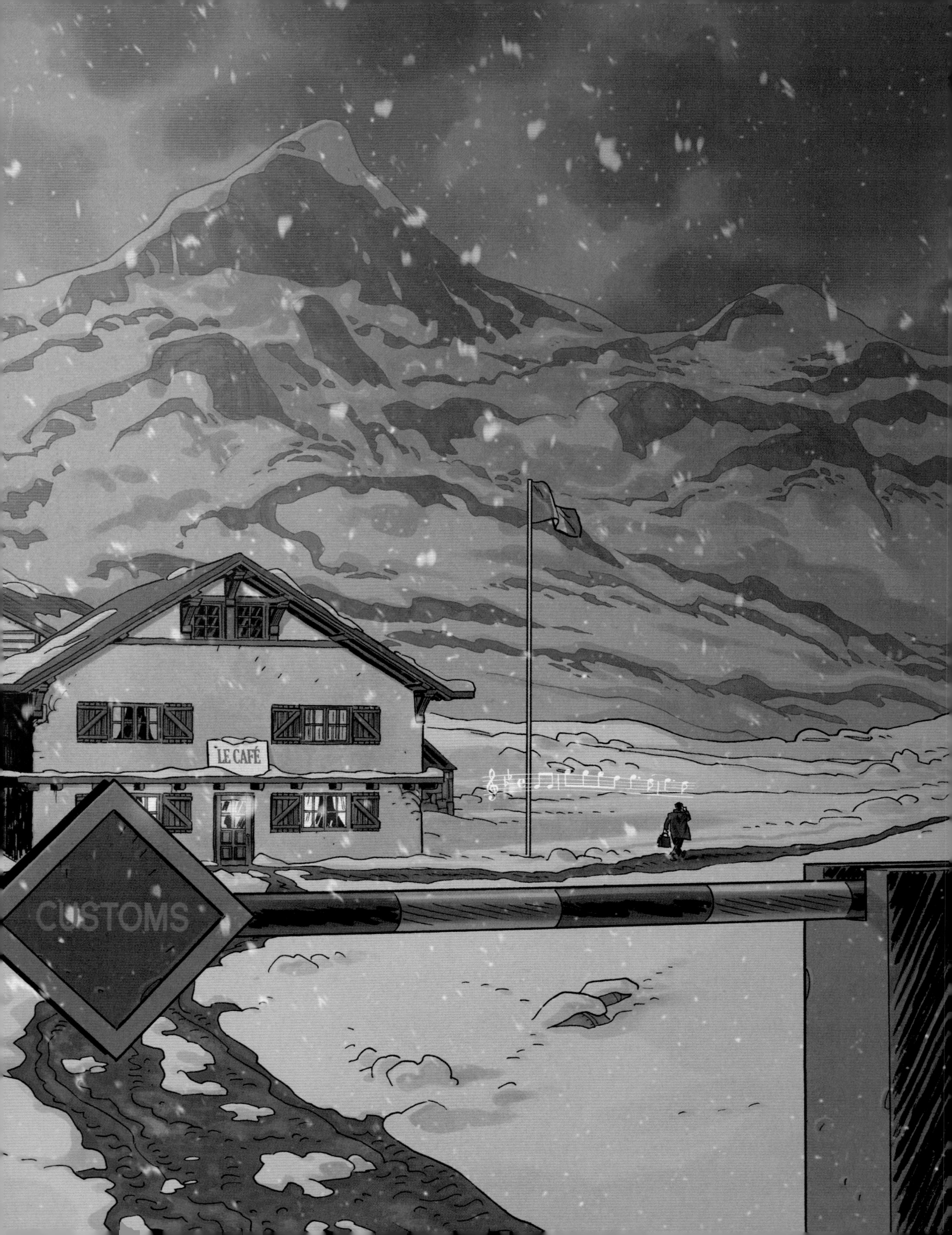
LE CAFÉ
CUSTOMS

Of the 9,328 Spaniards interned in concentration camps,
7,532 of them were at Mauthausen.
4,816 of them were killed.*

Of the 20,000 negatives smuggled out of the camp,
almost 19,000 of them are lost.

Francisco Boix died not long after,
at the age of 31.
He never did see his sister Núria again.

*It's worth bearing in mind that these numbers are merely the ones
that have been officially confirmed. It is therefore possible
that the actual numbers are higher.

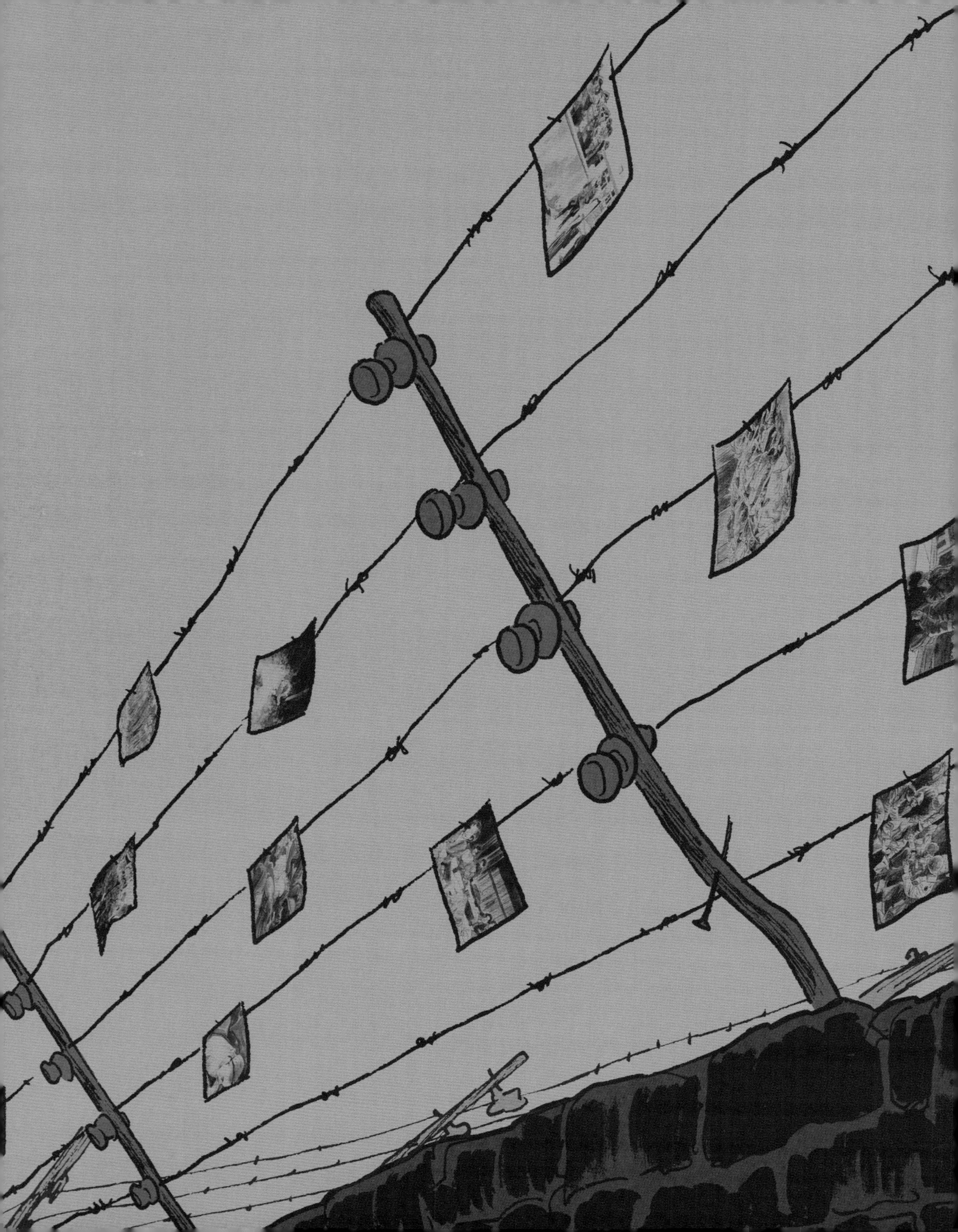

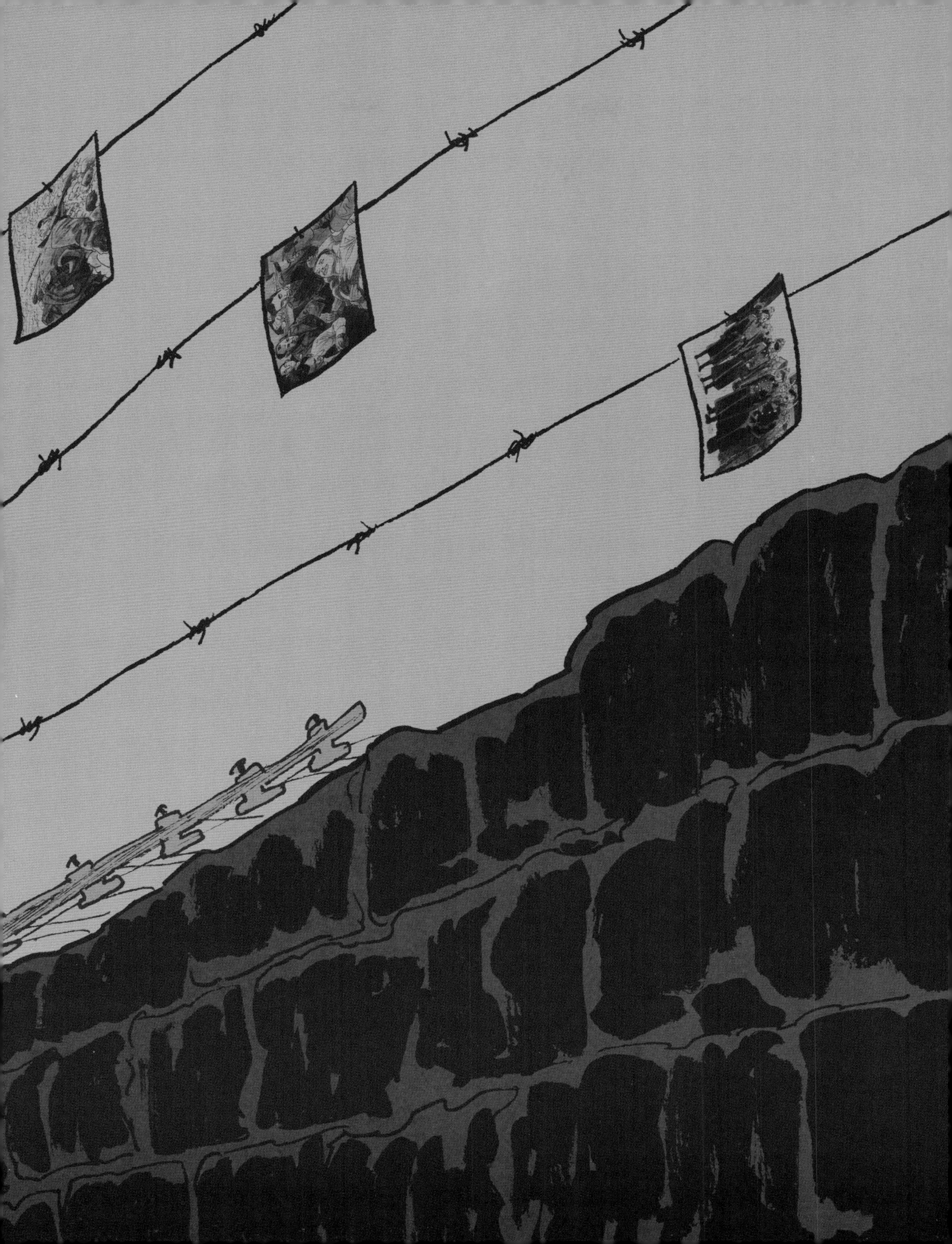

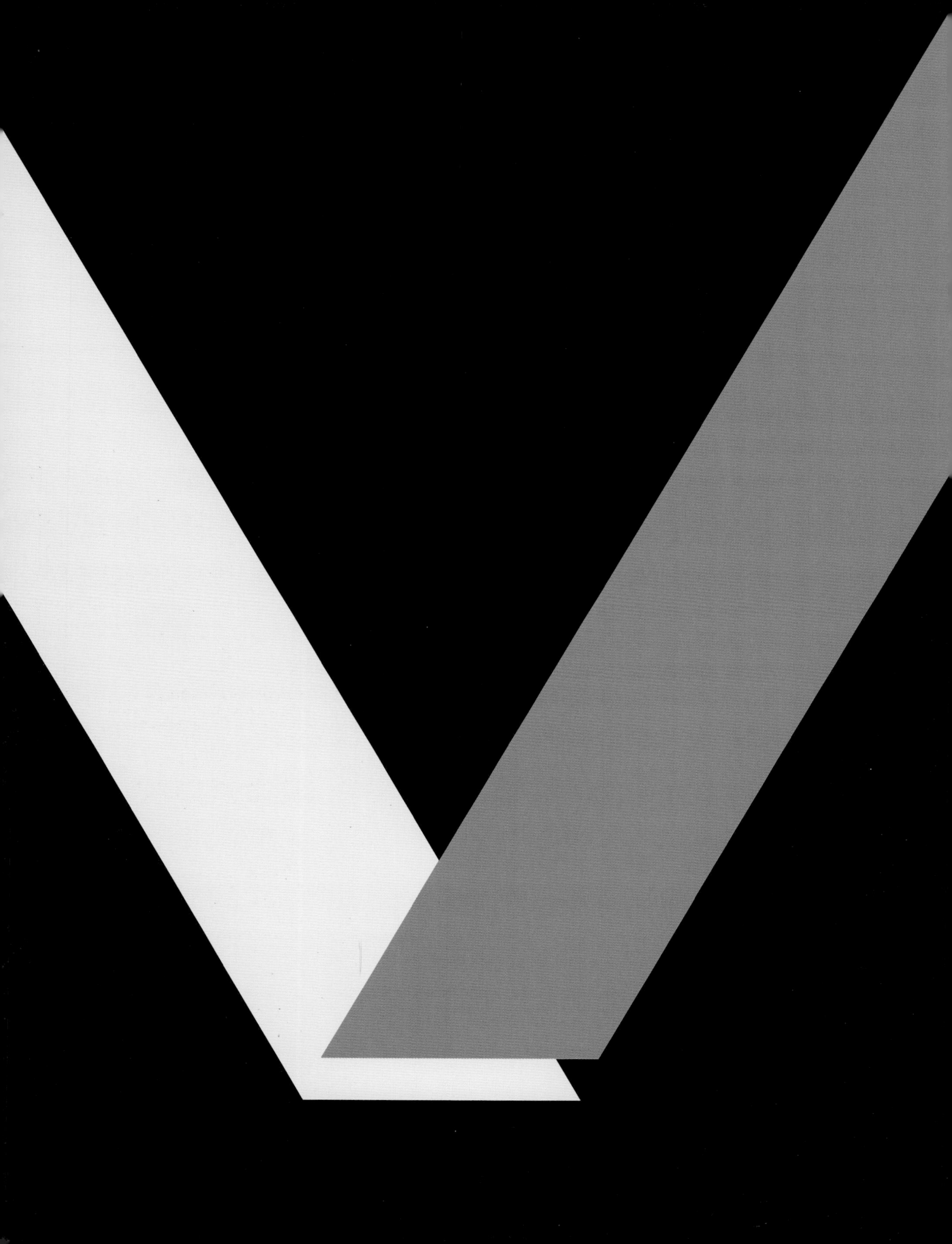

My thanks to Ralf Lechner, Gregor Holzinger, and Andreas Baumgartner of the Mauthausen Memorial for their patience and their documentary assistance; to Rosa Toran of the Amicale de Mauthausen (Spain) and to Margarida Sala of the Museu d'Història de Catalunya for generously agreeing to review my script; to Francesc Cardona of the Museu d'Història de Catalunya for the photos; to Josep Cruañas (Comissió de la Dignitat), Inma Navarro and Conxa Petit (Arxiu Nacional de Catalunya), and Ricard Marco (Fotoconexió), without whom we would not have been able to track down some of the photos; and to Pierrette Saez and Daniel Simon of the Amicale de Mauthausen (France) for their unconditional support.

Affectionate thanks to Benito Bermejo, without whom I would never have gotten to know Francisco Boix so intimately, for our endless conversations and for his valuable research on Boix and other deportees.

Thanks to Antoine Maurel of Lombard (who gave me my first big break with this story); thanks to Julie, Geneviève, Rebekah, Camille, Éric, Clémentine, and Gauthier for your hard work and dedication.

Thanks to François Pernot for believing in this project. Special thanks to Pedro and Aintzane for their work, their devotion, and their talent, through thick and thin.
And of course, thanks to Francisco.

SALVA

This book is dedicated to the memory of my father, whose absence I feel every day.

I'd like to thank my wife and colorist, Aintzane, for her support: without her this project could never have been completed. Thanks to Salva, who invited me on this voyage to Mauthausen and who introduced me to Boix; thanks, too, for his infinite patience and his words of encouragement. Thanks to Antoine, who believed in my drawing and who has always been able to see beyond my initial sketches.

Thanks to Julie for her untiring work and for her kindness; to Rebekah for her wonderful assistance on the cover; to Jaime Martin, who sent Salva and Boix my way; to Josep, who has always been there when I've needed him; to Lou and Veroh for their numerous WhatsApp messages; to Jordi for being there on that dark day; to Javi, who never hesitates to lend a helping hand when I ask him; and to those crazy *Rimbombancias y Monigotes* who enlivened the hours I spent at my drawing table.

Thanks to my family, I couldn't get by without them. And thanks to Broncano, Quequé and Ignatius of La vida moderna for their madness and laughter.

And thanks to Francisco Boix, to whom I hope I rendered the homage he deserves on every page. It's been a long and painful journey, but a gratifying one.

Pedro J. Colombo

To my parents, who took care of us. To my sister, who supported us and made us laugh. To Damian, who made us enter the dragon's lair.

To my husband for his silliness that I adore, for his sympathy as well as his tenderness, my thanks to him for always bringing the best out in me.

To my family and to my furry friends.

Thanks to Salva for having believed in us and for sharing his delight with each of our pages, an enthusiasm which was a great source of motivation for us.

Aintzane Landa

Published by Dead Reckoning
291 Wood Road
Annapolis, MD 21402

Library of Congress Cataloging-in-Publication Data
Names: Rubio, Salva, date, author. | Colombo, Pedro, illustrator. | Landa, Aintzane, date, colorist. | Madden, Matt, translator.
Title: The photographer of Mauthausen / writer, Salva Rubio ; artist, Pedro J. Colombo ; colorist, Aintzane Landa.
Other titles: Photographe de Mauthausen. English
Description: Annapolis, Maryland : Dead Reckoning, [2020]
Identifiers: LCCN 2020028540 (print) | LCCN 2020028541 (ebook) | ISBN 9781682476277 (paperback) | ISBN 9781682476284 (epub) | ISBN 9781682476284 (pdf)
Subjects: LCSH: Boix, Francisco, 1920–1951—Comic books, strips, etc. | Mauthausen (Concentration camp)—Biography—Comic books, strips, etc. | World War, 1939–1945—Photography—Comic books, strips, etc. | World War, 1939–1945—Atrocities—Austria—Mauthausen—Comic books, strips, etc. | Photographers—Austria—Mauthausen—Biography—Comic books, strips, etc. | Prisoners of war—Austria—Mauthausen—Biography—Comic books, strips, etc. | Prisoners of war—Spain—Biography—Comic books, strips, etc. | Holocaust, Jewish (1939–1945)—Comic books, strips, etc.
Classification: LCC D805.5.M38 R83513 2020 (print) | LCC D805.5.M38 (ebook) | DDC 940.53/185362—dc23
LC record available at https://lccn.loc.gov/2020028540
LC ebook record available at https://lccn.loc.gov/2020028541

♾ Print editions meet the requirements of ANSI/NISO z39.48-1992 (Permanence of Paper).
Printed in the United States of America.

28 27 26 25 24 23 22 21 20   9 8 7 6 5 4 3 2 1
First printing

© 2018 – ÉDITIONS DU LOMBARD (DARGAUD-LOMBARD S.A.) – RUBIO / COLOMBO / LANDA
Translation: Matt Madden
Lettering: Cromatik Ltd
Original title: Le Photographe de Mauthausen
All rights reserved.
http://www.lelombard.com

LE LOMBARD